BSCN
BUILDING SCALABLE CISCO® NETWORKS

BSCN
Building
Scalable Cisco®
Networks

Thomas M. Thomas II
Arjan Aelmans
Floris Houniet
Tan Nam-Kee

McGraw-Hill

New York   San Francisco   Washington, D.C.
Auckland   Bogotá   Caracas   Lisbon   London
Madrid   Mexico City   Milan   Montreal   New Delhi
San Juan   Singapore   Sydney   Tokyo   Toronto

McGraw-Hill

A Division of The McGraw·Hill Companies

P/N 0-07-212475-X
PART OF ISBN 0-07-212477-6

The sponsoring editor for this book was Steven Elliot, the associate developmental editor was Franny K elly, and the production supervisor was Clare Stanley. It was set in Century Schoolbook by D&G Limited, LLC.

Printed and bound by Phoenix Book Technology.

I dedicate this work to Jan Aelmans, my late grandfather whose role in my life becomes more and more significant every day. Thank you for being there!

Arjan Aelmans

I dedicate this book to my parents, Lambert and Irene. Their support was essential for the creation of this book.

Floris Houniet

To Mom and my two sisters, Sok-Ai and Sok-Thian.

Tan Nam-Kee

I would like to dedicate this book to my family for their support and understanding during all those times when I had to work on this series. There is no doubt in my mind that I could never have accomplished such a feat without their love and support.

Thomas M. Thomas II

CONTENTS

Contents

Contents

ACKNOWLEDGMENTS

I'd like to thank everyone who had to bear my presence during the writing of this book. Only when you're actually "on the road" with a couple of chapters, you realize that what you're really trying to do is fit two jobs and a research project in one life, while trying to tell yourself that there's time left for eating, sleeping and seeing your family and friends, which was hardly ever the case.

Most of all this goes for Yvonne Peper, the love of my life who took the biggest load on her shoulders, and carried it through until the end. Thanks forever, love! You're always in my heart.

The same goes for Harrie and Lies Aelmans, my parents who couldn't seem to comprehend what was going on in my appartment but never the less sponsored us often with late-night food deliveries (which was brilliant!) and loads of "try and get some sleep and a normal pace" advice that was hardly ever put to use. Thank you so much for all the support you gave me in my life, and for believing in me whenever I made yet another uncomprehendable decision. You're the best!

We owe a lot to Martin "Mighty Marty" van Delden's endless willingness and energy to produce the Visio figures for the book. Writing ended just minutes before the van Delden family actually got used to fax-reception beeps at 4 a.m. . . . thanks so much!

Someone else who had definitely earned credits is Franny Kelly at McGraw-Hill. Being not only an editor but a great manager as well, he proved to be invaluable during the writing of this book, especially in the final stages. Considering that Floris and myself are the only ones who have actually seen each other in real life and that all other communications took place using the Internet and of course the telephone, keeping everything together was quite a task to accomplish. Franny sure did. Thanks for all the support!

Last but certainly not least I'd like do say a big "thank you" to Floris who's spent over four months with me getting the bulk of the work done. Our late night/early morning round offs accompanied by great jazz, dimmed lights and Tullamore Dew were just fantastic and very inspirational. The result was yet another thousand new ideas, so God only knows what the future will bring. Thanks buddy . . .

ARJAN AELMANS

Here is a small list of some of the people who made it possible for me to write the book and who kept me from going any madder than I already am.

K. de Walle of AT&T solutions, P. Hotting of Infonet Europe. They lent me a tower of Cisco routers to play with and create the captures for the book.

K. Depijper (CCIE), for patiently listening to my questions and giving me some valuable technical tips on what to look out for.

M. Wessling, for lending me a few small hubs, and a huge switch that thinks it is a hub!

M. Beker, for letting me listen to fantastic jazz music, drink whiskey and complain as much as I wanted.

I also want to thank everybody in my family and my co-author, Arjan, for being supportive during the whole book-writing period, and calming me when my PC fell victim to the umpteenth catastrophic crash.

FLORIS HOUNIET

In addition, I would like to express my thanks to Francis Kelly, Jennifer Perillo, and all of the editorial staff at McGraw-Hill who make this book possible.

Special thanks to my family who put up with my extra work hours again. I would not have completed my chapters without their support and patience.

TAN NAM-KEE
CCIE #4307
JUNE, 1999

I would like to take a moment to acknowledge Franny Kelly and his talented staff at McGraw-Hill. It was his dedicated and drive that allowed this book to be the success that it is. I am certain that he achieved this through sheer willpower and other means. During this book's last days in development, the production people involved also should be recognized for their contribution in bringing together all the pieces into the truly awesome book you now hold.

THOMAS M. THOMAS II

ABOUT THE AUTHORS

Arjan Aelmans (The Netherlands) has worked for various IT contracting agencies in The Netherlands supporting their large-scale multivendor networks. After a year of doing research on Cisco Internetworking technologies, he is now CEO of Allied Network Research, a Dutch-based consulting company where he develops custom-made training programs and trains with the new Cisco curriculum. Arjan holds an MCSE and MCP+I certification.

Floris Houniet is a networking specialist working for major 'Blue Chip' companies within the European Union. He has worked in numerous enterprise environments designing, implementing and supporting complex environments. Currently based in The Netherlands, he has worked in the UK, Benelux, France and Scandinavia upgrading and redesigning International private Internetworks. He holds a Bachelor of Science in Aeronautical Engineering, CCNA, and is certified as an ISO 9001 Internal Auditor.

Tan Nam-Kee (CCIE #4307 and CCSI #98976) has provided extensive Cisco training and customized training to hundreds of networking professionals from multinational organizations such as Acer, Air Lanka, AT&T, Citibank, Compaq, Credit Suisse First Boston, Equant, GE Medical Systems, Hewlett Packard, IBM, Merrill Lynch, Telecom New Zealand, and others. He has more than 8 years of experience in the data communications industry specializing in the design, implementation, and management of multi-platform LAN/WAN environments.

Nam-Kee is the founding director of Couver Network Consulting, a consulting firm that provides consulting and training services to corporate and government clients in Asia Pacific.

Besides being a Cisco Certified Internetwork Expert (CCIE #4307) and Cisco Certified Systems Instructor (CCSI #98976), Nam-Kee is also a Microsoft Certified Systems Engineer (MCSE #926954), SCO ACE, HP Certified Consultant (OpenView), Bay Networks Certified Specialist (Routers, Optivity), and Sun Certified Administrator (System, Network). He also holds an M.S. in Datacommunications from the University of Essex, UK, and an M.B.A. from the University of Adelaide, Australia.

Thomas M. Thomas II, is a Certified Cisco Systems Instructor (CCSI), CCNA, CCNP & CCDA as well as the founder of NetCerts.com (www.netcerts.com), and the Cisco Professional Association Worldwide or CPAW for short (www.ciscopaw.org), a not-for-profit organization bringing together users of Cisco equipment to learn and network. He was previously a course developer for Cisco Systems and was a group leader of the Advanced Systems Solutions Engineering Team for MCI's Managed Network Services. In his spare time, he also has authored OSPF Network Design Solution & Thomas' Concise Telecom & Networking Dictionary. Tom is currently working as an Instructor/Consultant for Mentor Technologies (www.mentortech.com).

ABOUT THE REVIEWERS

Henry Benjamin CCIE, CCNA, CCDA, B. Eng., is a Cisco Certified Internet Expert under the CCIE program #4695. Henry is a network design engineer for Cisco Systems Inc. across Australia and Asia. He has more than 9 years of experience in Cisco networks including planning, designing and implementation of large IP networks running IGRP, EIGRP and OSPF. Henry holds a bachelor of Aeronautical Engineering degree from Sydney University.

John Vacca is an information technology consultant and internationally know author based in Pomeroy, Ohio. Since 1982, John has been the author of 26 books and more than 350 articles in the areas of Internet and Intranet security, programming, systems development, rapid application development, multimedia and the Internet. John was also a configuration management specialist, computer specialist, and the computer security official for NASA's space station program (Freedom) and the International Space Station Program, from 1988 until his early retirement from NASA in 1995. John can be reached on the internet at jvacca@hti.net.

1

Introduction

CHAPTER 1

Introduction to Building Scalable Cisco Networks

1.1 Preface

It's no secret that the networking industry is lucrative for manufacturers, service providers, investors, and employees. All the elements are in place to make a job market that will last for a long time to come. Unfortunately, the personal benefits do not come for free. The price we must pay is keeping up with the technology.

In the old economy, seniority and experience were the main components that defined an employee's position. In today's economy, knowledge is the key—not just any knowledge, but knowledge of current technology. Experience is valuable, but the best advantage is the willingness to put the past behind and forge on toward the future.

Those who choose to live in the past and not learn new technology will find themselves wondering why the younger crowd is making more money and is afforded more opportunities. It has little to do with age and much to do with staying current. If you are new to the field of networking, use your new-found enthusiasm to your advantage. Read everything networking-related that you can. If you have been in the computer, communications, or networking industry for a while, use your experience to your advantage. Your experience gives you an advantage that few have in this industry. You have seen the fast-paced changes that have swept through our industry time and time again. Hopefully, you have become successful and have advanced your career, as well. Regardless of your current position or experience, there is no substitute for diligent study, which is why you now hold this book in your hands.

So what now? You understand your position and know that you need to learn lots of new things, but you aren't sure where to start. That's where industry certification plays a roll. Industry certification is a great guide for your development in the fast-changing network field. Cisco Systems has developed an excellent road map to guide you through the broad field of networking. This road is known as the *Cisco Career Certification Program*.

This book offers you a great preparation and companion to Cisco's BSCN course, one of the required courses for the *Cisco Certified Networking Professional* (CCNP). This book covers topics from advanced

IP-address management to configuring high-level interconnections by using advanced routing protocols such as *Open Shortest Path First* (OSPF), *Enhanced Interior Gateway Routing Protocol* (EIGRP), and *Border Gateway Protocol* (BGP). Careful study of these topics will prepare you for success in passing the exam and will provide you with the opportunity to stay current in data communications—the key to success in your career.

1.2 Introduction

Building Scalable Cisco Networks is designed to give the reader a ground-up view of creating scalable IP networks by using Cisco equipment. Technology concepts, networking concepts, real-world configuration examples, and case studies will be provided throughout the book to build a strong understanding of the book's objectives. The practical nature of the book makes it applicable to networking professionals who need an understanding of Cisco-scalable IP networks and networking professionals who are working toward Cisco certification.

Here is an outline of each chapter:

■ Chapter 1, "Introduction to Building Scalable Cisco Networks"

The book is comprised of 12 chapters, with this first chapter being the introduction to the book. The remainder of the chapters are as follows:

■ Chapter 2, "Overview of Scalable Internetworks"

In this chapter, the key characteristics that make up a scalable Internetwork as defined by Cisco are discussed. You will learn the functionality that exists at each layer and learn which IOS features are available to optimally configure a Cisco router in a certain situation. We've also mapped specific layer requirements to actual router configurations and visualized this concept in a network diagram.

- Chapter 3, "Routing Protocols"

  This chapter is important to your overall understanding of routing principles, metrics, and distances. First, the basics of IP addressing are discussed, including classful and classless IP addresses. An introduction is made to subnetting, which will be discussed in greater depth in the next chapter.

- Chapter 4, "Extending IP Addresses"

  In this chapter, we will discuss some methods for conserving IP address space and how to spread the IP addresses wisely across an Internetwork. Various topics will be covered, such as *Variable Length Subnet Masks* (VLSMs), *Classless Interdomain Routing* (CIDR), and which pitfalls to anticipate. We will also look at some methods for solving specific problems that can occur in an Internetwork. One lesson to be learned here is that great caution should be taken when changing the IP addressing scheme for all or part of an Internetwork. A thorough understanding of the Internetwork in question should be gained before designing the changes, because one small mistake can cause havoc in minutes. In the next chapters, we will delve deeper into the routing protocols OSFP, EIGRP, and BGP.

- Chapter 5, "Configuring OSPF in a Single Area"

  In this chapter, you will learn about the basic communication process that occurs between OSPF routers within a single area. You also will learn about the stages in which a new router will learn about its surroundings and will eventually take part in the routing process.

  Because OSPF is a link-state protocol, it does not send out whole routing tables to neighboring routers; rather it uses a sophisticated method of communication that only tells surrounding routers about changes in the network. We will discuss how an OSPF router uses the SPF algorithm to build the routing table from this information and how updates are sent in a safe and secure fashion through the use of authentication and packet acknowledgement. This chapter also discusses the different roles that an OSPF router can play in an Internetwork.

■ Chapter 6, "Configuring OSPF in Multiple Areas"

In this chapter, we will discuss the hierarchical method that OSPF uses to subdivide large Internetworks into manageable parts. OSPF provides more scalability and stability and provides a large reduction in bandwidth use compared to distance-vector protocols. OSPF is an open standard, making it suitable for use in multi-vendor networks that require advanced features such as VLSM, fast convergence, and scalability. Different from the previous chapter, which introduced OSPF and its operation in a single area, this chapter's focus is configuring OSPF for operation in multiple areas.

■ Chapter 7, "Configuring Enhanced IGRP (EIGRP)"

In this chapter, we will look at the workings of Cisco's EIGRP. With this insight, it should be possible to understand, configure, and troubleshoot EIGRP within a scalable Internetwork. EIGRP is one of the most easy-to-implement IGPs around, because it supports many powerful features, is well supported by Cisco, and has an enormous installation base.

■ Chapter 8, "Basic Border Gateway Protocol"

Chapter 8 covers the basic principles behind BGP. BGP can run in two modes: *Internal BGP* (IBGP) and *External BGP* (EBGP). IBGP takes care of the communication between BGP routers within an *Autonomous System* (AS). In this way, BGP can route traffic through an AS or decide which EBGP router is best for sending traffic into a neighboring AS. IBGP uses the IGP within the AS to provide reliable routing between the IBGP routers. IBGP uses TCP/IP for all of its communication and usually uses a loopback interface defined on each BGP router as the source and destination IP addresses when communicating. IBGP must be logically and fully meshed, because IBGP routers never pass BGP routing information on to other IBGP routers. EBGP is the mode that BGP uses when it communicates between two different ASs. EBGP routers are normally connected over point-to-point links, so an EBGP router expects a peer router to be on the same subnet as itself. The exception is called *BGP multihop*, and we will discuss that concept as well.

■ Chapter 9, "Scaling Border Gateway Protocol"

BGP is the protocol of choice when it comes to linking large ASs. BGP offers the possibility of manipulating the way in which you advertise your network to the surrounding areas, as well as enables you to adapt the routing information coming into your AS. As Internetworks have become larger, ways have been found to reduce the burden of configuring and maintaining the BGP system as a whole. This chapter discusses the issues that can be encountered when using BGP in large Internetworks, such as interconnected *Internet Service Provider* (ISP) networks. We will show you how to use the appropriate Cisco IOS features and commands to configure and verify BGP operation in these situations.

■ Chapter 10, "Overview of Managing Traffic and Access"

In this chapter, you will learn how to deal with traffic in an IP environment by using access lists. We will also introduce the four principles that should be used when configuring access lists. Moreover, we will look at queuing and how you can use it to put expensive Wide-Area network (WAN) bandwidth to a more efficient use while assuring equal network access, so that time-critical traffic can still be supported on a heavy loaded network. Queuing, which stems from traffic prioritization, enables designated traffic to be forwarded before others. We will also discuss the different queuing options that Cisco IOS supports and how you can make decisions on which one to implement in a given situation.

■ Chapter 11, "Configuring IP Access Lists"

This chapter is about using access lists to manage and control IP traffic. Two types of IP access lists are available: standard and extended. IP standard access lists range from 1 to 99, and IP extended access lists range from 100 to 199. Access lists are like if-else (rule-based) statements, where the conditions for a standard access list are IP source addresses (and for an extended access list are IP source addresses, IP destination addresses, protocol numbers, and TCP/UDP port numbers). We will discuss the various applications for both standard and extended access lists and explain how they can be configured, as well as how their operation can be verified by using Cisco IOS.

■ Chapter 12, "Optimizing Routing Update Operations"

This chapter discusses the different ways of optimizing routing updates. The routing information overhead and the size of a routing table for OSPF, EIGRP, and BGP can be reduced significantly by using route summarization or route aggregation. With route summarization, routers can aggregate multiple route entries to a single advertisement, reducing the resource utilization (memory and *central processing unit*, or CPU) on the router and the complexity of the network. The capability to translate between heterogeneous routing protocols, different routing metrics, and update information is known as *route redistribution,* and this chapter covers in detail the route redistribution for OSPF, EIGRP, and BGP.

1.3 Who Should Read This Book?

The *Building Scalable Cisco Networks* exam focuses on introducing routing techniques and technologies for scaling a network. To fully benefit from this book, readers should ideally possess certain prerequisite skills using Cisco equipment. These skills include the following:

■ A working knowledge of the OSI reference model and the hierarchical model

■ An understanding of Internetworking fundamentals

■ Knowledge of how to operate and configure a Cisco IOS device

■ Working knowledge of the TCP/IP stack and how to configure a routed protocol, such as IP

■ An understanding of the Distance Vector Routing Protocol operation and how to configure the Routing Information Protocol (RIP) and IGRP

- Knowledge of when to use static and default routes and how to enable them on a Cisco router
- How to display and interpret a Cisco router routing table
- How to enable a WAN serial connection
- How to configure Frame Relay *Permanent Virtual Circuits* (PVCs) on interfaces and subinterfaces
- How to configure an IP standard and extended access list
- How to verify router configurations with available tools, such as *show* and *debug* commands

1.3.1 CCNP Candidates

CCNP candidates will receive valuable information for CCNP certification. This book will cover the concepts you will be tested on in the *Building Scalable Cisco Networks* (BSCN) exam. The next section covers the type of material that will appear on the BSCN exam.

We break the information down into sets of concepts that are covered in great detail. These concepts will then be reinforced with real-world examples of how to implement the concepts. This information will help you better understand the concepts, as well as the Cisco command syntax that is necessary for configuring your network. The best approach for taking the BSCN exam is to fully understand the concepts and then to drill down to the details of the implementation.

1.3.2 CCIE Candidates

Those working toward *Cisco Certified Internetworking Expert* (CCIE) certification will get a valuable distillation of the issues surrounding the concepts involved in building scalable networks using Cisco technology. The practical hands-on approach of this book will prove invaluable in understanding many of the concepts you will be grilled on in the CCIE exam.

The CCIE exams are long, grueling, full of detail, and cover a broad range of concepts. This book will help you understand the concepts and configurations of IP-based Internetworks that are built to offer reliability, availability, responsiveness, efficiency, and adaptability while remaining accessible, yet secure.

1.4 Topics Covered on the Exam

BSCN prepares you for taking the newly developed routing exam that is part of the *Cisco Certified Network Professional* (CCNP) 2.0 curriculum. The routing exam's objectives are the last to be released by Cisco and are currently not yet available. Please check the following URL for a complete overview of current Cisco Career Certification exams and their respective exam objectives: `www.cisco.com/warp/public/10/wwtraining/certprog/testing/exam_list.htm`.

In order to successfully pass the exam, a student must be able to select and implement the appropriate Cisco IOS services and features that are required to build a scalable, routed network. For a given network specification, the exam objectives can be subdivided into the following tasks:

- Select and configure the appropriate Cisco IOS services to simplify IP address management at branch offices by centralizing addresses
- Implement the appropriate technologies for a scalable, routed network that includes link-state routing protocols and redistributions
- Configure edge routers to effectively interconnect into a BGP cloud by using either a single or a multi-homed interconnection into an ISP's BGP network

- Select and configure the appropriate access-list features for controlling access to networks or devices or for minimizing overhead traffic
- Implement case studies that reflect a scalable Internetwork that uses multiple routed and routing protocols

1.4.1 ACRC Exam Changes

Many changes have been made to the ACRC Exam, and this book addresses them in the following ways:

- Scalability issues are addressed in the same fashion as in ACRC 11.3, but with some new information.
- *Non-Broadcast Multi-Access* (NBMA) issues are addressed in the OSPF and EIGRP chapters.
- Redistribution continues to be addressed through the discussion of access lists.
- Policy-based routing using route maps is discussed.
- *Not-So-Stubby Areas* (NSSAs) are added to the OSPF discussion.
- BGP is now included, adding an advanced overview of ASs, peering, synchronization, route reflectors, policy control, communities, multi-homing, redistributions with IGPs, and configuring BGP for single or multiple connections to an ISP and within the BGP cloud.
- Materials on the *Internet Packet Exchange* (IPX) protocol and AppleTalk have been removed, because this exam will focus on IP only.
- Bridging, *Dial-on-Demand Routing* (DDR), *Integrated Services Digital Network* (ISDN), and T1/E1 have also been completely dropped from the exam.

 1.5 BSCN Course Objectives

The BSCN course objectives covered in this book are outlined in this section:

Chapter 2:

BSCN Objective

Understand the key requirements of a scalable internetwork

Describe the characteristics of a scalable internetwork

Select the appropriate Cisco IOS features for a given set of internetwork requirements

Chapter 3:

BSCN Objective

Understand the IP addressing model

Understand subnetting methodology

List the key requirements for routing IP traffic

Describe characteristics and operation of Distance-Vector protocols

Describe characteristics and operation of Link-State protocols

Compare operation of distance-vector and link-state protocols

Describe the contents of a routing table

Chapter 4:

BSCN Objective

Understand IP addressing issues

Describe IP addressing solutions

Understand hierarchical addressing in an internetwork

Understand *Variable Length Subnet Masks* (VLSM)

Understand *Classless Inter Domain Routing* (CIDR)

Understand route summarization

Chapter 5:

BSCN Objective

Understand OSPF operation in a single area

Describe OSPF operation in a Multi Access network, a Point-to-Point network and a *Non Broadcast Multi Access* (NBMA) network

Understand OSPF configuration in a single area

Understand verifying OSPF operation in a single area

Chapter 6:

BSCN Objective

Understand the issues involved when configuring OSPF for operation in multiple areas

Understand differences between area types, router roles and LSA types

Understand configuration of Stubby, Totally Stubby and Not-So-Stubby Areas

Understand OSPF verification in a multi area network

Chapter 7:

BSCN Objective

Describe Enhanced IGRP features

Describe operation of Enhanced IGRP

Describe how Enhanced IGRP can be configured for usage in a scalable internetwork

Verify Enhanced IGRP operation in a scalable internetwork

Chapter 8:

BSCN Objective

Understand when to use and when not to use BGP

Understand BGP terminology

Understand BGP operation

Understand the differences between Internal BGP (IBGP) and External BGP (EBGP)

Understand BGP configuration

Understand BGP operation verification

Chapter 9:

BSCN Objective

Understand Internal BGP (IBGP) scalability problems

Configure and understand BGP Route Reflectors

Configure and understand BGP policy control by using prefix lists

Understand usage and configuration of BGP Communities and Peer Groups

Describe how to configure BGP routes to multiple ISP networks

Understand the usage of Internal Gateway Protocol (IGP) between BGP redistribution

Configure and verify operation of a multi-homed BGP network according to a given network design specification

Chapter 10:

BSCN Objective

Describe causes of network congestion

List solutions for controlling network congestion using Cisco IOS services

Describe the function and applications of Access Lists

List solutions for optimizing routing updates

Chapter 11:

BSCN Objective

Describe IP Traffic Management concepts

Describe operation and configuration of Standard IP Access Lists

Describe operation and configuration of Extended IP Access Lists

Configure restricted Virtual Terminal, HTTP and SNMP access

Verify Access List configuration

Describe an alternative to Access Lists

Chapter 12:

BSCN Objective

Describe redistribution between multiple routing protocols

Describe configuration of redistribution

Describe controlling routing update traffic

Verify redistribution operation

Describe operation and configuration of policy-based routing using route-maps

Verify policy-based routing

1.6 Additional Support Forums

In addition to this book, a network professional can access many other sources for additional peer support. This support can come in many forms and can take on several different variations. If you are interested in pursuing a Cisco certification, two listservs run from www.groupstudy.com and can provide an additional perspective on the technologies covered within this book. The first listserv is for candidates who are pursuing their *Cisco Certified Network Associate (CCNA)* certification, CCNP, and/or CCIE. This place is great for reading other people's questions and answers (known as *lurking*), asking questions, or imparting the wisdom you've found after reading this book to others. Although the last method might not seem worthwhile, remember that by explaining a topic to someone else, you gain a greater understanding of the topic. You can solidify the knowledge you know, but also you can gain a friend who can help you understand a topic in the future.

These are definitely exciting times. The industry is young and growing by leaps and bounds every day. By working hard now to study and learn these concepts, you are on your way toward understanding the fundamentals required to understand new technologies as they are developed. Now let's get started with *Building Scalable Cisco Networks*. Enjoy.

PART

2

Scalable
Networks

CHAPTER 2

Overview of Scalable Internetworks

2.1 Objectives Covered in This Chapter

To better understand what is necessary to build a scalable network, the following objectives will be covered.

Table 2-1

BSCN objectives

BSCN Objective
Understand the key requirements of a scalable internetwork
Describe the characteristics of a scalable internetwork
Select the appropriate Cisco IOS features for a given set of internetwork requirements

2.2 Introduction

The effort required to build or maintain a corporate network has increased dramatically over the last few years. Companies are moving away from legacy networks, often out of necessity when clearing up Y2K problems, and using bandwidth-hungry applications that have evolved, courtesy of powerful desktop computers.

Whereas the networks used to be highly meshed and the traffic flowed directly from one site to another, nowadays that has become too expensive and difficult to manage. What is needed is a system whereby the whole network can manage itself to a large extent, and where changes can be implemented with a minimum of effort and disruption to users.

To make this possible, routers are needed to guide the traffic from source to destination, and to provide backup when one or multiple circuits fail. For the routers to be able to do this work, they need information about the network, and that is where the routing protocols come in. They gather information about the network world around them and, if properly configured, create a robust environment in which data is transported efficiently from source to destination.

2.3 Scaling Large Internetworks

A scalable network is one that can be changed to suit the demands placed on it without major disruptions. Most Internetworks need to be scalable because of the speed at which new technologies are being introduced, and because people are demanding connectivity outside the office, from home or remote office locations.

So, what is a scalable Internetwork? Which decisions must be made, and what are the critical factors that influence the health and growth of a scalable Internetwork?

Scalability is a term used to describe networks that are built to be dynamic. Any network that experiences growth must adapt easily to—and expand with—new demands.

The best examples of such Internetworks are of a hierarchical design. This makes robust address and device management possible and allows one to tackle problems, expansion, and redesigns in one part without affecting the whole Internetwork.

Figure 2-1 illustrates a typical three-layer hierarchical Internetworking model as is generally applied to Cisco and other networks. The layers are defined as the following:

1. *Core layer*   The core is the center of the Internetwork for the entire enterprise and includes the highest-level backbones. This part of the Internetwork is built to provide reliable transport within the backbone structure and to the distribution layer.

   Therefore it should be made using redundant elements to ensure maximum reliability. High performance and manageability are of the utmost importance.

   It should contain the links (if they exist) to networks outside the enterprise, and here the security issues should be addressed.

2. *Distribution layer*   The distribution layer of the Internetwork connects the access layers of the network to the core layers while retaining high routing efficiency.

   It controls access to the core layers, redistributes core layer routing protocols into optimized access layer protocols, and summarizes routes, if necessary.

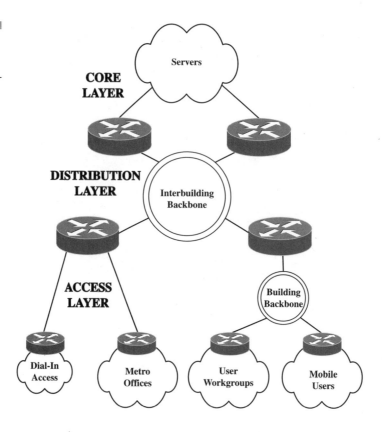

Maintaining efficient security, involving connections to third-party networks, also is tackled at this layer.

3. *Access layer*   The access layer provides the infrastructure to transport data between the local segments and transport it to the higher layers. In the case of remote sites, this layer can consist of technologies such as *Integrated Services Digital Network* (ISDN), using *Dial on Demand Routing* (DDR), frame relay, and leased lines to provide the connectivity to the distribution layer routers.

Locally, the layer can consist of routers, switches, bridges, or hubs to connect and control the traffic.

The importance of defining these layers stems from the fact that each layer has its own specific needs. Although these demands can overlap, it is important to know the requirements of the layer that a router is to be part of when building the configuration.

In a typical situation, the core routers will have to be deployed redundantly. Any failure will impact a large part of the network or seriously impact performance. Traffic should be forwarded with minimum delay, as trouble in this area could impact the routing and stability of the rest of the Internetwork.

For this role, one would choose a router from the Cisco 7000 or 12000 series, depending on the requirements.

The distribution layer is responsible for routing to the different parts of the Internetwork and therefore should be optimized to efficiently choose between the available paths. They must be capable of processing changes in the network quickly to reduce convergence time.

Distribution layer routers include the Cisco 3000 and 4000 series routers, although in smaller networks, one might consider using the modular 2600 Cisco router.

The Access routers are the barriers between the core network and the workgroup networks. They therefore should supply security and filter unwanted traffic from the rest of the Internetwork.

Table 2-2

Essential characteristics of the layer model

Core	Optimize routes between different areas
	Provide maximum availability and reliability
	Provide redundancy within the core routers
Distribution	Control access to Core layer resources
	Use bandwidth efficiently
	Form an isolation layer between Core and Access layer areas
Access	Restrict local traffic to Access layer, such as broadcasts
	Authorization of access to distribution layer

The routers available for access can range from the Cisco 800 for very small sites to 2600, or even the 3600 routers for larger sites.

Although these are general guidelines for what to expect in the different layers, it is possible to interchange the types in the different layers. It might be possible to find a 3640 router in the Core later, for example, if it has the capacity necessary. Due to the common software, Cisco IOS, the configurations can be set up independently of the router hardware used.

2.4 Defining a Scalable Internetwork

When managing or creating a scalable Internetwork, it is useful to be aware of the factors that influence it, the quality perceived by the users, and the budget required for maintenance and operation.

The following paragraphs summarize the requirements of a modern Internetwork and offer a method for subdividing networking issues into manageable parts that can be tackled with the features offered by Cisco's IOS software.

2.4.1 Reliability and Availability

Companies are coming to rely on networks for their critical business needs. Internet shops obviously cannot sell without being available to the shoppers on the Internet. But more critical services, such as hospitals, also rely on the continuous availability of networks to offer life-saving services. Factories and distribution centers rely on networks to provide information from the main offices on what to load onto trucks and trains. A broken network connection can cause huge queues and create logistical nightmares for companies that rely on fast and efficient delivery of goods. Such outages can run into the millions of dollars in damage in a very short time.

For these reasons, it is becoming increasingly important that nasty surprises be avoided and, if they do occur, that they be contained quickly and solved by a process invisible to the user.

Different techniques can be used according to the budget and criticality of the service to provide a reliable and highly available Internetwork. In the critical core layer, for example, redundancy probably is necessary to avoid large interruptions to the service. Redundancy of links also should be considered, and here multiple paths (meshing) or *Dial on Demand Routing* (DDR) backup is used.

With all such backup measures, fast convergence is essential to minimize interruptions to the traffic flow while the routers are computing alternative routes. This is where advanced routing protocols such as Cisco's *Enhanced Interior Gateway Routing Protocol* (EIGRP) or *Open Shortest Path First* (OSPF) can be used to good avail.

These protocols offer the following features:

- *Reachability*   EIGRP and OSPF can dramatically increase the reachability in large networks as they are not bound to the hop count limit of simpler routing protocols. This enables networks to be built with greater flexibility and therefore enhances the availability.

- *Fast convergence*   EIGRP and OSPF use mechanisms that detect network failures much faster than other routing protocols. Also they use methods to rebuild a routing table using less bandwidth and less time. This speeds up network convergence time and reduces the chances of outages causing routing traffic overloads.

2.4.2 Responsiveness

The Internetwork must be scaled to accommodate different types of traffic that pass through it. Interactive *Systems Network Architecture* (SNA) traffic, for example, is typically rather delay sensitive, and this can lead to problems when making use of WAN connections. This might work fine if the WAN is dedicated to this type of traffic, but when combined with bursty or high-bandwidth protocols, the SNA-reliant systems can be brought to their knees very easily.

To enable the coexistence of traffic with very different delay versus bandwidth needs, one can introduce quality of service into the Internetwork. Each protocol will be analyzed and the requirements translated to Cisco router features.

Features that scalable protocols can use to increase network responsiveness are the following:

■ *Alternative paths and backup circuits*   EIGRP and OSPF can keep lists of feasible alternative paths to switch to in the case that a transit network goes down or becomes congested. These circuits can be fixed, but can also be circuits used only when needed, such as backup circuits.

■ *Load balancing*   A router can use an alternative route to help alleviate congestion problems on a circuit. Through the use of advanced metrics, the routing protocol can determine how to best send traffic to the destination network, whether it be over one circuit of spread or over multiple.

2.4.3 Efficiency

Computer networks are becoming more and more intelligent. They can be tuned to give higher priority to critical data; they can block traffic that is unwanted and provide security from intruders. They have become far more than just a method to connect computers together and transport data. The reason for this development has been the enormous increase in data generated by modern applications and the diversity of the types of data. One cannot rely on every application to politely minimize the amount of traffic it puts on the network, or to determine the best way to connect to the destination.

The cost of transporting data over great distances is enormous, and every saving that can be made in bandwidth is a bonus. This is where routers come into play and can create efficiency in the transport of multiple protocols—by blocking unnecessary broadcasts, minimizing routing updates, and caching service advertisements locally.

Features used to increase network efficiency are the following:

■ *Access lists*   Access lists will be explained in detail later in the book, but it is useful to know that they can be used to block unwanted traffic, allowing the tuning of the network, and resulting in a network that only transports the traffic which it was designed to transport. Access lists are available in many tastes, and can range from simple and quick to long, detailed and processor intensive.

■ *Summarizing routing information*   Routing information swapped between routers can consume a large part of a network's available bandwidth, as a network becomes larger, and more information needs to be fed to all the routers. Using route summarization offers the possibility of reducing the granularity of the updates in favor of smaller updates. For example, if an Internetwork spans the USA and Europe, and there are a small amount of transatlantic links, then the routers in Europe do not need to know exactly how to reach every individual network in the USA. A summary will suffice, telling the router to send data destined for the USA to one of the transatlantic links.

■ *Less routing updates*   OSPF and EIGRP do not send periodic updates of their whole routing table, they simply send information about anything that changes. This is an enormous saving in bandwidth in comparison with older routing protocols.

■ *Reducing costs*   Reducing costs can be accomplished through a number of means. Basically the idea is to reduce the amount of bandwidth being paid for but not used.

■ For this, *Dial on Demand Routing* (DDR) can be used, only dialing out when bandwidth is needed. This works well for links with low volume, infrequent traffic. Also here snapshot routing comes into play. It is a dynamic routing method, but one that only sends routing updates at predefined intervals. This offers the flexibility of a dynamic protocol but allows the use of DDR.

■ Using switched access such as Frame Relay, provide a minimum guaranteed rate of traffic, but adds a burst possibility, which can be used to transport non-time-critical data.

■ *Compression*   With Cisco routers, compression is possible, for TCP headers and data. This obviously can reduce bandwidth need, and therefore the efficiency of the network.

2.4.4 Adaptability

Adaptability can be seen in much the same way as responsiveness, but in the longer term. Whereas responsiveness should be built into the network so that a responsive network will react to predefined situations, an adaptable network is one that can easily be changed within the scope of the original Internetwork-wide design. It should accommodate new features, protocols, and user locations.

If a company decides that more employees should work at home, for example, the network should be able to accommodate the extra remote dial-in users without major changes to the distribution or core layers.

On the other hand, if an Internet gateway is physically relocated because of a change of service provider, the core network should be able to offer the same service to the users as was the case before the move, without interruptions to the users.

A summary of what a typical Internetwork should be able to adapt to follows:

- *Different types of traffic and protocols* Some protocols will be nonroutable (needs to be encapsulated), some are time sensitive, and others create great bursts of traffic. The internetwork should be able to adapt to accommodate such different traffic types.
- *Protocol adaptability* Where company takeovers, or legacy networks are integrated into other networks, it must be possible to allow the different routing protocols to talk together, or have the 'strange' protocol encapsulated so it can run over the existing network. The tools to accomplish this are redistribution, tunneling and possibly EIGRP's support for various network layer protocols (IP, IPX and Appletalk).

2.4.5 Accessibility and Security

These terms often seem contradictory when it comes to actually implementing them. Roving users want to be able to log into the network wherever they are and expect the same in terms of responsiveness as they would get on their desktop systems in the office. The network must control and check such connections, however, and eliminate any connections that are deemed dangerous for the company. This is often where access lists come into play, but often, in an effort to make certain areas of the Internetwork accessible, secure parts of the Internetwork are unwittingly opened up.

To avoid such situations, it is important to design the interface between the access layer and distribution layer well. This is where one often can find huge access lists, which try to accommodate all the security rules necessary. Access lists require processor power, however, and the further down the list the matching rule is located, the longer the traffic must wait before it is forwarded to the correct interface or dropped.

As a rule, access lists must be avoided if possible and kept as short as possible when necessary. Too often, they are seen as a simple and quick fix to the alternative of adapting the network to the new circumstances. In the long term, however, access lists are hard to manage, easy to forget, and can become a nightmare when troubleshooting.

Accessibility can be enhanced by using the correct type of data carrier for the application, using fast dedicated circuits to build a core layer that meets the requirements, and using switched services such as Frame Relay, ATM, X25 and SMDS for flexibility at a slight performance cost. These are no strict rules however, and data carriers can be mixed if the situation requires. Each type of carrier has its own security advantages or problems.

Accessibility also means that connections to other Internetworks should be possible. Cisco supports redistribution between protocols, and for policy based Interdomain routing Cisco offers BGP support.

2.5 Summary of Cisco Features

Tables 2-3 through 2-7 are subdivided in the five key requirements Cisco uses to define scalable Internetworks. You will find IOS features and technology listed, along with practical examples of how to use them in a live network environment. We've also added extra study references to chapters in this book.

Table 2-3

Reliability and availability

Features Offered by Cisco/IOS	Example	Further Reference in Chapter
Reachability: Because the actual path costs are determined after analyzing a combination of factors (depending on the protocol used), very large Internetworks can be supported by IOS-based routers.	By using scalable routing protocols such as EIGRP or OSPF, extended metrics become available. Rip and hoplimits become a thing of the past. Using dial backup enhances reachability when congestion or outages occur.	5, 6, 7
Fast convergence	Implementation of scalable protocols.	5, 6, 7
Alternate paths routing	OSPF and EIGRP build an independent map of the Internetwork and can quickly find new routes when link problems occur.	5, 6, 7
Load balancing	OSPF and EIGRP can decide whether two links are suitable to share traffic to a common destination.	5, 6, 7
Tunneling	Unroutable protocols can be encapsulated in a routable protocol by the router and then sent over the WAN. The destination router recovers the original data from the routable protocol and sends it to the destination network.	*
Dial-backup	This technique uses temporary circuits to reduce peak traffic on main links and can serve as backup circuits if the main circuit fails.	*

* This subject falls outside the scope of this book.

Table 2-4

Responsiveness

Features Offered by Cisco/IOS	Example	Further Reference in Chapter
Weighted fair queuing	By using weighted fair queuing, bandwidth is fairly allotted to all users, so one single user, network device, or application no longer can claim all the Internetwork's available bandwidth.	10
Priority queuing	By using priority queuing, certain traffic can be tagged as important. This ensures that important data is delivered without timing out because of other, less-important traffic that is claiming too much bandwidth. The downside of this technology is that less-important traffic may not reach its destination on time.	10
Custom queuing	Custom queuing allows for highly detailed traffic shaping by allowing bandwidth to be divided up into slots. These slots can be configured according to business/QoS requirements of various types of traffic.	10
Dial on demand routing (DDR)	A small site might encounter peak loads at certain times, although the general level of traffic is very low. Use Dial on Demand Routing (DDR) to alleviate the temporary bandwidth shortage.	*

Table 2-5

Efficiency

Features Offered by Cisco/IOS	Example	Further Reference in Chapter
Access lists	These lists are used by the router to permit or deny packets based on selectable variables. Cisco has different types of access lists to fulfill different filtering requirements.	10, 11
Snapshot routing	Often used over slow links to conserve bandwidth, it enables routers to take part in the routing process fully, but without sending the regular updates required by most protocols. The administrator can set the update interval manually.	*

Table 2-5

Continued

Features Offered by Cisco/IOS	Example	Further Reference in Chapter
Compression over WANs	This feature allows the router to compress header and/or data information to reduce bandwidth usage. This process is CPU intensive.	*
Dial on demand routing (DDR)	DDR routing is used when a link only needs to be available for specific traffic. The traffic that enables the link is specified in an access list. This feature often is used for backup links, SOHO sites, and Internet connections.	*
Reduction in routing update traffic	Using route summarization and incremental updates, the load on the Internetwork for routing purposes can be reduced. Summarization binds contiguous networks together in one update. Incremental updates only send information that has changed, as opposed to sending all information at every update interval.	7, 8
Switched access	Cisco supports most switched access types, including Frame Relay, ATM, and SMDS which allow for far more efficient use of the available bandwidth.	5,6,7

Table 2-6

Adaptability

Features Offered by Cisco/IOS	Example	Further Reference in Chapter
Capability to pass both routable and nonroutable network protocols	Tunneling can be used to aid in the adaptability of the whole Internetwork.	*
Capability to enable islands of networking protocols to exploit each protocol's strengths	Using *Border Gateway Protocol* (BGP) to handle interdomain traffic and using EIGRP for the internal routing	3, 8, 9
Balance between multiple protocols in a network	Each protocol works differently, so the Internetwork must be able to adapt to accommodate the characteristics of each one.	3

* This subject falls outside the scope of this book.

Table 2-7	Features Offered by Cisco/IOS	Example	Further Reference in Chapter
Accessibility and security	Dedicated and switched WAN support	Cisco offers a very wide range of interfaces. This enables a router to connect to dedicated services such as T1s. Switched services such as X25, ISDN, and Frame Relay also are supported.	*
	Support of exterior protocols	Both *Exterior Gateway Protocol* (EGP) and BGP are supported by Cisco.	8,9
	Access lists	Very powerful tools used to restrict and redirect traffic	10, 11
	Authentication protocols	Both *Password Authentication Protocol* (PAP) and *Challenge Handshake Authentication Protocol* (CHAP) are supported by the PPP implementation of Cisco's IOS. The use of Tacacs(+) or Kerberos also is supported.	*

* This subject falls outside the scope of this book.

2.6 Chapter Summary

This chapter discussed the key characteristics that make up a scalable Internetwork as defined by Cisco. It described which functionality lives at each layer and what IOS features are available to optimally configure a Cisco router in a certain situation. It also mapped specific layer requirements to actual router configurations and visualized this in a network diagram. The most important thing to remember is that in order for an Internetwork to be truly scalable in every way, it has to meet the following characteristics: responsiveness, reliability, availability, efficiency, adaptability, and accessibility (while still providing security). These aspects should be considered when making a design or configuration decision that could affect the functioning of the Internetwork(s) involved. The next chapter, "Routing Protocols," discusses routing principles and protocols in more detail and provides the knowledge required to decide which technology to use in a given situation.

2.7 Frequently Asked Questions (FAQ)

Question: Is it possible to quantify the quality of a whole Inter-network?

Answer: When assessing the quality, there are a number of interesting issues to look at. The assessment of these issues determines the perceived quality—in other words, how the user perceives the quality of the network.

Obvious is the uptime, which is quantified as a percentage. An uptime of 99.98 percent or higher is good for the core level. This maps to about two minutes of downtime a week.

The *mean time between failure* (MTBF) also is important. This records how often a problem occurs.

The *network delay* is a measure of how congested the network is and can be of great influence to the perception of network quality.

Question: Which is the best routing protocol to use if I want a network that performs well?

Answer: It is impossible to mark one single protocol as being the best. Choosing between the protocols involves an in-depth investigation in the Internetwork. Bandwidth requirements, router types, router protocol, topology, future growth, and budget all play a role.

2.8 Case Study

A large distributor of car parts acquires 30 percent of its stock from a foreign supplier. For more efficient administration, the distributor and supplier connect their networks. They use ISDN-BRI to interconnect each other's Cisco routers. Although both were aware from the beginning that this would not be a smart move from an economical point of view, it was essential for them to be connected as soon as possible. Consider the network diagram of the Internetwork in Figure 2-2.

1. What Cisco IOS feature could be configured to prevent this network from having to be constantly connected while maintaining the capability to send routing updates?

   (Configure Snapshot Routing and Dial on Demand Routing: The link is only triggered when either routing updates or data is being sent. This results in a minimal impact on performance and achieves maximum savings using the current implementation.)

2. What Cisco IOS feature is to be configured on R1 to ensure security when R-A dials in, thereby creating one large network where all LAN recourses are exposed?

   (A properly configured access list on R1 can prevent unauthorized data coming from network B to cause problems on network A.)

3. What would be a good alternative in order to increase the available bandwidth by at least 50 percent without choosing a dedicated connection such as Frame Relay or X.25?

   (Add another BRI interface to both routers and configure load balancing that triggers extra channels when bandwidth use reaches a predefined threshold.)

4. A small number of heavy users on both networks is clogging up the link between network A and B. As a result, network responsiveness for all other users has become very poor. What Cisco IOS feature can be configured to prevent this from happening?

(Configuring weighted fair queuing will fairly allot bandwidth to all users.)

Or:

(Configuring custom queuing will allow highly detailed traffic shaping.)

Figure 2-2
Case study example

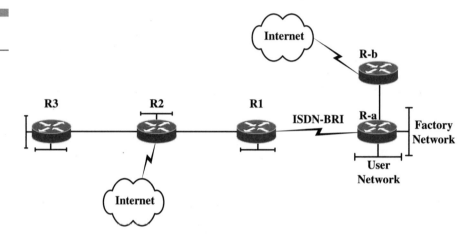

2.9 Questions

1. According to Cisco's method, when considering the design of a hierarchical network, where would you **not** place access lists?

2. Describe what the access layer does in Cisco's hierarchical design.

3. What are some of the characteristics of a scalable Internetwork?

4. Describe the primary function of the core layer.

5. Describe the primary function of the distribution layer.

6. Describe the primary function of the access layer.

7. Which router layer provides access to core resources that reside on the core layer?

8. Name three features in Cisco IOS that can be used to reduce bandwidth over a link.

9. Name three features in Cisco IOS that can be used to enhance stability and availability.

10. What is the core function of the distribution layer in a hierarchical network?
    a. Provide services that optimize communication between routers
    b. Provide OSPF area summarization
    c. Control broadcasts
    d. Control access to resources that are in the core, and efficiently use bandwidth
    e. This is an OSI function defined by a standards committee.

11. What are the key features of a scalable network?
    a. Reliable, responsive, efficient, adaptable, accessible, but not secure
    b. Reliable, responsive, efficient, adaptable, accessible, and secure
    c. Reliable, responsive, efficient, routable, and accessible
    d. Reliable, responsive, efficient, bridgeable, and accessible
    e. Reliable, responsive, efficient, nonadaptable, and accessible

12. PAP and CHAP are IOS authentication options available when which of the following WAN protocols is in use?
    a. Frame Relay
    b. X.25

    c. Tacacs

    d. ISDN

    e. PPP

13. Reducing the number of routes in a routing table can be accomplished by using which of the following?

    a. Snapshot routing

    b. DDR

    c. Route summarization

    d. RIP version 1

    e. IGRP

14. What are the three layers of a hierarchical network?

    a. Core, access, distribution

    b. Core, access, redistribution

    c. Access, core distribution, core

    d. Core and distribution only

    e. Core, access lists, distribution

15. Which of the following is used to control network congestion?

    a. Access lists

    b. Snapshot routing

    c. Compression techniques over the WAN

    d. Filter broadcast traffic

    e. All of the above

    f. List solutions for controlling network congestion

16. Which of the following are possible causes of network congestion in an IP network?

    a. DNS requests

    b. DHCP requests

    c. Routing protocol updates

    d. User applications

    e. All of the above

17. You have been asked by an organization to provide connectivity only as required and when data is transferred. Which IOS feature will perform this task?

    a. Access lists

    b. Snapshot routing

    c. DDR

    d. Switching fabric

    e. Both a and b

18. Which statement describes a scalable network?

    a. It is a network that cannot adjust to new users' requirements.

    b. It is a network that requires an administrator to constantly redesign the network.

    c. It can adjust to growth and demands for connectivity.

    d. Both a and b

    e. RFC 1798 describes all functions.

19. Which one of the following is not available as a configurable queuing option?

    a. WFQ

    b. Custom

    c. Priority

    d. GTS

    e. CSMD/CA

20. What are the three layers of a hierarchical network?

2.10 Answers

1. In the core layer. This layer is dedicated to transporting data in a quick and efficient manner. Decisions about traffic should have been made in the distribution and access layers.

2. The access layer is the lowest layer in the design and connects the end nodes to the Internetwork. It also applies filtering to stop unnecessary (local) traffic from entering the rest of the Internetwork.

3. ■ Efficiency

   ■ Responsiveness

   ■ Reliability

   ■ Adaptability

   ■ Scalability

   ■ Accessibility

4. The core layer delivers a fast, efficient, and reliable transport structure.

5. The distribution layer ensures the reliable transport of data between the corporate resources and the end users.

6. The access layer connects local networks to the Internetwork and filters traffic.

7. Routers on the distribution layer.

8. ■ Snapshot routing

   ■ *Dial On Demand* (DDR)

   ■ Compression

   ■ Access lists

9. ■ Tunneling

   ■ *Dial On Demand* (DDR)

   ■ Alternative path routing

   ■ Snapshot routing

10. **d.**

11. b.
12. e.
13. d.
14. d.
15. d.
16. d.
17. d.
18. c.
19. e.
20. ▪ Core
    ▪ Access
    ▪ Distribution

CHAPTER 3

Routing Protocols

3.1 Objectives Covered in This Chapter

To better understand what is necessary to build a scalable network, the following objectives will be covered.

Table 3-1

BSCN objectives

BSCN Objective
Understand the IP addressing model
Understand subnetting methodology
List the key requirements for routing IP traffic
Describe characteristics and operation of Distance-Vector protocols
Describe characteristics and operation of Link-State protocols
Compare operation of Distance-Vector and Link-State protocols
Describe the contents of a routing table

3.2 Introduction

This chapter starts with a short recap of IP v4 addressing and subnetting. Those who already have a good knowledge on the subject can skip this part; for others, though, a quick refresh might be useful.

The rest of the chapter dives into the concepts of routing. What is routing, why do we need routing, and how do routers find the necessary information to be able to route traffic? Readers will also get an overview explaining the differences among the routing concepts to prepare them for the more in-depth discussions in the following chapters.

3.3 IP Addressing

This section is based on the most widely used protocol at this time: IP v4. Although IP v6 is already being used in certain cases, it falls outside the scope of this book.

Before tackling the following chapters, it is important to have a firm grasp of the following concepts:

- Basic IP addressing and classful subnets
- Classless subnetting, using *variable-length subnet mask* (VLSM).

3.3.1 Basic IP Addressing

IP addresses are 32-bit numbers, commonly written in dotted decimal notation of 8 bits each.

Therefore an IP address will be noted as A.B.C.D. (for example, 192.168.0.1).

This number is a unique identifier for a network and node. The first part of the IP address is used to define the network. The second part is used to define the node on that particular network. In the rest of the chapter we will refer to the network part of an IP address by using the letter 'n.' The node as described is also called the host, and will be referred to using the letter 'h.'

An IP address is the sum of two identifying numbers rolled into one.

It should be obvious that as more bits of the IP address are assigned to the network part of the IP address, less bits are available to hand out to individual nodes on the chosen network.

So, using the preceding example, the network number is 192.168.0.h. The node number is 1. In this case, only the last eight bits (one byte) are used to define the node, so this network can accommodate eight bits worth of nodes. Eight bits represent 255 numbers, but in practice, two node addresses are reserved: the value 0 and 255. So in this case, 253 addresses could be supplied for nodes on this particular network. All devices that use IP to communicate use this IP address to find the device they are trying to send information to. IP nodes can only talk to other IP nodes that have the same network number. If they want to talk to nodes on other networks, they need a router that knows about the other networks in the Internetwork to forward the information to.

3.3.2 Subnets

So how does a node know which parts of its IP address define the network and node, and why does it need to know? This is where *subnets* come into play. Subnets are used to define where the split is between the network part and the node part of the IP address. A node that wants to communicate with another node first checks the IP address of the destination node and checks whether the network part of the address is the same as its own.

If the address is the same, the node assumes that the destination is attached to the same wire as itself. It then proceeds to pass the data down the OSI model to layer 2 (data link), which in turn, sends the information on to layer 1 (physical) and transmits it to the wire.

If the network number is different from its own network address, the host sends the data to a router defined as the default gateway in the host. The router forwards the packets to the destination network or replies with an ICMP `unreachable` statement if it does not know the destination network.

Those who find it difficult to thoroughly understand IP addressing may want to take some time to write the IP addresses in binary notation. The Microsoft Windows software offers a scientific calculator that can convert decimal to binary, although those who do it themselves may find it helpful in understanding the system.

3.3.3 Classful Subnets

Initially, subnets were defined statically—called *classful subnets*. Five subnet ranges were defined: class A, B, C, D, and E. To find which IP address belongs to which class, look at the first four bits of the IP address:

3.3.3.1 Class A Subnets These subnets are defined by a zero (0) in the first bit. The first eight bits (including the zero at the beginning) represent the network part of the IP address, and the following 24 bits represent the host part.

So seven bits for the network part (eight bits minus one that must be zero), offer 128 (2^7)combinations. Because all 0s and all 1s are reserved addresses, 126 combinations are left for assigning to networks.

Because 24 bits are reserved for hosts, 16,777,214 addresses can be handed out on each of the 126 networks.

The first octet of the IP addresses ranges from the value of 1 to 127. The binary notation follows:

```
0nnnnnnn.hhhhhhhh.hhhhhhhh.hhhhhhhh.
```

3.3.3.2 Class B Subnets   These subnets are defined by a 1 in the first bit and a 0 in the second bit. In this case, the first 16 bits are used for the network portion, and the last 16 bits are used for the hosts part.

So taking into account that all 1s and all 0s are not allowed in the network or host part, and that the first two bits already have been reserved in the network part, 14 bits can be used for the network part (giving 16,384 networks) and 16 bits for the hosts part (giving 65,532 hosts).

The first octet of the IP addresses ranges from the value of 128 to 191.

The binary notation follows:

```
10nnnnnn.nnnnnnnn.hhhhhhhh.hhhhhhhh
```

3.3.3.3 Class C Subnets   These subnets are defined by a 1 in the first and second bits, and a 0 in the third bit. In this case, the first 24 bits are used for the network portion, and the last eight bits are used for the hosts part.

This gives 2,097,152 networks and 254 hosts per network.

The first octet of the IP addresses ranges from the value of 192 to 223.

The binary notation follows:

```
110nnnnn.nnnnnnnn.nnnnnnnn.hhhhhhhh
```

3.3.3.4 Class D Subnets   The first four bits are 1110. This is a special case, where all remaining 28 bits are reserved for multicast use. These special addresses fall outside the scope of this book.

The first octet of the IP addresses ranges from the value of 224 to 239.

The binary notation follows:

```
1110mmmm.mmmmmmmmm.mmmmmmmmm.mmmmmmmmm
```

3.3.3.5 Class E Subnets   The first four bits are 1111. This is also a special case, where all remaining 28 bits are reserved for experimental use.

The first octet of the IP addresses ranges from the value of 240 to 255.

The binary notation follows:

```
1111eeee.eeeeeeee.eeeeeeee.eeeeeeee
```

3.3.4 Classless Subnets

In classless subnetting, the split between the host and the network part can be located just by looking at the IP address. In the case of a company having a network with 200 PCs and printers, this is easy. It can allot a class C network, and all is fine. However, if a company happens to have a network of 300 hosts, it would have to assign a class B network to encompass all the hosts on the network, or split the network into two class C networks.

In the first case, this is obviously a great waste of IP addresses, because the company only uses 300 of the 65,532 available IP addresses.

Table 3-2

Subnet examples

Class	Address	Default Subnetmask	Network Address	Host Address
A	122.32.54.6	255.0.0.0	122.0.0.0	0.32.54.6
A	11.42.96.4	255.0.0.0	11.0.0.0	0.42.96.4
B	191.64.6.32	255.255.0.0	191.64.0.0	0.0.6.32
C	211.46.5.36	255.255.255.0	211.46.5.0	0.0.0.36
C	192.48.204.4	255.255.255.0	192.48.204.0	0.0.0.4

In the second case, the fact that the two networks can only talk to each other through a router can cause problems, increase costs for administration, and increase network complexity.

This problem is tackled by adding *variable-length subnet mask* (VLSM) information to the IP addresses. When routing protocols can convey the extra VLSM information, this is called *classless interdomain routing* (CIDR). For more information, see Chapter 4, "Extending IP Addresses."

Remember that certain older hosts and routing protocols only use the classful IP addresses, as described earlier, and do not understand the VLSM method.

If a router is running a non-VLSM capable routing protocol, such as RIP, it does not mean that the router cannot have classless networks attached to the interfaces. However, this situation can cause problems, because the routing protocol will send only the classful information to other routers.

For a more thorough discussion on IP addressing and subnetting, please refer to Chapter 9.

3.4 Routing

This chapter gives a basic view on routing protocols. First it is important to know the difference between networks, Internetworks and autonomous systems (AS's), which must be understood, as they will be used extensively in this book.

- A network is a data link layer definition. Hosts on a network can send data to each other by using the hardware address (MAC address) as destination address. Bridges and basic switches are used to extend and manipulate traffic on a network.

- An Internetwork is the name for a group of networks that are attached to each other using network layer devices such as routers. Here, the hardware address (MAC) is not visible to all hosts, and therefore a routed protocol such as IP is necessary to allow the routers to find the correct destination network. The public Internet is the obvious example of a huge Internetwork.

- An autonomous system (A.S.) is a group of routers in an Internetwork, which exchange information on which networks they know about, and how to reach them. Autonomous systems are used to define logical groups of routers in a large Internetwork.

So, what does a router have to do to be able to route traffic? It comes down to 3 major decisions, which each routing protocol makes in its own way.

1. The protocol of the hosts must be recognized by the router that is sending or receiving traffic. Such protocols include TCP/IP, IPX, Appletalk, DECNET etc.

2. The router must have an entry in its routing table indicating that the destination network exists and is reachable. If there is no mention of the destination network in the routing table, or if the network is not reachable, then the router will either discard the packet, and produce an error message, or send the packet to a predefined location. This last option is called a default route, and is used to have a router send unknown data to a router that has a fuller overview of the Internetwork.

3. If the router has found that it can route the packet, then it must know over which interface to send the packet to get it closer to the destination network. Routing protocols use metrics as a method to find the best route to a destination network. A small metric indicates a fast route, a higher metric indicates a slower route. Obviously the router will send the packet over the interface which forms the start of the fastest route. Routers can also send data over multiple circuits if programmed to do so. This is called 'load balancing' and makes it possible to use bandwidth from multiple circuits to route traffic to one and the same destination. The packet will then have to be encapsulated for the media it is to be sent over, such as Ethernet, Token Ring, Serial circuits, etc.

What does a routing table look like?

Using the command 'show ip route' will show routing entries similar to the following;

```
D    168.109.60.0 [90/742239] via 10.45.17.254, 4:32:44
Serial 0
```

Although all the routing protocols have the job of finding routing table information, they use different mechanisms to obtain this information. Basically, routing protocols use two methods to discover the world around them: distance vector and link state protocols. There are also protocols that are a combination of the two, or hybrid routing protocols. An example of this is Cisco's EIGRP protocol. The pros and cons of both distance vector and link state routing protocols are discussed here.

As the previous section explained, when a host tries to connect to a host that is on a different network, it sends the data to the router defined in the host as the default gateway. The host can forget about the processes necessary for getting the data to the remote host, even if the host is thousands of miles away.

When a router gets a data packet, it checks the destination IP address in the packet and uses this information to check its own routing table to find a link over which to forward the packet.

The routing table contains a list of networks the router knows it can send packets to, as well as links over which to send the packets. These can be static routes (entered by a system administrator), default routes (a special static route to send unknown destination IP addresses to), or dynamically discovered routes found by using a routing protocol.

Distance vector routing protocols include

- *Routing Information Protocol* (RIP)
- *Interior Gateway Routing Protocol* (IGRP)

Link state routing protocols include

- *Open Shortest Path First* (OSPF)
- *Intermediate System-Intermediate System* (IS-IS)

- *Netware™ Link-Services Protocol* (NLSP) (used in IPX environments)

All routing protocols need to perform these tasks:

- Find neighbors—in other words, routers—that are adjacent to the router, and to which the router can forward packets.

- Find routes to fill the routing table (found from attached networks or learned from information passed on from adjacent routers).

- Assign the best routes, figuring out which route is the best one to take if there is more than one way to get to the destination network.

- Maintain the routing information, so that when the Internetwork changes, the router still makes the right decisions about where to forward packets.

3.4.1 Router Packet Switching

Although this might seem like a contradiction, a router does switch. When a router receives a packet, the packet is led through the router from the inbound interface to the outbound interface. The way in which this works will be explained.

The switching process uses the output of the routing protocol, the routing table, to determine which interface to use to send the packet on its way. This is done in four steps.

1. When a packet arrives on the inbound interface, it is checked to see if it is not corrupted (CRC), and then stored in router memory.

2. The router checks the destination address in the packet, and tries to find a match in the routing table. If this is successful, it finds the next hop address to send the packet to, and the interface in the router that is used to connect to the next hop.

3. The router now finds the OSI layer 2 address of the next hop device. For example on IP LAN environments this can be found in the ARP table (show ip arp), or be found using the ARP protocol. WAN connections can have varying methods for finding the hardware address to send to.

4. The router now uses the found information to rewrite the header of the packet, creates a new CRC checksum, and sends the packet to the outbound interface. The outbound interface puts the packet on the wire, and the cycle is complete.

Cisco routers can make use of dedicated hardware, or differing software strategies to speed up this process. Most of these try to reduce the time spent looking through the routing table for the destination address. Others try to optimize the speed at which packets enter and leave the same physical interface. A full discussion of these features falls outside the scope of this chapter.

3.5 Distance-Vector Routing Protocols

Distance-vector routing algorithms keep track of how to reach destination networks by receiving the routing tables from adjacent (neighbor) routers.

A router examines the networks to which it is directly connected and puts them in its routing table with a metric (distance) of 0. The router then passes on all the routes it has discovered to all the neighbor routers it knows of, by sending its routing table to each neighbor.

A neighbor router reads the routing table, increases the metric to show that an additional router needs to be crossed to get to the destination network, and adds the routing information to its own routing table. This routing table then is sent off to all the neighbors it knows of.

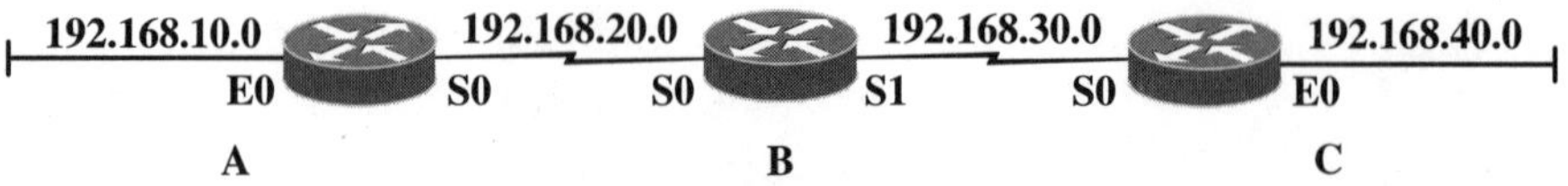

Figure 3-1
Hops in a routing
table

Figure 3-1
Hops in a routing
table

INT.	Network	Hop
E0	192.168.10.0	0
S0	192.168.20.0	0
S0	192.168.30.0	1
S0	192.168.40.0	2

A

INT.	Network	Hop
S0	192.168.10.0	1
S0	192.168.20.0	0
S1	192.168.30.0	0
S1	192.168.40.0	1

B

INT.	Network	Hop
E0	192.168.10.0	2
S0	192.168.20.0	1
S0	192.168.30.0	0
S0	192.168.40.0	0

C

The distance a router puts in its routing table is called a *hop count* or *metric* (see Figure 3-1). Usually the word *hop count* is used for the older routing protocols, where they simply counted the number of routers (hops) necessary to get to the destination network. RIP, for example, is such a routing protocol. It uses the hop count as the only method for determining the best route to a destination network. However, RIP will use multiple paths to reach a single destination if the hop counts of the routes are the same. More modern protocols add more information than just the hop count, and there the word *metric* is used. Information about the way in which Cisco's IGRP protocol uses metrics is discussed later in this chapter.

The routers must maintain a routing table with the following information:

- The destination network address that has been learned.
- Information on where to send the packets for that network (the vector).
- The metric for the destination network over that particular link (the distance). See Table 3-3.

Not everything is perfect, though, and routing loops are the main problem of distance vector protocols. Because the router does not have a complete view of the network, it cannot decide whether a packet is being looped.

Table 3-3

Routing table entry

Routing Table Variable	Explanation
D	Shows which routing protocol was used to learn about this route (D=EIGRP)
168.109.60.0	The IP network address of the destination network
90	The administrative distance of this route (assigns a priority level to the route, see Chapters 3–10)
742239	The metric (a number indicating the distance and speed to the destination)
10.45.17.254	The ip address of the interface of the next hop router
4:32:44	The age of this routing entry
Serial 0	The interface on this router to send the data over

If router A sends its routing table to router B, and it sends it on to router C, and vice versa, then each router knows about all the networks in the Internetwork. Figure 3-2 indicates the stages from a converged network to a count-to-infinity situation.

This method does have some drawbacks, though:

1. The Internetwork is converged. The tables show that the network 192.168.40.0 is correctly entered into all the routing tables. Then the link to network 192.168.40.0 breaks!

2. Router C removes the network entry from its routing table and starts looking for an alternative path to the network. Router A still thinks it can send packets to network 192.168.40.0 through router B with a hop count of 2.

3. Router C gets Router B's routing table in an update and sees the 192.168.40.0 network with a hop count of 1. This is put into router C's routing table with an incremented hop count of 2.

4. Router B gets a routing update from router C with the increased hop count of 2 (was 0) and therefore increments its own routing table entry to 3.

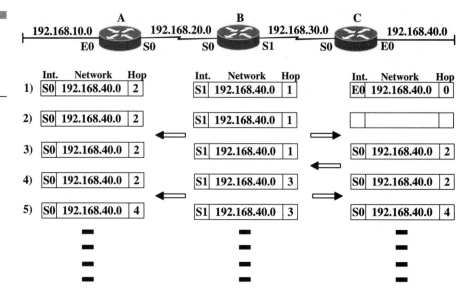

5. Router C and router A get an update from router B and update their hop counts to 4.

This keeps on bouncing back and forth until things go horribly wrong. This situation is called *count to infinity.*

Luckily, there are some solutions to the problem, as the following sections explain.

3.5.1 Hop-Count Limit

IP RIP protocol defines a maximum of 16 hops within an Internetwork. This does not stop the preceding problem from occurring, but when it does, and the hop count increments, it stops at 16, and the RIP protocol assumes the route is unreachable. The problem is that if the network really is so large that it has more than 16 hops from one end to another, RIP cannot route over the complete Internetwork.

3.5.2 Split Horizon

Split horizon is used to avoid routing loops by not allowing routes learned through a certain interface to be advertised out through the same interface again.

A problem occurs when multilink interfaces are used, such as ISDN or Frame Relay multipoint.

A router with an ISDN Bri interface, for example, can connect to two routers—such as router A and router B—over the two data channels offered by the Bri circuit.

When split horizon is enabled, it does not return the routing updates learned from the ISDN interface back to the interface. So updates sent by router A are not sent to router B, and updates from router B are not sent to router A.

Creating virtual point-to-point interfaces—one for each link to a router—can solve this problem. In this way, the router treats each virtual interface as a dedicated link to another router, enabling split horizon operation. The virtual interfaces are mapped to the multipoint physical interface, such as the ISDN Bri, which simply forwards the traffic from the virtual interfaces.

For ISDN connections, Cisco's dialer interfaces can be used to accomplish this. For Frame Relay point-to-point, subinterfaces can be used.

3.5.3 Hold-Down Timers

Hold-down timers keep routers from accepting route updates that would erroneously re-enable an invalid route by disabling the acceptance of new routing information for that specific route. During the hold-down period, the network can converge and eliminate all invalid routes to the faulty network.

When the hold-down state is in effect, the router accepts only two types of routing updates for the specific route before the hold-down timer expires:

- A router advertises a route with a better metric than the one it originally had. This enables topology changes in a network to be accepted without too much convergence delay.

- The router that sent the original message indicating that the network was inaccessible sends a message that the network is reachable. The hold-down timer is removed and the route reinstated. This type of routing helps avoids problems when a link is unstable and frequent route updates are sent through the network about its status.

3.5.4 Triggered Updates

A triggered update is an update that is sent by a router when an important change is detected, such as a link failure or a change in metric. Normally, routers only send updates after a specific time (for example, 30 seconds for RIP), but triggered updates happen as changes arise.

Triggered updates allow routers to learn about important events quickly, and they help avoid the generation of routing loops. However, without the help of hold-down timers, this method is not infallible. A triggered update can get dropped in a busy network, or a router could get the update after it has sent its regular routing update, with the faulty or changed route still intact.

3.5.5 Poison Reverse

Poison reverse is a method that helps the network converge more quickly and helps remove large routing loops, working together with the triggered updates and hold-down timers.

When a router finds that it cannot reach a destination network, it sends out a triggered update. In this update, the router tells surrounding routers that the route is still available, but with the highest metric possible, "poisoning" the route. This special case means that the route is unreachable. The routers typically react to this by removing the route from the routing table and putting it in hold-down mode. The high metric also is propagated to the routers downstream, so the faulty route is quickly passed through the network.

3.5.6 Link State Protocols

Link state routing protocols work using the link state algorithm. This system works by informing each router in an *autonomous system* (AS) about all the other routers in the same AS and to which networks they are directly connected. In this way, each router can build a complete picture of the whole AS and determine the best routes to all networks itself. Instead of passing whole routing tables to each other, link state-based routers only send link change updates to each other. To build the picture of an AS, the routers must complete the following tasks:

1. Each router finds information about any connected routers (adjacencies). When an adjacency is defined, the router regularly sends Hello packets to these neighbors to be sure they are still reachable.

2. The router sends out *link state packets* (LSPs) to all these neighbors, informing them about all the networks it is attached to. One LSP is generated for each network the router knows of. The receiving routers forward these LSPs to all their neighbors and so on, until all the routers in the AS have received the information.

3. Each router stores the information it receives from all the LSPs, and with this, it builds a topology database. Because all routers should receive all the LSPs, all the topology databases should be the same.

4. The *shortest path first* (SPF) process calculates the best (shortest) routes to all networks based on the topology database. If this information were presented graphically, it would look like a tree, with the router as root.

5. The router uses this information to feed routing information to the routing table.

3.6 Topology Changes

When a change in the network occurs, the first router to notice builds an LSP packet containing the changes to the links or neighbors and sends it to the network.

As soon as a router receives an LSP packet, it stores this information. The SPF algorithm then is rerun to completely recalculate the topology table and insert the correct information into the routing table.

This mechanism avoids routing loop problems like the distance vector system has and is generally more stable, because all routers have a complete view of the Internetwork.

There are also some downsides to the link state protocol. If a link goes down, for example, and two routers report the link as inoperative in an LSP, but one sends the update over a slow link and the other over a fast link, problems can occur.

Suppose that a link failure lasts only a short while, and an LSP receiving router has just recalculated the topology table, based on the LSP that was received over a fast link. Then it receives two new LSPs—one coming over the fast link, telling it that the link has been restored, and the other coming over the slow link telling it that the link has failed. What must the router do? Reinstate the route, or leave it as inoperative.

This problem can cause major problems. The larger the network becomes, the larger the risk of such problems (see Figure 3-3).

Another problem is what happens during network instability. In this case, the topology tables will be updated frequently, but to guarantee a reliable delivery of the LSPs to enable convergence in an Internetwork, a stable network is necessary. The Internetwork will not become stable without the prompt delivery of the LSPs, however. One way to partially avoid this problem is to have the router forward a received LSP packet to the neighboring routers before it recalculates the topology.

To solve these problems, a number of techniques can be used:

■ There is a configurable LSP timer for the periodically sent LSPs. Increasing this timer makes the Internetwork less susceptible to instability due to short failures.

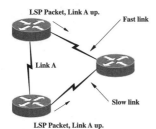

Figure 3-3
A sequencing problem when receiving routing update packets.

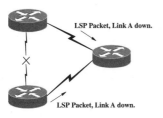

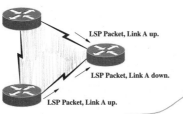

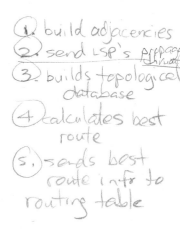

(handwritten notes)
1. build adjacencies
2. send LSP's propagate throughout net
3. builds topological database
4. calculates best route
5. sends best route info to routing table

(handwritten notes)
① you
⓪ builds adjacencies
② sends LSP's
Router says "I have network 1"
LSP 1 "I have network 1"
LSP 2 "I have network 2"
LSP 3 "I have network 3"

(handwritten notes)
③ Each router takes all LSP's from all the routers and builds a topological database. All routers receive all LSP's

■ For routers connected to a common network, such as a LAN, one router can be designated as a target router for LSP updates. Instead of all the routers talking to each other, they send their updates to this *designated router* (DR), which in turn updates all the routers with one and the same Internetwork overview.

■ A large Internetwork can be split into smaller autonomous systems, so the routers in each separate system only receive and send updates to members of the same AS. This decreases the amount of update traffic and decreases the amount of processor power required to perform the SPF algorithm.

■ In some versions of link state protocols, it is possible to time stamp the LSP packets so that out-of-sequence updates can be ignored.

These techniques and the mechanisms behind these enhancements are discussed in greater detail in Chapters 5, "Configuring OSPF in a Single Area," and 6, "Configuring OSPF in Multiple Areas."

3.7 Comparing Distance Vector to Link State

Table 3-4

Distance vector-link state overview

Distance Vector	Link State
Does record neighbor routers, only records network IP addresses.	Discovers neighbors, and communicates with them to ensure that they are reachable using Hello packets.
Detects failures when a routing table entry is not received within a certain period.	Discovers failures when a neighbor does not respond to a predefined amount of Hello packets.
Low overhead for the router CPU and memory.	Higher overhead for the router, because topology tables must be stored and SPF algorithms must be run for every topology change.
Higher bandwidth use due to routing whole tables.	Lower bandwidth use, although the amount needed increases dramatically on large or unstable Internetworks.
Fixed-period update timing gives slow convergence.	Updates only the information that has changed, as it happens. Faster convergence.
Routers assimilate all route information from their neighbors into their own routing tables. These routers only learn about directly connected networks.	Routers receive LSPs from all other routers in the Internetwork and build a database of all the best routes to all networks. In this way, routers have a complete view of the network.
When a router detects a change in the Internetwork, it updates its routing table and passes this information on during periodic routing table updates.	When a router detects a change in the Internetwork, it sends updates to all the routers on the network.
In the case of no changes, the route updates are performed at periodic intervals (usually, one minute).	If no changes are detected, the updates are sent out after 30 minutes to two hours.

Table 3-5

Routing protocol
scalability overview

Feature	RIP v1	RIP v2	IGRP	EIGRP	OSPF	IS-IS
Link State/ Distance Vector	DV	DV	DV	Hybrid	LS	LS
Classless (CL) / Classful (CF) routing	CF	CL	CF	CL	CL	CL
Metric, Hop count/ Composite/Cost	Hop	Hop	Comp	Comp	Cost	Cost
Load balancing over equal cost paths	Yes	Yes	Yes	Yes	Yes	Yes
Load balancing over unequal cost paths	No	No	Yes	Yes	No	No
Metric limit	16	16	255	255	200	1024
Scalability, typicalon a scale of 1-10	1	3	5	7	7	10

Table 3-6

Classless/classful
routing comprison

Feature	Classful	Classless
Routing protocols	RIPv1, IGRP	RIPv2,EIGRP, OSPF, IS-IS, BGP
Subnet mask includedin routing update	No	Yes
Subnet mask consistent throughout Internetwork	Yes	Not necessarily
Summarization possible anywhere in the Internetwork	No	Yes

A complete description of EIGRP and OSPF will be given in the following chapters.

3.8 IGRP Routing Metrics and Cisco Administrative Distances

This section covers IGRP's five possible variables on which it makes its routing metric decisions. It covers how the two main variables (bandwidth and delay) are used and why the others often are considered a liability to network stability. This section ends with a discussion on the concept of administrative distances and the way Cisco implements them.

You can configure IGRP to consider up to five variables when making routing decisions.

3.8.1 Bandwidth

Bandwidth is a measure of the speed of the physical network connected to an interface. A 64KB serial connection has a bandwidth of 64,000 bits per second. Cisco uses a factor of 1,000 in the bandwidth command. Entering the command `bandwidth 64` on a serial interface results in a configured bandwidth of 64KB. Although it is a static number used for metric calculation only, it does not necessarily reflect the actual bandwidth of the link, because the bandwidth is not measured dynamically. Cisco's default bandwidth of a serial link is 1544, for example, whether you are using an ISND-BRI line or a T1 interface. You can change the bandwidth value by using the `bandwidth` command. Bandwidth is displayed as BW in the output of the `show interface` command.

3.8.2 Delay (Latency?)

Delay is a measure to indicate how much time a packet spends in the switching fabric that forms the link between two routers. Slower links have longer delays, and faster links have shorter delays. A Frame Relay link, for example, often has a higher value for delay than a leased line link; this is caused by the larger amount of active switching components between source and destination. The number used on the interface is not determined dynamically; it is configured to a static value by a network administrator or left at the Cisco default. Because it is arbitrary, this variable also can be used to influence the routing protocol in the way it chooses a best route. It's important to realize that this number is *not* generated by the router; it has a standard default value that can be changed by the administrator. Delay is displayed as `DLY`, in units of milliseconds, in the output of the `show interface` command.

3.8.3 Load

In Cisco terms, load is a measurement that is taken over a period of time and averaged. It doesn't reflect an exact instant in time but is meant to reflect link use. Being an eight-bit number, load is represented in the output of the `show interface` command as a fraction of 255, such as 30/255. The minimum of this value is 1, reflecting a minimally loaded link. The maximum is 255, which is a 100 percent loaded link.

3.8.4 Maximum Transmission Unit (MTU)

MTU represents the largest frame a link can accept. The IOS implementation of IGRP tracks the smallest MTU along each route. MTU, however, is *not* used in the composite metric calculation for IGRP.

3.8.5 Reliability

In Cisco lingo, reliability is a measurement that is taken over a period of time and averaged. It doesn't reflect an exact instant in time but is meant to reflect the condition of a link. It can incorporate how often the link transitions from an up state to a down state, as well as the error rate of frames arriving on the link. In contrast to bandwidth and load, reliability is measured dynamically and is expressed in an eight-bit number, where 255 reflects a 100 percent reliable link, and 1 represents a minimally reliable link. In the output of the `show interface` command, reliability is shown as a fraction of 255—for example, 204/255.

3.8.6 Considerations on Load and Reliability

Load and reliability are useful values to include in the metric of a link. It would be dangerous to include them as bursty traffic, however, without averaging the values over a certain amount of time, or short bursts of circuit errors could make the metric change wildly, destabilizing the network in the process.

If a link has a burst of traffic or errors, for example, and therefore the metric increases enormously, the router would react by deciding that the route is invalid and start the whole process of recalculating a better route. As soon as the next metric is recalculated, the router finds that the link is fine and has to recalculate again.

To avoid this problem, the router records the five-second load and reliability values, and averages them over a five-minute period. This effectively removes any peak values.

3.8.7 IGRP Metric Calculation

IGRP's composite metric to determine the best route is calculated as the following:

$$\text{metric} = [k1*BW_{IGRP(min)} + (k2*BW_{IGRP(min)})/(256-LOAD) + K3*DLY_{IGRP(sum)}] * [k5/(RELIABILITY+k4)]$$

where $BW_{IGRP(min)}$ is the minimum BW_{IGRP} of all the outgoing interfaces along the route to the destination, and $DLY_{IGRP(sum)}$ is the total $DLY_{IGRP(sum)}$ of the route.

The values k1 through k5 are configurable weights; their default values are k1=k3=1 and k2=k4=k5=0. These defaults can be changed with this command:

```
metric weights tos k1 k2 k3 k4 k5
```

if k5 is set to zero. The k5/(RELIABILITY+k4) term is not used.
Given the default values for k1 through k5, the composite metric calculation used by IGRP reduces to the default metric:

$$\text{metric} = \text{BW}_{\text{IGRP(min)}} + \text{DLY}_{\text{IGRP(sum)}}$$

To find the value for BW, find the smallest of all the bandwidth values from outgoing interfaces and divide 10 million by that number (the bandwidth is scaled by 10 million in kilobits per second).

To find the delay, add all the delays from the outgoing interfaces and divide this number by 10, because the delay is entered into the router in tens of microseconds (usecs).

Based on this formula and experience, Cisco recommends that only bandwidth and delay be used because of the following factors:

- Load can cause routing instability. Rerouting around a heavily loaded link reduces the load on that link. This causes the router to reconverge on the link it just rerouted around, and the cycle starts all over again.

- Reliability also is a feature that should not be used extensively; errors on a link can come and go in bursts. If a link is very unreliable, consider shutting it down and waiting for it to be repaired instead of risking the stability of the whole Internetwork.

- The process of convergence is in itself something to be avoided. While reconvergence is in progress, some routers might have an incomplete routing table and drop packets that have unknown destination network addresses. Using many variables in the routing process can cause frequent recalculations of best routes and therefore frequent reconvergence.

- When using the *maximum transmit unit* (MTU) to aid in the routing decisions, be aware that modern protocols such at FTP and HTTP are not bound to a fixed-packet size. So using this variable can complicate the process and create more confusion than necessary. In certain cases, however, it can be useful, such as when trying to avoid sending known amounts of traffic with a large MTU over a small MTU-type media.

We have now seen how IGRP determines its metric.

Using these metrics, IGRP is able to load balance over a maximum of 6 paths. For this to happen the metrics of the routes must lie within 1% of each other. This feature is enabled by default.

3.8.8 Manipulating IGRP's Bandwidth and Delay Variables

This section provides examples of how manipulating the router's delay and bandwidth variables can significantly influence IGRP's routing decisions. It includes a practical example of IGRP's superiority to RIP when it comes to building flexible networks. Apart from this one comparison, RIP will no longer be mentioned, because the Cisco IOS does not provide any means of manipulating RIP tables to override the default hop-based metric used by this protocol. Now consider the network shown in Figure 3-4.

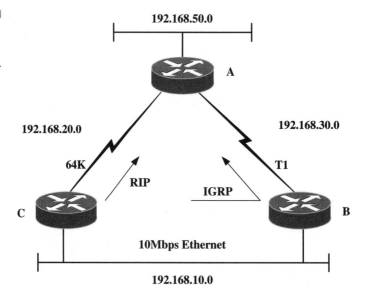

Figure 3-4
A network running
RIP and IGRP

In this particular network, despite the speed difference between the links C -> A and C -> B -> A, RIP would still choose the slower ("less desirable," in Cisco terminology) path from router C to router A, being the one-hop route. To overcome this inconvenience, a more advanced routing protocol was developed—IGRP.

As discussed earlier in this chapter, IGRP combines five variables to form a metric that replaces RIP's simple hop count: bandwidth, delay, load, reliability, and MTU. Complying with Cisco's recommendation of only using bandwidth and delay variables, the overall metric calculation for any path between a router and remote network is based on two conditions:

- The minimum bandwidth of any link in the path to the destination network
- The sum of all delays in the path to the destination network

3.8.9 Using the Delay Variable to Influence the Routing Process

The next example proves the concept, because router C can be configured to load share traffic destined for network 192.168.50.0 over its links to router A and router B. Router C is led to believe that it has two equal-cost routes to 192.168.50.0 by administratively changing the delay parameter.

In the next output example, router C has only one route installed to 192.168.50.0 (see Figure 3-5). To enable this initial situation, all the variables on the router interfaces have been adjusted so that they are the same, regardless of the media type.

To have router C install the alternative path to the 192.168.50.0 network via router B, you can manipulate the `delay` command on interface serial 0 of router C. This is because you want to make router C believe that its link to 192.168.50.0 via router A has a total delay that equals the total delay of the link to 192.168.50.0 when routing through router B.

Recall that router C is not aware of the fact that router B is not connected to 192.168.50.0 and therefore forwards packets intended

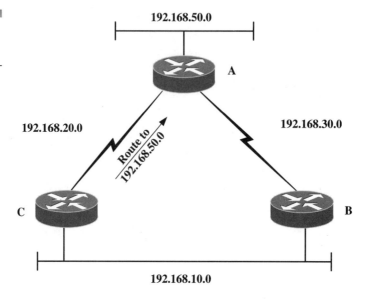

Figure 3-5
Router C with one
route to router A

for 192.168.50.0 through router A. The thing to do is to make router
C believe that router B is just as far away from the 192.168.50.0 network as router A. Figure 3-6 shows where the delay must be
increased to accomplish this.

As this example illustrates, these variables are quite powerful. The
next series of IOS examples shows how to enforce routing decisions.

The following example shows the routing table of router C, where
the single route to network 192.168.50.0 is visible:

```
C#show ip route
Codes: C - connected, S - static, I - IGRP, R - RIP, M -
mobile, B - BGP
     D - EIGRP, EX - EIGRP external, O - OSPF, IA - OSPF
inter area
     N1 - OSPF NSSA external type 1, N2 - OSPF NSSA external
type 2
     E1 - OSPF external type 1, E2 - OSPF external type 2, E
- EGP
     i - IS-IS, L1 - IS-IS level-1, L2 - IS-IS level-2, * -
candidate default
     U - per-user static route, o - ODR

Gateway of last resort is not set
```

Figure 3-6
Increasing the delay
variable on the router

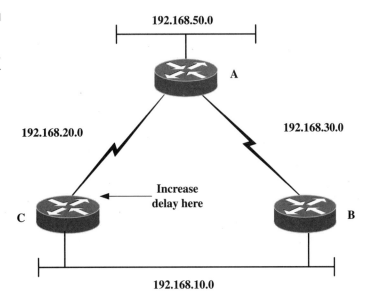

```
I       192.168.50.0/24 [100/80225] via 192.168.20.1, 00:00:21,
        Serial0
C       192.168.10.0/24 is directly connected, Ethernet0
I       192.168.30.0/24 [100/82125] via 192.168.10.253,
        00:00:22, Ethernet0
            [100/82125] via 192.168.20.1, 00:00:21, Serial0
C       192.168.20.0/24 is directly connected, Serial0
```

Then the delay variable on serial 0 is adjusted to give the route directly to router A and the route through router B the same total delay.

```
C#configure terminal
Enter configuration commands, one per line.   End with
CNTL/Z.
C(config)#interface serial 0
C(config-if)#delay 4000
C(config-if)#end
C#
```

After the reconvergence period, the output of the show ip route command can be viewed to verify that the router now sees two routes to the destination network:

```
C#show ip route
Codes: C - connected, S - static, I - IGRP, R - RIP, M -
mobile, B - BGP
    D - EIGRP, EX - EIGRP external, O - OSPF, IA - OSPF
inter area
    N1 - OSPF NSSA external type 1, N2 - OSPF NSSA external
type 2
    E1 - OSPF external type 1, E2 - OSPF external type 2, E
- EGP
    i - IS-IS, L1 - IS-IS level-1, L2 - IS-IS level-2, * -
candidate default
    U - per-user static route, o - ODR
Gateway of last resort is not set
I    192.168.50.0/24 [100/82225] via 192.168.20.1, 00:00:12,
Serial0
        [100/82225] via 192.168.10.253, 00:00:18, Ethernet0
C    192.168.10.0/24 is directly connected, Ethernet0
I    192.168.30.0/24 [100/82125] via 192.168.10.253,
00:00:18, Ethernet0
C    192.168.20.0/24 is directly connected, Serial0
C#
```

The variables can be checked in the following section of router C's configuration using the show interface serial 0 command: The delay on serial 1 is increased to 40,000. The units are expressed in units of milliseconds, so 4,000 equals 40,000.

```
C#show interface serial 0
Serial0 is up, line protocol is up
  Hardware is QUICC Serial
  Internet address is 192.168.20.2/24
  MTU 1500 bytes, BW 128 Kbit, DLY 40000 usec, rely 255/255,
load 1/255
  Encapsulation PPP, loopback not set, keepalive set (10 sec)
    .
    .
    .
```

If the command show ip route is issued, followed by a network address (in this case, 192.168.50.0), the router limits the output of the routing table to information relevant to the requested network address. This can be very useful when dealing with a router that has a large routing table. In the output of this command, router C now has two equal-cost paths, or parallel routes, to 192.168.50.0:

```
C#show ip route 192.168.50.0
Routing entry for 192.168.50.0/24
  Known via "igrp 10", distance 100, metric 82225
  Redistributing via igrp 10
  Advertised by igrp 10 (self originated)
  Last update from 192.168.20.1 on Serial0, 00:00:10 ago
  Routing Descriptor Blocks:
  * 192.168.20.1, from 192.168.20.1, 00:00:10 ago, via
Serial0
    Route metric is 82225, traffic share count is 1
    Total delay is 41000 microseconds, minimum bandwidth is
128 Kbit
    Reliability 255/255, minimum MTU 1500 bytes
    Loading 1/255, Hops 0
    192.168.10.253, from 192.168.10.253, 00:00:22 ago, via
    Ethernet0
    Route metric is 82225, traffic share count is 1
    Total delay is 41000 microseconds, minimum bandwidth is
    128 Kbit
    Reliability 255/255, minimum MTU 1500 bytes
    Loading 3/255, Hops 1
  C#
```

The next example shows the output of the `debug ip igrp transactions` command on router C, which shows both routes to 192.168.50.0 being advertised to router C with the same metric. The first message in the output is from router A; the second is from router B. This explains the reason why the previous routing table has both routes in it.

Note that when debugging when connected to the router using Telnet, the `terminal monitor` command must be issued to see the results. This is not necessary when connected to the physical console port of the router. Also, the `undebug all` command at the end stops the debugging process and frees up the processor for other tasks:

```
C#terminal monitor
C#debug ip igrp transactions
IGRP protocol debugging is on
IGRP: sending update to 255.255.255.255 via Ethernet0
(192.168.10.252)
    network 192.168.20.0, metric=82125
IGRP: sending update to 255.255.255.255 via Serial0
(192.168.20.2)
    network 192.168.10.0, metric=80125
```

```
       network 192.168.30.0, metric=82125
IGRP: received update from 192.168.10.253 on Ethernet0
       network 192.168.50.0, metric 82225 (neighbor 80225)
       network 192.168.30.0, metric 82125 (neighbor 80125)
       network 192.168.20.0, metric 84125 (neighbor 82125)
IGRP: received update from 192.168.20.1 on Serial0
       network 192.168.50.0, metric 82225 (neighbor 1100)
       network 192.168.30.0, metric 84125 (neighbor 80125)
C#undebug all
```

NOTE: *The most important point to understand is that a router uses the delay on an interface over which it receives a routing advertisement to determine the metrics for the routes being advertised. In other words, delay is applied on inbound advertisements, not outbound. The delay variable was not changed on router A. Instead, it was changed on router C to force router C to accept router A's advertisement for 192.168.50.0 with a higher metric than the default.*

Router C now load balances over the two links on a session-by-session basis or a packet-by-packet basis. This may result in better use of the links between router C and router A. However, if router B is already sending enough traffic to router A to keep the link nearly full, the extra traffic from router C may cause it to be oversubscribed. Care should be used when manipulating routing tables and changing the routing in a way that is different from their default behavior. Sometimes the end results may not be what was expected.

3.8.10 Issues with Manipulating the Delay Variable

Contrary to what was just covered, it is not possible to have *both* router B and router C load balance their traffic to 192.168.50.0.

The total delay on both paths from router B's perspective has to be equal in order for router B to accept router C's *and* router A's advertisements for 192.168.50.0.

The delay on router C's serial 0 interface was changed to 40,000 usecs to force router C to load share. So router B's serial 0 interface delay would have to be changed to 60,000 usecs (20,000 usecs for the link to router C and 40,000 for the link between router C and router A). As a result, this would affect the total delay that router C's path to 192.168.50.0 via router B encounters. Router C now would have a path to 192.168.50.0, via router A, with a delay of 40,000 usecs and a path to 192.168.50.0 via router B with a total delay of 80,000 usecs (20,000 for the link to router B and the additional 60,000 usecs for router B's link to router A).

As with most problems in the networking world, there is a solution. Using the bandwidth variable, this problem can be solved. Read on to find out how!

3.8.11 Understanding the Effects of Manipulating the Bandwidth Variable

This example will illustrate that there is a difference when manipulating the routing process using the bandwidth variable. In contrast to the delay variable, the bandwidth is not cumulative. Only the lowest bandwidth over any hop path is taken into account when determining a metric for a route.

Observe how changing the bandwidth on router B's serial interface 0 affects the metric that router B advertises out for network 192.168.50.0.

Consider the previous situation, where router C has two routes of identical metric to network 192.168.50.0. Changing the bandwidth on the link between router B and router A changes router C's routing decisions.

The capture `igrp transactions` shows what router B advertises before changing the bandwidth:

```
B#debug ip igrp transactions
IGRP protocol debugging is on
B#
```

```
06:38:05: IGRP: sending update to 255.255.255.255 via
Ethernet0 (192.168.10.253)
06:38:05:         network 192.168.50.0, metric=80225
06:38:05:         network 192.168.30.0, metric=80125
b#
```

The following output from router B shows how to change the bandwidth variable. This example tells the router that it has a 64 Kbit circuit connected to the serial 0 interface instead of a 128 Kbit circuit:

```
B#configure terminal
Enter configuration commands, one per line.  End with
CNTL/Z.
B(config)#interface serial 0
B(config-if)#bandwidth 64
B(config-if)#end
B#
```

This can be checked using the show interface serial 0 command:

```
B#show interface serial 0
Serial0 is up, line protocol is up
  Hardware is HD64570
  Internet address is 192.168.30.2/24
  MTU 1500 bytes, BW 64 Kbit, DLY 20000 usec, rely 255/255,
load 1/255
  Encapsulation PPP, loopback not set, keepalive set (10 sec)
```

The following outputs are from the debug ip igrp transactions and show ip route commands on router C. These examples show the changes in the routing information that router B sends to router C before and after the change in bandwidth variable.
Before:

```
C#debug ip igrp transactions
IGRP protocol debugging is on
IGRP: received update from 192.168.20.1 on Serial0
    network 192.168.50.0, metric 82225 (neighbor 1100)
IGRP: received update from 192.168.10.253 on Ethernet0
    network 192.168.50.0, metric 82225 (neighbor 80225)
```

```
C#sh ip route
Codes: C - connected, S - static, I - IGRP, R - RIP, M -
mobile, B - BGP
    D - EIGRP, EX - EIGRP external, O - OSPF, IA - OSPF
inter area
    N1 - OSPF NSSA external type 1, N2 - OSPF NSSA external
type 2
    E1 - OSPF external type 1, E2 - OSPF external type 2, E
- EGP
    i - IS-IS, L1 - IS-IS level-1, L2 - IS-IS level-2, * -
candidate default
    U - per-user static route, o - ODR
Gateway of last resort is not set
I    192.168.50.0/24 [100/82225] via 192.168.20.1, 00:00:38,
Serial0
                        [100/82225] via 192.168.10.253,
00:00:09, Ethernet0
```

After:

```
C#debug ip igrp transactions
IGRP protocol debugging is on
IGRP: received update from 192.168.20.1 on Serial0
    network 192.168.50.0, metric 82225 (neighbor 1100)
IGRP: received update from 192.168.10.253 on Ethernet0
    network 192.168.30.0, metric 160250 (neighbor 158250)
C#show ip route
Codes: C - connected, S - static, I - IGRP, R - RIP, M -
mobile, B - BGP
    D - EIGRP, EX - EIGRP external, O - OSPF, IA - OSPF
inter area
    N1 - OSPF NSSA external type 1, N2 - OSPF NSSA external
type 2
    E1 - OSPF external type 1, E2 - OSPF external type 2, E
- EGP
    i - IS-IS, L1 - IS-IS level-1, L2 - IS-IS level-2, * -
candidate default
    U - per-user static route, o - ODR
Gateway of last resort is not set
I    192.168.50.0/24 [100/82225] via 192.168.20.1,
00:00:33, Serial0
```

These variables can be useful to alleviate specific problems on routers and are easily controlled on the tiny Internetwork used in the examples. Caution must be used on larger networks, however, where changing these parameters could lead to major instability.

3.9 Command Review IGRP

Table 3-7

Command
overview IGRP

Command	Description
Bandwidth *kilobits*	Specifies the bandwidth parameter, in kilobits per second, on an interface. Used by some routing protocols (such as IGRP) to calculate metrics. Has no influence on the actual bandwidth of the data link.
Delay *tens-of-milliseconds*	Specifies the delay parameter, in tens of milliseconds, on an interface. Used by some routing protocols to calculate metrics. Has no influence on the actual delay of the data link.
ip address *ip-address mask* **[secondary]**	Specifies the IP address and address mask of an interface.
Maximum-paths *maximum*	Specifies the maximum number of parallel routes an IP routing protocol can support, from one to six, with a default of four.
Metric holddown	Toggles the IGRP holddown on/off
Metric maximum-hops *hops*	Specifies the maximum number of hops IGRP can advertise before a route is marked as unreachable, with a maximum of 255 and a default of 100.
Metric weights *tos k1 k2 k3 k4 k5*	Specifies how much weight the bandwidth, load, delay, and reliability parameters should be given in the IGRP and EIGRP metric calculations.
Neighbor ip-address	Defines a unicast address to which a RIP, IGRP, or EGP routing update should be sent.
Network network-number	Specifies the network address of one or more directly connected interfaces on which IGRP, EIGRP, or RIP processes should be enabled.
Offset-list {access-list-number | name}{**in** | **out**} *offset* [*type number*]	Specifies a number of hops (for RIP) or additional delay (for IGRP) to be added to the metrics of incoming or outgoing route advertisements.
Passive-interface type number	Disables the transmission of routing updates on an interface.
Router IGRP autonomous-system	Enables the indicated IGRP routing process on a router.

Command	Description
Show interface [type number]	Displays the configured and monitored characteristics of an interface.
Show ip route [*address* [*mask*]] [*protocol*[*process-ID*]]	Displays the current routing table as a whole or by entry.
Timers basic *update invalid holddown flush* [*sleeptime*]	Adjusts EGP, RIP, or IGRP process timers.
Traffic-share {**balanced** | **min**}	Specifies whether an IGRP or EIGRP routing process should use unequal-cost load balancing or equal cost only.
Validate-update-source	Toggles the source address validation function of RIP and IGRP routing processes.
Variance *multiplier*	Specifies a multiplier by which a route metric can vary from the lower-cost metric and still be included in an unequal-cost load balancing group.

3.10 Administrative Distances

Earlier in this chapter, the term *metric* was described as the overall desirability of a route to a remote (not locally attached) network.

Within Cisco technology, however, there is another concept called *administrative distance,* which is "a subjective analysis of the believability of a routing protocol." In other words, if a router running more than one routing protocol learns about the same network from multiple protocols, the protocol that has the lowest distance associated with it will be the one whose entry is installed in the router's routing table. There are two special types of administrative distance:

- *Connected interface (administrative distance = 0)* This is a network that has been assigned to an interface in a router. Because the distance is 0, it always takes precedence over a route

Figure 3-7
Connected versus
learned distances

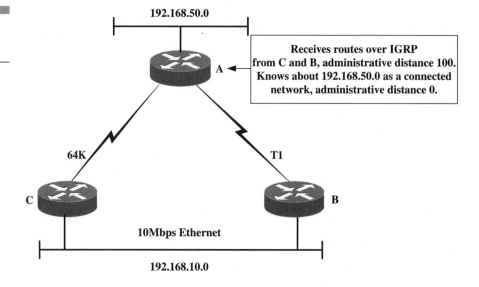

advertised through some other method for the same network. If router B advertises a route to network 192.168.50.0, router A ignores it, because it already has a connected (better) route to this network (see Figure 3-7).

■ *Static routes (administrative distance = 1)*   This is a route that has been manually entered into a router by the system administrator. Router C has a static route configured, indicating that 192.168.50.0 is reachable via router B's interface IP address of 192.168.10.253. This route will be seen to be better than any dynamic route that router C receives from router A, even though Figure 3-8 shows that the path through router A is actually shorter!

There are different types of routing protocols, and Cisco has assigned administrative distances to them (see Table 3-8). The network administrator can give a certain protocol more or less importance in the Internetwork by changing these values. In the following table, the word *internal* means that the route was advertised from within the AS. *External* means it was advertised from a different AS.

Figure 3-8
Static versus dynamic
distances

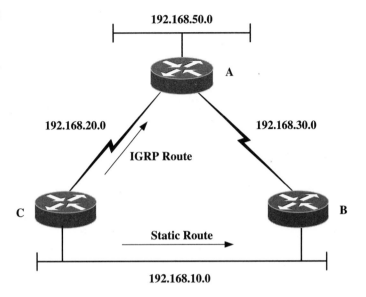

Table 3-8

Administrative
distances overview

Routing Protocol	Administrative Distance
Connected interface	0
Static route	1
Enhanced IGRP summary route (EIGRP)	5
External BGP	20
Internal enhanced IGRP	90
IGRP	100
OSPF	110
IS-IS	115
RIP	120
EGP	140
External Enhanced IGRP	170
Internal BGP	200
Unknown	255

3.11 Chapter Summary

This chapter is important to an overall understanding of routing principles, metrics, and distances. First the basics of IP addressing were discussed, including classful and classless IP addresses. Subnetting was introduced, which is discussed in greater depth in the next chapter.

Distance vector and link state routing protocols were discussed. It is important to understand these principles well, because they will be built on as the book progresses. The process of convergence was also discussed, in which all the routers in an Internetwork try to learn the correct paths to the destination networks. The primary activities of convergence are updating the routing table, removing invalid or bad routes, and preventing bad routes from propagating through the Internetwork. Parallel paths and creating them in IGRP using the delay and bandwidth commands also were discussed.

Finally, this chapter explained the method Cisco uses to decide which routing protocol to believe if multiple protocols are used.

 # 3.12 Frequently Asked Questions (FAQ)

Question: When I attach two networks to my router, I find that both networks can communicate, even without having a routing protocol configured on the router. Is this normal?

Answer: Yes. A router sees networks attached to its interfaces and will route between those interfaces. The routing protocol, such as RIP or IGRP, is there only to learn about networks from other routers and how to send data so it will get there as efficiently as possible.

Question: When I change the `bandwidth` command on a router interface, will I change the speed of the link?

Answer: No. Cisco uses the bandwidth command purely as an indication for various calculations. Because a router is usually a *data terminal equipment* (DTE) device, it receives a clock signal from a modem, which determines the actual bandwidth of a link.

3.13 Case Study

Consider the Internetwork in Figure 3-9.

1. Assuming that all routers have RIP configured, what path will be used to get from network 144.64.198.20 to 152.40.34.12? Write down the path using the router names.

   (A, B, E, G, H, I)

2. What made RIP decide to take that path?

   (RIP calculates its routing decision based only on hop count. So despite the slower links used in the path A-B-E-G-H-I, according to RIP, it's the fastest route because of the lower hop count.)

3. Assuming that all routers have IGRP configured, what path will be used to get from network 144.64.198.20 to 152.40.34.12? Write down the path using the router names.

   (A, B, C, D, F, H, I)

4. What made IGRP decide to take that path?

   (IGRP combines five variables to form a metric that replaces RIP's simple hop count: bandwidth, delay, load, reliability, and MTU. Despite the fact that the path A-B-C-D-F-H-I uses more hops, IGRP sees the speed advantage it has when this path is chosen.)

Figure 3-9
Case study example

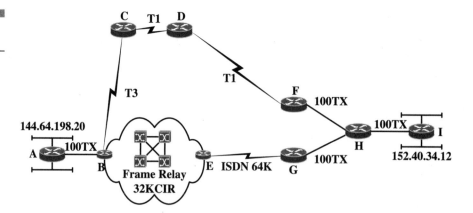

3.14 Questions

1. Which of the following are link state protocols?

    a. IP RIP, AppleTalk, RTMP

    b. IPX RIP, RTMP, NLSP

    c. OSPF, NLSP, IS-IS

    d. IGRP, EIGRP

    e. EIGRP, OSPF, TCP/IP

2. Which statement is *not* true about link state protocols?

    a. Link state advertisements are sent to all routers in an area.

    b. Each router executes the SPF algorithm.

    c. Link state routers keep a topological database of the network.

    d. Link state routers include the originating router's routing table.

    e. Link state routers know of possible alternative paths to a particular network.

3. What is the maximum hop count with most distance vector applications, such as IP RIP?

    a. 14

    b. 12

    c. 13

    d. Configurable

    e. 16

    f. Infinite

4. Which of the following protocols use a composite metric?

    a. IGRP

    b. RIP

    c. EIGRP

    d. OSPF

5. What is the basic function of a router?

    a. Forwarding of packets based on network address

    b. Assembling and disassembling of packets to and from Frame Relay networks

    c. Connecting two networks using a nonrouting protocol

    d. Extending the logical network to get around the maximum Ethernet cable length of 100 meters in 10BASE-T

6. Name two important benefits of using link state routing protocols.

    a. They use several components to calculate the metric of a route.

    b. They only send updates when changes occur in the network.

    c. They are better protocols than distance vector protocols.

    d. They are the only routing protocols supported by Cisco IOS.

    e. They converge faster.

7. Which of the following protocols uses a topology table?

    a. RIP
    b. EIGRP
    c. OSFP
    d. IGRP

8. What command do you use on a Cisco router running EIGRP, to show all the ways that the router learned a given route?

    a. `show eigrp topology`
    b. `show ip route`
    c. `show route`
    d. `show ip eigrp topology`
    e. `show all route`

9. Fill in the blanks by identifying the type of routing protocol that is described by each sentence. Possible answers are DV or LS.

    ■ _LS_ send out updates to other routers if a change in the network occurs.

    ■ _DV_ is the easiest routing protocol to configure.

    ■ RIP and RTMP belong to this group of protocols. _DV_

    ■ _LS_ learns about neighbors to ensure bi-directional communication.

    ■ OSPF is an example of this protocol. _LS_

    ■ _LS_ uses the shortest path first algorithm.

10. List the five variables IGRP uses to compute metrics.

11. On which two conditions does IGRP base its overall metric calculation for any path between a router and remote network?

12. What is the difference between a network and an Internetwork?

13. What is the main difference between classful and classless subnetting?

14. Why were VLSM and CIDR introduced?

15. What are a routing protocol's main tasks?

16. What is the unit of distance that distance vector protocols calculate?

17. How would you define the term *vector* in the context of distance vector protocols?

18. What is the purpose of split horizon?

19. What is the purpose of poison reverse?

20. What is the term to describe a logical group of routers running a link state protocol? *autonomous system*

10. (delay) (bw) bad, mtu, reliability

11. delay + bw

12. network (LAN)
    Internetwork (WAN) group of networks

13. classless subnetting passes the subnet ~~in the~~ it takes bits from the ~~network~~ host and allows the user to create more networks

14. VLSM + CIDR were introduced to alleviate a growing shortage of IP's

15. ~~recognize traffic~~ relay data,
15

3.15 Answers

1. **c**
2. **d**
3. **e**
4. **a** and **c**
5. **a**
6. **b** and **e**
7. **b** and **c**
8. **d**
9. LS, DV, DV, LS, LS, LS
10. ■ Reliability
    ■ Load
    ■ Bandwidth
    ■ MTU
    ■ Delay
11. ■ Cumulative delay over the whole path to the remote network
    ■ Smallest bandwidth value on any hop between the router and remote network
12. A network is a group of hosts that share the same OSI layer 2 infrastructure. In other words, they do not need a router to communicate. An Internetwork is a group of interconnected networks.
13. In the case of classful subnetting, bits are "borrowed" from the host portion of the classful address to create a group of bits used to expand the network potion of the IP address.

    Classless subnetting uses a prefix value that simply assigns a certain amount of bits to the network and host portions of the IP address.
14. VLSM was introduced to increase the amount of usable IP addresses through subnetting. CIDR went on to implement classless subnetting to routing protocols.

15. ■ To gather information about networks not directly connected to the router

■ To find the most efficient path to those networks

■ To maintain and update the information when the network topology changes

16. Metric

17. Distance vector protocols determine two things: where to send data to (the vector) and how far its destination is (distance).

18. Split horizon stops a router from sending route information out the interface from which that route information was learned. This is one of the ways distance vector protocols avoid routing loops.

19. Poison reverse is another way in which routers prevent routing loops. When a route becomes unreachable, the router sends out a routing update with a metric of infinity. This keeps the router from learning about the network from a routing loop.

20. An *Autonomous System* (AS)

CHAPTER 4

Extending IP Addresses

4.1 Objectives Covered in This Chapter

To better understand what is necessary to build a scalable network, the following objectives will be covered.

Table 4-1

BSCN objectives

BSCN Objective
Understand IP addressing issues
Describe IP addressing solutions
Understand hierarchical addressing in an internetwork
Understand Variable Length Subnet Masks (VLSM)
Understand Classless Inter Domain Routing (CIDR)
Understand route summarization

4.2 Chapter Introduction

This chapter goes into some depth on the subject of IP addresses and how they can be used effectively. As the use of the IP protocol has increased dramatically over the past years, it has become increasingly important not to waste the addresses available. The first step to accomplish this was introduced by finding a solution for the wasteful classful addresses. By not grouping IP addresses together into class A, B, and C subnets, and instead allowing network ranges to be "made to fit," it is possible to reduce the amount of wasted space. This flexibility in subnetting is called *variable-length subnet masking* (VLSM).

Another method was devised by assigning a couple of private IP address ranges. These are free for anybody to use but may not be routed across the Internet. So these are fine to use for company-internal Internetworks (intranets), but they can cause problems when reaching outside the boundaries of the company.

As the Internetworks get larger, the amount of routing information the routers must store increases in size also. Here, *classless interdomain routing* (CIDR) helps. Routers can group a number of networks together and advertise them as one network to their neighbors, reducing the routing table size and the size of routing updates.

RFCs, or "request for comments" are well known papers that explain about agreements made, protocols and other IT related subjects. These are free to read, and can be downloaded from various sites on Internet.

A few RFC's that contain the agreements around the subject in this chapter are as follows.

RFC 950 : Subnet Masking : This RFC was the first to describe the use of Subnet masks.

RFC 1518 : Route summarization : A description of using a single IP network address to represent a group of hierarchically organized set IP network addresses.

RFC 1812 : Variable length subnet masking : This RFC goes on where RFC 950 left off. It describes variable length subnet masking, and discusses the pitfalls involved in subnetting in the presence of classful devices.

RFC 1918 : Address allocation for private internets : This RFC describes the use of IP addresses within private networks. These are specially assigned IP addresses which are not forwarded over the Internet, but which can be used within organizations for devices that do not access the Internet directly, or use NAT (network address translation).

RFC 2050 : Classless inter-domain routing. Replaces RFC 1466, which discusses CIDR. This is a method by which Internet routing tables are to be reduced by assigning blocks of IP addresses to Internet service providers (ISPs).

These subjects will be covered in the following chapter, starting with the basics and going on to the more complicated tricks possible with a group of IP addresses.

4.3 Variable-Length Subnet Masks

To better understand the principles discussed in this section, we will first have a look at a common everyday network, the telephone system. These networks are in some ways very similar to IP networks, in that they work with numbers to identify end nodes, and are hierarchical in design. We will have a quick look at how a telephone number is split into various parts, each of which inform a certain layer of the telco's network where the call has to be forwarded to.

As mentioned, a telephone number is split into multiple parts, where numbers lowest in the hierarchy (i.e., nearest the telephone) are placed most to the right, and the numbers higher in the hierarchy are placed more to the left. As we have seen, this is the same case with IP addresses.

When a person makes a local call, the local exchange will notice that the call is being placed to the same 'area' as the call originated, and will know that it does not need to forward the call to a remote exchange. However, if the number includes a different exchange number, and the exchange does not have a direct link to the other exchange, then the call will be forwarded an exchange higher in the hierarchy. This exchange will then find a route all the way back down the hierarchy to the called phone.

See Figure 4-1 for a graphical view.

Figure 4-1

A telephone system, similar to an network

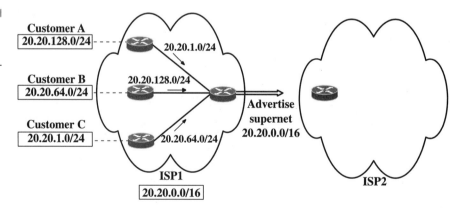

In the figure the telephone with number 555-1234 makes two calls. One to a neighbor with number 555-1235, and another to a distant friend with number 666-2345.

When the first call is received by the local exchange it finds that caller and called areas (555) are the same so it can pass the call straight on.

However, if the area code is different, then it can immediately see that it needs to send the call on to another exchange to be connected to the called party. To do this it does not need to keep a list of all the telephone numbers in the whole world, but only a list of area codes that it has links to, such as the 666 exchange. If the 555 exchange finds that it does not know how to reach a certain exchange (such as an international call), it will send the call on to an exchange higher in the hierarchy. This exchange, which has an even larger overview of the whole network and possibly even has connections to other telco networks, will try and find a way to reach the called party.

Keeping this split number, hierarchical system in mind when reading the rest of the chapter will help in getting an overview of the methods used.

Variable-Length Subnet Masks (VLSM) is a technique that allows the network administrator to split large classful IP address ranges into multiple smaller ones.

Suppose that an Internetwork uses the class A 10.0.0.0 network.

Looking at this address from a classful point of view, the number 10 is the network part of the IP address, and the remaining three octets are reserved for the hosts. (See Chapter 3, "Routing Protocols.")

Hosts see the class A address and assume that address to talk to any other host with an IP address in the 10.0.0.0 range over their local network. This is not a great method, because all the possible 16 million hosts try to talk to each other directly.

So subnets were introduced, where the large 10.0.0.0 network is split into smaller, more manageable parts. A host that understands VLSM on a subnetted network will not just look at the IP address and find a class A, B, or C network address; it will check the subnet mask to see which part of the IP address is actually the network

part, the subnet part, and the host part. In this way, the host determines whether it will send the data straight to the host or to the
router for forwarding.

So what is the so-called subnet?

4.3.1 Subnetting

Subnetting works by using part of the host address bits to create
additional networks within the classful (class A, B, or C) network.

These *subnets,* as they are called, act just like network addresses,
because they split the large classful networks into smaller, more
manageable parts.

Looking at the basic class A IP address, the first octet (8 bits) is
assigned to the network ID, and the remaining 24 bits are assigned
to the host ID (see Table 4-2).

The bits contained in the subnet ID are used to form the new network numbers, or subnets. Each subnet is considered a separate network inside the class A network. So how does a host know which part
of the IP address is network, subnet, or host?

A subnet mask is used to convey this information. This is a 32-bit
number, just like the IP address, and it contains binary 1s to indicate
network and subnet parts, and 0s for host parts.

In the case of a class A address, the subnet mask looks like this
(see Table 4-3):

Binary: 11111111.00000000.00000000.00000000

Decimal: 255.0.0.0

Bit count or prefix: 8

Table 4-2	**8 Bits**	**24 Bits**
Class A network: 10.0.0.0	Network ID = 10	Host ID

Table 4-3	8 Bits	8 Bits	16 Bits
Class A network with 8-bit subnet	Network ID = 10	Subnet ID	Host ID

This subnet mask also is called the *default mask,* because it is no different to the classful method of looking at a class A network. The eight binary 1s tell the device that the first eight bits of the IP address are the network part, and the zeros indicate the host part. Now people are no longer restricted to looking at the first few bits in the IP address, as is used in the classful method, described in Chapter 3.

Now deviate from the default class A mask and add an eight-bit subnet. The subnet mask looks like this:

Binary: 11111111.11111111.00000000.00000000

Decimal: 255.255.0.0

Bit count or prefix: 16

This eight-bit subnet can be used to create 255 subnets within the class A network, each with 16 bits for hosts on each network. In this way, the same possibilities exist to assign IP addresses that would exist in a class B, but within the class A defined address space (the first bit is 0).

It is important to realize that subnet bits are taken from the host part of the subnet mask and used to subdivide the default mask into multiple subnets.

Here are some examples:

A class A network has a default subnet mask of eight bits.

A class A network with an eight-bit subnet has a subnet mask with 16 bits. This subnet mask is then the same as a class B subnet mask.

Later in the book, the *bit count* or *prefix* method is used on many of the newer systems; this is simply the total of the binary 1s in the subnet mask. This can be used only if the subnet bits are set to the highest-order bits possible (starting on the left and moving to the right).

In the early implementations of VLSM, this was not a prerequisite, but with the introduction of CIDR and changes in philosophy concerning subnetting, it is required nowadays.

In Figure 4-1, a class A network is depicted (8 bits subnet mask, 0 bits subnet) with one host communicating with two others. All the host addresses are part of the same network, so the hosts can talk directly to each other.

In Figure 4-2, there is a 16-bit subnet. Therefore, the second and third octet of the IP address form a subnet and are no longer part of the host address.

As long as the network and subnet parts of the IP address are the same, the hosts can communicate directly, but if there is a difference in the network or subnet parts (or both), the host forwards the data to the router for forwarding.

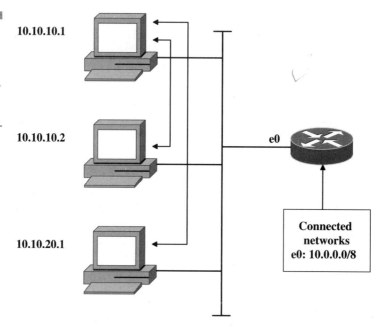

Figure 4-1
Classful 10.10.10.0 network-hosts 10.10.10.x can communicate directly with hosts 10.10.20.x.

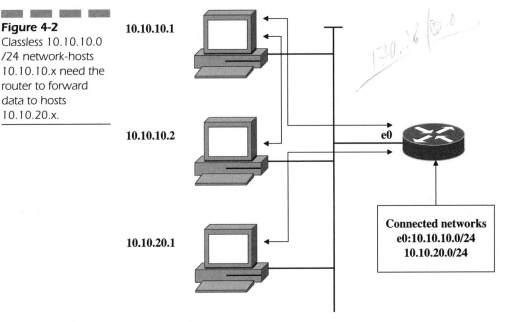

Figure 4-2
Classless 10.10.10.0
/24 network-hosts
10.10.10.x need the
router to forward
data to hosts
10.10.20.x.

4.3.2 Special Cases in Subnetted IP Addresses

4.3.2.1 Host Part All Zeros This indicates the "wire" or subnet itself. This is what the router stores in its routing table, because it is not interested in actual hosts-only the networks. Non-VLSM routing protocols (RIPv1, IGRP) are incapable of storing and communicating anything but classful IP addresses, and so can only look at the host and subnet parts together. This need not be a problem, as long as the subnets are contiguous. In other words, if *all* the subnets with the same network address are attached to one router running RIPv1 of IGRP, then it is not a problem if they are advertised with only the network address. Because the router itself does recognize the subnets, it has them advertised in its routing table as "connected" and can complete the packets' final hop to the subnet.

Figure 4-3 demonstrates the confusion possible when router A and B have subnetted class B addresses, and the routing updates only send the class B network address to router C.

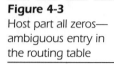

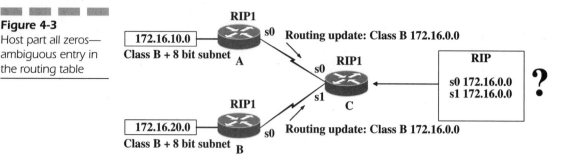

Router C will not be able to make a routing decision based on the information it has in its routing table.

4.3.2.2 Subnet Part All Zeros   In the early days of subnetting, it was found that some hosts became confused if the subnet bits were all 0s. This is because the subnet was seen as a network within a network, and the all-0s subnet indicated a wire address. Also, there were systems that used all 0s as a broadcast address, instead of using all ones. So to avoid confusion, RFC 950 states that using subnets with a value of 0 is not recommended.

For those who are positive that all the routers, routing protocols, and devices on the network can understand the subnet value 0, Cisco offers the option of enabling this on its routers.

The commands follow:

```
B#configure terminal
Enter configuration commands, one per line.  End with
CNTL/Z.
B(config)#ip subnet-zero
```

4.3.2.3 Subnet Part and Host Part All Zeros   This is the classful method of looking at a network or "wire" address. Classless routing protocols such as OSPF and EIGRP use the subnet mask to determine whether this is a wire address on a subnet with all 0 bits, or the wire address for the whole network. Table 4-4 shows how classful RIPv1 and EIGRP would advertise the network address.

Table 4-4

Advertisement of
network addresses
for RIPv1 and
EIGRP

Protocol	Network	Subnet
Class B with 8-bit subnet mask, subnetted bits all zero	172.16.0.0	255.255.255.0
Rip reports: class B with default mask	172.16.0.0	255.255.0.0
Eigrp reports: network address with subnet	172.16.0.0	255.255.255.0

4.3.2.4 Network, Subnet, and Host Parts All Zero This is used
by hosts on a subnet to indicate themselves. For example, if a host
is booted and does not know its own IP address, it sends a broadcast
onto the network with a host address of all zeros, asking for an IP
address and subnet mask. A DHCP or BOOTP server answers to the
MAC address, supplying the necessary information.

4.3.2.5 Host Part All Ones This indicates a directed broadcast to
a specific subnet (see Figure 4-4). If a router sees this address in the
destination field, it forwards the message to the network and subnet indicated in the IP address and broadcasts it on that network.

4.3.2.6 Subnet and Host Parts All Ones This is a directed
broadcast to all the subnets within the network indicated in the IP
address (see Figure 4-5). In theory, the router will behave as
described in the preceding section, but it will broadcast the message
onto all the subnets within the network. Because this option can

Figure 4-4
A directed broadcast
to a single subnet

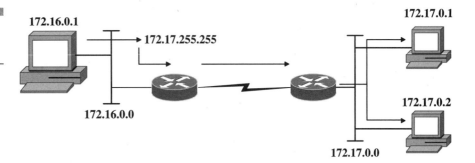

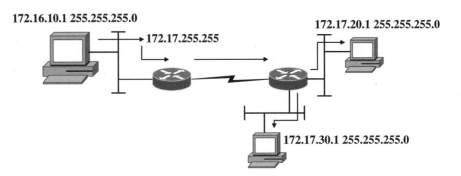

Figure 4-5
A directed broadcast
to multiple subnets

cause problems if the IP address and subnet are configured incorrectly, and because the option is practically never used, most routers do not forward such data.

4.3.2.7 Network, Subnet, and Host All Ones This is a local broadcast (see Figure 4-6). These are never forwarded by routers and are used on local area networks by hosts to get information about other hosts on the same subnet.

4.4 Subnetting in Practice

The previous section discussed the theory of subnetting. This section presents an example of how to subnet an IP network or subnet an existing subnet into smaller subnets.

4.4.1 Example 1

Suppose that you have a private class B IP network with an address of 172.20.0.0. You will use this address to populate 10 separate subnetworks, giving each a range of IP addresses to supply to the hosts on each subnet.

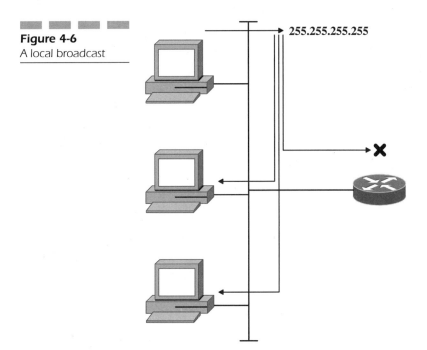

Figure 4-6
A local broadcast

255.255.255.255

What to do?

First figure out how many bits are needed in the subnet mask to be able to make the amount of subnets required.

You have decided that you want 10 subnets within this network. Don't forget that if you want to stay compatible with older implementations of IP, you should discard the all-1s and all-0s subnets.

You can make two combinations with one binary bit, four with two bits, eight with three bits, and so on. Mathematically, this can be calculated by using powers of 2.

You must subtract 2 from whatever amount of subnets you find to comply with RFC 950, or 1 if you decide to use Cisco's `ip subnet-zero` command. Comply with RFC 950 to be on the safe side (as most people do).

Table 4-5 shows the amount of subnets available for a certain amount of bits used to form the subnet.

Table 4-5

Subnet bits
mapped to
available subnets

Subnet	Bits	# Combinations	# Subnets
1	2^1	2	0
2	2^2	4	2
3	2^3	8	6
4	2^4	16	14
5	2^5	32	30
6	2^6	64	62
7	2^7	128	126
8	2^8	256	254
9	2^9	512	510
10	2^{10}	1,024	1,022
11	2^{11}	2,048	2,046
12	2^{12}	4,096	4,094
13	2^{13}	8,192	8,190
14	2^{14}	16,384	16,382
15	2^{15}	32,768	32,766
16	2^{16}	65,536	65,534

As this table shows, one subnet bit is pretty useless, because it cannot be used effectively to create subnets.

Also, 15 and 16 bits are useless when applied to class B subnets. Because the class B network has 16 bits in its default mask, adding 16 subnet bits gives a subnet mask of 32 bits. That means that the whole IP address is the network part, and there are no bits left for the host!

Also, 15 bits are not possible for a class B, because this results in one bit for the host part. One bit offers two host-part combinations, and those then would be the broadcast address and wire address, again leaving nothing for the host itself.

Now write the network address that has been assigned in binary notation:

172.20.0.0 = 10101100. 00010100.00000000.00000000

Default subnet mask (class B, 16 bits):
11111111.11111111.00000000.00000000

You want 10 subnets, so checking the table, you find that you need four subnet bits, giving 14 possible subnets.
Add the four bits to the subnet mask:

Subnetted subnet mask total 16 + 4 bits:
11111111.11111111.11110000.00000000

Converted back to decimal notation, this gives you
255.255.240.0.

Table 4-6 shows the possible subnet combinations.
Here are a few things to notice in Table 4-6:

- The first and second octets always stay the same. This is because you were assigned the 172.20.0.0 network to subdivide.
- The third octet is split into two parts:
  - The first part contains the four subnet bits you need to assign to the desired 10 subnets. In this part, you can see that you have all possible binary combinations, including the illegal values discussed earlier. Looking at the subnet bits, you see that #1 and #16 are illegal.
  - The second part is what is left over for the host part after you snip off the four subnet bits.
- The fourth octet remains unchanged—eight bits for hosts.
- The subnet of wire address:
  - When you write the default classful class B address, you use all zeros in the host part to indicate that you are referring to the whole network. In this case, this is 172.20.0.0. This is also the number you would find in a router's routing table indicating that it knows a route to that network.

Table 4-6 Possible subnet combinations

#	Octet 1 Network	Octet 2 Network	Octet 3 Subnet		Octet 4 Host	Subnet (Wire) Host	Broadcast Address
1	10101100	00010100	0000	0000	00000000	172.20.0.0	172.20.15.255
2	10101100	00010100	0001	0000	00000000	172.20.16.0	172.20.31.255
3	10101100	00010100	0010	0000	00000000	172.20.32.0	172.20.47.255
4	10101100	00010100	0011	0000	00000000	172.20.48.0	172.20.63.255
5	10101100	00010100	0100	0000	00000000	172.20.64.0	172.20.79.255
6	10101100	00010100	0101	0000	00000000	172.20.80.0	172.20.95.255
7	10101100	00010100	0110	0000	00000000	172.20.96.0	172.20.111.255
8	10101100	00010100	0111	0000	00000000	172.20.112.0	172.20.127.255
9	10101100	00010100	1000	0000	00000000	172.20.128.0	172.20.143.255
10	10101100	00010100	1001	0000	00000000	172.20.144.0	172.20.159.255
11	10101100	00010100	1010	0000	00000000	172.20.160.0	172.20.175.255
12	10101100	00010100	1011	0000	00000000	172.20.176.0	172.20.191.255
13	10101100	00010100	1100	0000	00000000	172.20.192.0	172.20.207.255
14	10101100	00010100	1101	0000	00000000	172.20.208.0	172.20.223.255
15	10101100	00010100	1110	0000	00000000	172.20.224.0	172.20.239.255
16	10101100	00010100	1111	0000	00000000	172.20.240.0	172.20.255.255

- This is also the case for subnetted addresses. Because the boundary between the subnet and the host part does not necessarily fall on an octet boundary, however, it can be more difficult to recognize.

■ The broadcast address of the subnet:

- Every subnet needs a broadcast address for hosts to be able to do ARP requests, etc. In a broadcast address, all host bits are set to 1.

Here is an example of the #5 subnet in Table 4-7 to show how the IP addresses are mapped to it. The grayed bits form the host part.

Just in case you forgot how you managed to convert 79 into binary 01001111, here's how it is done.

Each octet is a combination of 8 bits. Each bit has a decimal multiplier mapped to it; the leftmost bit is the most-significant bit (worth the most in decimal) and the rightmost bit is the least-significant bit (worth 1).

Written outright, the following multipliers correspond to the bits:

128-64-32-16-8-4-2-1

When converting a binary number to the decimal equivalent, multiply the multiplier with the corresponding binary bits, and add up the results.

Table 4-8 shows what this example produces.

One last question that remains is how many hosts can you now put on each subnet?

Table 4-7	**Description**	**Octet 1**	**Octet 2**	**Octet 3**	**Octet 4**
Example of a subnet and broadcast address mapped to their binary equivalents	Subnet/wire address	172	20	64	0
	Binary equivalent	10101100	00010100	01000000	00000000
	Broadcast address	172	20	79	255
	Binary equivalent	10101100	00010100	01001111	11111111

Table 4-8

Example of a binary number conversion

<- Most Significant				Least Significant ->				Bit Significance
0	1	0	0	1	1	1	1	Binary number
128	64	32	16	8	4	2	1	Decimal multiplier
0	64	0	0	8	4	2	1	Results, add up to 79

As you can see in the example, you have four bits in the third octet and the whole fourth octet to use for hosts. This gives you $4 + 8 = 12$ bits. Solving 2^{12} gives 4,096 combinations. Because you reserve two host addresses for the all 0s (subnet/wire address) and all ones (broadcast), you can supply 4,094 hosts with an IP address on each subnet.

4.4.2 Tips and Tricks

All these steps were mapped to binary notation to make it easier to understand the system.

Here are a few shortcuts:

- To determine how to build the list of network or subnet addresses (wire addresses), take the amount of host bits you have chosen to use, and find the amount of binary combinations possible with that amount of bits. That is the number to increment the decimal network addresses within the octet that has the subnet/host part split. In this case, you have four host bits, $2^4 = 16$, so you increment with 16.

- When you look at the subnet (wire) addresses, you can see that they increment in steps of 16, starting at 0. In this way, you can quickly build the table without a lot of binary-to-decimal conversions!

- There is also a way of easily determining the broadcast address, because it is simply the subnet address of the next subnet minus one and all ones for any remaining host octets.

4.4.3 Subnetting Steps in Short

Subnetting consists of the following steps:

1. Define the network (or subnet) address and subnet mask that will be subnetted.
2. Define the amount of bits needed for the desired amount of subnets, or the amount of bits for the desired amount of hosts on each subnet.
3. Write the subnet mask from 1 in binary, and create the new subnet mask by finding where the split is between subnet and host bits. Work left to right if you know the amount of subnet bits, and right to left if you know the amount of host bits. Write down the new subnet mask that you have created.
4. Using the new subnet mask, work through all binary combinations of the subnet bits to find the subnetwork addresses (host bits all 0), for each subnet. You might be able to use the method described in "Tips and Tricks."
5. Remove all the subnets where the subnet bits are all zeros or all ones, unless you decide that your network can handle `ip subnet-zero`.
6. Determine the broadcast addresses for each subnet by entering all ones for the host parts, or use the "short" method described in "Tips and Tricks."
7. Supply the hosts on each subnet with the IP addresses between the subnet address and the broadcast address.

4.4.4 Example 2

In this example, nothing new will be introduced. Instead of subnetting a class B network, however, you will subnet one subnet into smaller subnets.

In Example 1, you created 14 subnets with each 4,094 hosts from a class B address. What happens if you have a few special LANs with only a few hosts? Take 15 hosts for this example. If you assign the 4-bit subnet from Example 1 to each LAN, you lose 4,079 IP addresses on each LAN.

So you can create a few subnets by using only one of the subnets from Example 1 to accommodate 15 hosts each.

Following the previous steps, you should start by finding the "mother" network. In this case, you will use one of the subnet #10 you created in Example 1.

1. This subnet has a wire address of 172.20.144.0 and a subnet mask of 255.255.240.0

2. Because you want 15 hosts per subnet, you might think that four bits would do, because four bits make for 16 binary combinations ($2^4 = 16$). However, because all 1s and all 0s are reserved addresses, you can only effectively use 14. So you need to include one bit extra, giving 5 bits in total and 30 usable hosts.

3. In Table 4-9 the original subnet mask is 255.255.240.0; this is shown in the first row. In the second row, you see the 5 host bits you need to accommodate the 15 hosts per subnet. The third row shows the new subnet mask, with the new subnet bits shown in gray. In decimal, this address is 255.255.255.224.

4. Using the quick method, you see that you have 5 bits for the host part. $2^5 = 32$, so you must increment in steps of 32 in the fourth octet, because that is the octet with the subnet/host split. Building the list of subnet numbers is straightforward now, although be aware that when one of the multiples reaches 256, you must increment the more significant octet by 1 and start back at 0. See

Table 4-9

The original subnet mask 255.255.240.0

Decription	Octet 1	Octet 2	Octet 3	Octet 4
Original subnet mask	11111111	11111111	11110000	00000000
Host bits needed for 15 hosts (5)				00000
New subnet mask	11111111	11111111	11111111	11100000

Table 4-10	Subnet Addresses	Third Octet Binary	Fourth Octet Binary
Using the "quick" method to find subnet addresses	172.20.144.0	10010000	00000000
	172.20.144.32	10010000	00100000
	172.20.144.64	10010000	01000000
	172.20.144.92	10010000	01100000
	172.20.144.128	10010000	10000000
	172.20.144.160	10010000	10100000
	172.20.144.192	10010000	11000000
	172.20.144.224	10010000	11100000
	172.20.145.0	10010001	00000000
	172.20.145.32	10010001	00100000
	172.20.145.64	10010001	01000000
	172.20.145.92	10010001	01100000
	.	.	.
	.	.	.
	.	.	.
	172.20.159.92	10011110	01100000
	172.20.159.128	10011111	10000000
	172.20.159.160	10011111	10100000
	172.20.159.192	10011111	11000000
	172.20.159.224	10011111	11100000

Table 4-10. (The more significant subnet is the one to the left of the one you are working on.) The binary equivalents for octet three and four have been added for clarity. Subnet bits are gray.

How do you know when to stop incrementing with 32? There are two ways:

- In this case, you are using seven subnet bits. This means there are $2^7 = 128$ possible combinations, so there are 128 possible subnets.

- You can look at the broadcast address of the network of subnet you started out with. Because the broadcast address is the highest address available, you would be encroaching on the 172.20.160.0 subnet if you continued.

5. Because this example must comply to RFC 950, you will remove subnets with subnet bits of all 0s and all 1s. This leaves you with 126 subnets on which you can supply 5 bits worth of host addresses ($2^5 = 32$, leaving 30 effective addresses).

6. You can determine broadcast addresses by using the fast method. In Table 4-9, the first column contains the subnet address determined earlier, and you can use it by subtracting one from the next row's subnet address to find the broadcast address. In the second and third columns, the binary values of the broadcast addresses have been added for clarity. Notice that the only difference between these columns in Table 4-7 and the Table 4-9 are the binary values for the host part, which are all 1s (broadcast) instead of all 0s (wire).

7. For example, take the third subnet address found: 172.20.144.64 (See Table 4-10).

    As you can see, there are a few pitfalls to watch out for when subnetting, but if you practice a bit using binary notation, you will get a feel for the system (see Table 4-11).

    One big mistake that is made often is to get mixed up in the number of combinations possible with a certain number of bits and the decimal multiplier that corresponds to a certain bit in an octet.

    For example, the most significant bit in an octet corresponds to the decimal multiplier of 128, but with 8 bits, you can make $2^8 = 256$ combinations.

    Remember that when converting an octet from binary to decimal, you count up all the results of multiplying the multiplier with the binary bits (see Table 4-12).

Table 4-11

Third subnet
address

Description	IP Address	Subnet Mask
First IP address (subnet address of wire address)	172.20.144.64	255.255.255.224
Second IP address assigned to a host	172.20.144.65	255.255.255.224
.	.	.
.	.	.
.	.	.
Thirtieth IP address assigned to a host	172.20.144.90	255.255.255.224
Broadcast address for this subnet.	172.20.144.91	255.255.255.224

When finding out how many IP addresses can be made with a certain amount of bits, raise the 2 to the power of the amount of bits.

4.5 Classless Interdomain Routing

Classless Interdomain Routing (CIDR) was devised to merge the many updates and partially solved issues that were the result of many years of tweaking the method by which IP addresses were managed.

One problem was that Internet routers had to cope with ever-increasing routing table sizes because of the large amount of networks being built. Another problem was the complexity of the subnetting method, which still had links to the old classful network divisions.

A number of recommendations were made.

Subnet addresses would be allowed to contain all 0s and all 1s. The philosophy behind this was that instead of defining a separate subnet between the classful network part and host part of an IP address, the whole classful concept would be dropped.

In the CIDR world, each device looks at the IP address and the subnet mask, ignoring the class A, B, and C implications. It then is typical to express the network part of the address as a prefix, or the

Table 4-12

Determining the broadcast addresses

Subnet Addresses	Broadcast Addresses	Third Octet Binary	Fourth Octet Binary
172.20.144.0	172.20.144.31	10010000	00011111
172.20.144.32	172.20.144.63	10010000	00111111
172.20.144.64	172.20.144.91	10010000	01011111
172.20.144.92	172.20.144.127	10010000	01111111
172.20.144.128	172.20.144.159	10010000	10011111
172.20.144.160	172.20.144.191	10010000	10111111
172.20.144.192	172.20.144.223	10010000	11011111
172.20.144.224	172.20.144.255	10010000	11111111
172.20.145.0	172.20.145.31	10010001	00011111
172.20.145.32	172.20.145.63	10010001	00111111
172.20.145.64	172.20.145.91	10010001	01011111
172.20.145.92	172.20.145.127	10010001	01111111
.	.	.	.
.	.	.	.
.	.	.	.
172.20.159.92	172.20.159.127	10011110	01111111
172.20.159.128	172.20.159.159	10011111	10011111
172.20.159.160	172.20.159.191	10011111	10111111
172.20.159.192	172.20.159.223	10011111	11011111
172.20.159.224	172.20.159.255	10011111	11111111

amount of bits that form the network part of the address (see Table 4-13).

Subnetting becomes a lot easier, because a 16-bit network address (what used be the size of a class C) can be subnetted into two 17-bit networks just by adding a bit to the subnet mask. This is easiest to

Table 4-13

Number of bits used to make up network address

Decription	Octet 1	Octet 2	Octet 3	Octet 4
Class B network address, 8 subnet bits	172	16	10	0
Subnet mask, 24 bit prefix	255	255	255	0
Pre CIDR	Network	Network	Subnet	Host
CIDR	Network	Network	Network	Host

Table 4-14

Example of subnetting

Address	CIDR	Prefix	Subnet Mask
Network (wire)	172.20.0.0	/16	255.255.0.0
Broadcast	172.20.255.255	/16	255.255.0.0
Split into two networks	.	.	.
First network (wire)	172.20.0.0	/17	255.255.128.0
Broadcast	172.20.127.255	/17	255.255.128.0
Second network (wire)	172.20.128.255	/17	255.255.128.0
Broadcast	172.20.255.255	/17	255.255.128.0

visualize by thinking of subnetting as enlarging the network part of the subnet mask instead of introducing a separate subnet part.

Table 4-14 shows an example.

Here it is obviously very important that all devices understand subnet masks. You can see that without the help of the prefix number, there is no way to see that the broadcast, 172.20.255.255, is for the /16 of /17 network.

4.5.1 Supernetting (Route Summarization)

The previous example of subnetting also works the other way around. If a router has two contiguous networks attached to it that have 17-bit prefixes, it can advertise both networks as one network with a 16-bit subnet mask.

This is called *supernetting,* and is used to decrease the size of routing tables (see Figure 4-8).

For example, if an *Internet service provider* (ISP) has a large lump of IP addresses to use for its customers (for example, 20.20.0.0 / 16), it can advertise all these subnetted addresses as the one lump to its neighbors and work out internally to which exact customer packets should go. In this way routers will not have to use so much memory and processor time to look through large lists of small subnets. Also, the routing updates will be smaller, reducing bandwidth usage.

There are some considerations to look at, however:

Supernetting works fine if the ISP is really connected to all the networks contained in the supernet. If one of the ISP's customers decides to leave and move to another ISP keeping its IP addresses, a hole will appear in the range of IP addresses that the ISP is advertising.

This range of IP addresses will be advertised from another ISP, and routers could have difficulty deciding whether to send packets to the old ISP or the new ISP.

Having routers always choose the route with the longest subnet or the most accurate match solves this problem.

Figure 4-8
Supernetting

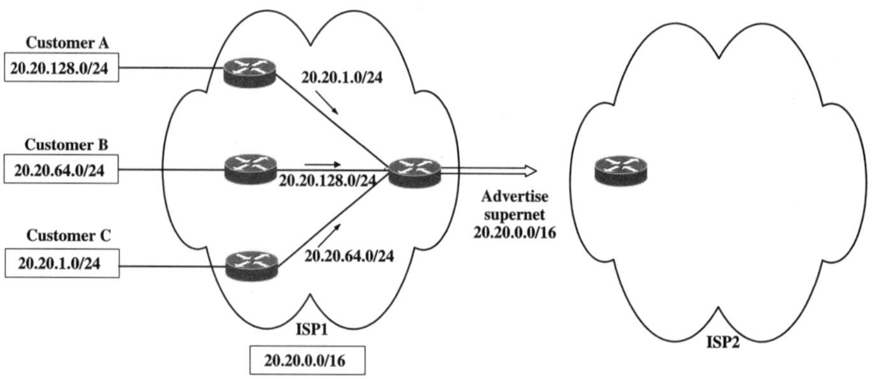

For this reason, you should be very careful when deciding to summarize routes.

4.5.2 Noncontiguous Networks

A noncontiguous network can be defined as a network with two or more instances of the same network ID that is separated by a network with a different network ID (see Figure 4-9). Such a situation can occur when the network topology breaks, or by an intended (re)design decision. The main problem that arises in the case of a noncontiguous network is that a router doesn't know where to forward traffic destined for the (previous contiguous) network. The reason for this is that when the router tries to resolve an IP address down to the network part, it appears as a duplicate address, because it has no way to distinguish between the two. In other words, the same network ID appears multiple times but in different locations. The result is unre-

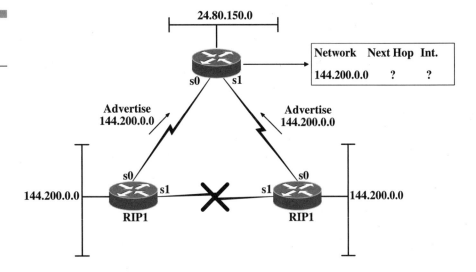

Figure 4-9
A noncontiguous
network

liable in most cases—for example, in a situation in which all the paths in question are of equal cost. In that case, the router will erroneously start load balancing between the paths, causing intermittent connectivity.

As a result, it is vital that summarization is either turned off or not configured when noncontiguous networks exist in an organization. It is unlikely that summarization can provide the information needed for the router on the other side of the intervening network ID to be able to make the appropriate routing decisions in order to forward to the destination subnets. This is especially the case when EIGRP is used, because EIGRP *automatically* summarizes the network portion of an IP address, which would cause total chaos in such a situation.

Summarization cannot always be achieved, because it depends greatly on the implemented addressing scheme. Chapters 5, "Configuring OSPF in a Single Area," and 7, "Configuring Enhanced IGRP," demonstrate that in order to improve a network design, manual configuration can be required.

An important condition to keep in mind when considering the use of summarization is to check for common high-order bits in the implemented addressing scheme. This might not always be the case if an addressing scheme is already in place, however, because many pre-classless network designs obviously did not take a possible development such as summarization into consideration. By now, it may be obvious that in the majority of cases, detailed analysis of the addressing scheme is required before the decision can be made to implement summarization. VLSM, for example, may not always offer the desired flexibility when it comes to allocating the required bits for addressing a network.

When the results of such an analysis are negative for summarization, a couple of conclusions can be drawn:

- Recognize the fact that there are scalability limitations, and therefore do not summarize at all.
- You may want to redesign the currently implemented

addressing scheme. Depending on the size of the Internetwork in question, this task is not to be taken lightly—it often requires an experienced specialist. However, it may be obvious that the advantages of a completely new scalable addressing scheme could be numerous.

4.5.3 IP Unnumbered

There is a special case of subnet that requires some attention. Most routers are connected through serial point-to-point links of some kind or another. These links have only two hosts—the two routers on each side of the link.

Because these router interfaces need IP addresses, the /30 or 255.255.255.252 subnet is often used. This subnet offers four combinations, but only two are usable.

There is a downside to this. On large Internetworks, there can be many serial links, and each of them has its own subnet, which needs to be advertised by the routing protocols. This can cause large routing tables and increase convergence time. It also can deplete the already scarce IP address space available.

A solution was devised: IP unnumbered.

When using this, the IP address of another interface in the router is "borrowed." IP-wise, this makes the serial interface in the router transparent and combines it with the other interface (usually, a loopback interface or Ethernet interface). The routers on each end of the serial link route to each other's "donor" interface, where the packet is routed and forwarded.

The downside to this is that for network management and troubleshooting reasons, the interface itself is not visible for `ping`, `traceroute`, or `telnet`.

To implement this on a Cisco router, enter the following commands:

```
C#configure terminal
C(config)#interface serial 0
C(config-if)#ip unnumbered <donor interface id>
```

4.5.4 IP Helper Addresses

Remember that routers do not forward broadcast messages. This is to prevent broadcast storms, although broadcasts are not good things to have bouncing around an Internetwork. This can prove to be troublesome for some protocols that rely on broadcasts to work properly.

Table 4-15 lists such IP protocols supported by Cisco and their port numbers.

To understand how Cisco supports these protocols, take a look at the TFTP.

Many devices, including Cisco routers, have the option to search for a TFTP server at boot time to load software. Because the devices do not have an IP address at boot time, they send out a broadcast asking whether any TFTP servers are on their local network.

So what happens if the TFTP server is not on the local network, but on another network? The router connecting the booting device's local network to the rest of the Internetwork will not forward the broadcast. By using the IP helper address, however, you can tell the router to forward the broadcast to a specific IP address or a network address (see Figure 4-10). In essence, the broadcast is turned into a unicast (a single IP address) or directed broadcast (a network or subnet address).

Table 4-15

IP protocols supported by Cisco and their port numbers

Port	Protocol
37	Time
49	TACACS
53	DNS
67, 68	BOOTP client, server
69	TFTP
137, 138	NetBIOS name, datagram

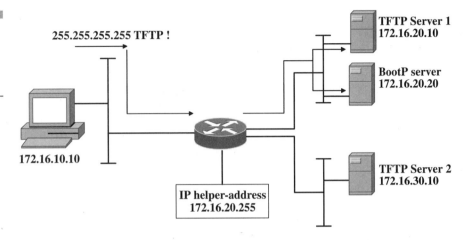

Figure 4-10
Forwarding
broadcasts using the
IP helper address
command

Figure 4-9 shows that the broadcast is transformed into a directed broadcast aimed at the 172.16.20.255 whole network. Therefore, TFTP server 2 on the 172.16.30.0 network will not get the TFTP request.

4.6 Chapter Summary

This chapter discussed some methods for conserving IP address space and how to spread the IP addresses wisely across an Internetwork.

Topics such as VLSM and CIDR were covered, as well as pitfalls to avoid. Also, methods for solving specific problems that can occur in an Internetwork were examined.

This chapter demonstrated that great caution should be used when changing the IP addressing scheme for all or part of an Internetwork. A thorough understanding of the Internetwork in question should be gained before designing the changes, because one small mistake can cause havoc in minutes.

The next chapter delves deeper into the routing protocols OSFP, EIGRP, and BGP.

4.7 Frequently Asked Questions (FAQ)

Question: If I want to use my own IP addresses for my private network, what makes these addresses different from "normal" IP addresses?

Answer: There are a few ranges that can be used, as described in RFC 1597. These ranges are

```
     10.0.0.0  to  10.255.255.255
  172.16.0.0  to  172.31.255.255
192.168.0.0  to 192.168.255.255
```

Many people use these ranges, but they are not allowed on the Internet. Routers on the Internet will be configured to drop packets containing such addresses. To "translate" between the private and public addresses Cisco uses a feature called *Network Address Translation* (NAT).

4.8 Case Study

Consider the network in Figure 4-10.

1. What address class could be used on this network?

   (A class C addressing scheme could be used.)

2. Could VLSM be implemented on this network?

   (VLSM cannot be implemented on this network, because the configured routing protocols do not support the propagation of subnet masks.)

3. Write down the subnet masks in bit notation for this network, assuming that all routers are running EIGRP and VLSM is used.

   (The bits in the subnet masks could be allocated like this:

Remote Subnet Part	Host Part
000	00000

This approach allows for six remote subnets ($2^3 - 2 = 6$) and 30 hosts on each of the subnets ($2^5 - 2 = 30$).)

Figure 4-11
Case study example

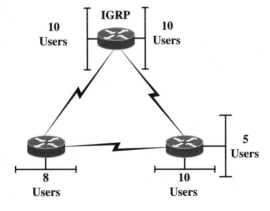

4.9 Questions

1. Suppose that you are faced with a group of 6 networks, each with 30 hosts. How can you subnet a class C network to supply IP addresses for each subnet and host? Show the subnet mask.

2. Give a short description of what route summarization does.

3. What does VLSM stand for?

4. List the ranges of host addresses available by using a /28 prefix on the following network address: 172.168.10.128 /27.

5. What question is important to ask when determining the amount of subnet bits in a subnet mask?

6. Convert the following IP address into binary notation: 192.168.45.17.

7. Define a noncontiguous network.

8. What characteristic must a routing protocol have in order to be able to use VLSM in an Internetwork?

9. What is another name for *route summarization* in a CIDR environment?

10. If a network is to use IP address summarization, what essential criterion must the addressing scheme meet?

11. What networks does RFC 1918 provide, and which prefixes do they use?

12. Describe a situation in which route summarization would not qualify.

13. Why is it wise to use a hierarchical IP addressing scheme?

14. If a host station is situated on LAN A, which does not have a DHCP server, which command can you use to allow the host to reach a DHCP server on LAN B?

15. Which Cisco IOS command allows the use of subnet values of 0?

16. What is indicated by an IP address in which the subnet and host part are all binary 1s?

17. What are the decimal ranges of the first octet of the class A, B, and C addresses?

18. How does a router distinguish between the network and host part of an IP address in a VLSM environment?

19. What is the subnet mask of an IP address with a prefix of /26?

20. When subnetting a network address, are the subnet bits taken from the network part of the address or the host part?

4.10 Answers

1. 255.255.255.224, which is the same as the CIDR /27 prefix

2. Route summarization combines multiple subnets into one routing entry by adjusting the subnet bits.

3. VLSM stands for *variable-length subnet mask.*

4. 172.168.10.129 - 158

5. The amount of nodes per subnet or number of subnets needed

6. 11000000.10101000.00101101.00010001

7. A network is noncontiguous when a group of network addresses belonging to the same subnet is split into two groups by a differently addressed network.

8. The routing protocol must be able to send the subnet mask or prefix in a routing update.

9. Supernetting

10. The structure must be hierarchical, allowing the IP addresses to be grouped together higher in the hierarchy.

11. Private network addresses

    Prefixes: /8 /12 /16

12. ■ Noncontiguous networks are present.

    ■ Specific subnets need to be advertised.

    ■ The addressing scheme is incompatible.

    ■ Detailed information is required for security issues.

13. ■ Less IP address space is wasted.

    ■ Route tables are smaller.

    ■ A less-powerful router is needed to run the routing protocol.

14. On the LAN A router interface:

    ```
    IP helper address <IP address of DHCP server>
    ```

15. Global command:

    ```
    ip subnet-zero
    ```

16. This is a *directed broadcast.* It is a broadcast sent out to all the hosts of the subnets of the specific network address.

17. ▪ A: 1–127 (127 is reserved for local host)
    ▪ B: 128–191
    ▪ C: 192–223

18. By using a subnet mask

19. 255.255.255.192

20. The host part provides the subnet bits.

3

Scalable
Routing
Protocols

CHAPTER 5

Configuring OSPF in a Single Area

5.1 Objectives Covered in This Chapter

To better understand what is necessary to build a scalable network, the following objectives will be covered.

Table 5-1

BSCN objectives

BSCN Objective
Understand OSPF operation in a single area
Describe OSPF operation in Multi Access networks, a Point-to-Point networks and *Non-Broadcast-Multi-Access* (NBMA) networks.
Understand OSPF configuration in a single area
Understand verifying OSPF operation in a single area

5.2 Chapter Introduction

OSPF offers many improvements over RIPv1 and other classful routing protocols in large Internetworks. The most distinctive ones follow:

- OSPF does not have a maximum hop-count limitation of 15. Because OSPF is a link state protocol, each router has a full understanding of all the networks in its area. Therefore, the danger of routing loops is no longer present, making the hop-count limitation unnecessary.

- Bandwidth use is more efficient, because OSPF is a link state protocol and therefore sends incremental updates instead of full updates.

- Because of its neighbor relationships, combined with incremental updates, OSPF propagates network changes more quickly.

- OSPF fully supports VLSM and route summarization and noncontiguous networks.

- A number of security options can be set to enable routing updates to be sent using encryption.

■ Path determination is improved because the metric value can be set manually.

■ OSPF is very flexible in addressing and in design changes.

These characteristics make OSPF well suited for large-scale Internetworks and more responsive to network topology changes.

OSPF's open standard design offers flexible solutions in various situations. Its flexible character ensures interoperability with other routing protocols while maintaining its scalability options. While answering to the characteristics that are demanded by such specifications, OSPF's design is rather complex compared to other protocols. To fully understand this, an examination of OSPF's main ingredients is necessary. This chapter starts off with a summary of OSPF's main characteristics, followed by a more detailed discussion on how OSPF puts these characteristics to use. The key attributes in this summary appear in bold in the following list:

■ Routers running OSPF maintain a **connection-oriented** relationship with routers on the same physical segment they reside on. In OSPF lingo, these particular routers are called *adjacent neighbors*.

■ Instead of sending a full routing update to every router in the network when a change occurs, OSPF sends an *incremental update* to its adjacent neighbors, which in turn will do the same.

■ OSPF is not limited to segmenting only by IP address or subnet; it uses *areas* to designate groups of networks.

■ OSPF can exploit the features offered by VLSM and manual route summarization.

■ Because specific tasks can be assigned to all the different routers in the network, inter-router communication in the network is improved.

■ Although OSPF can be implemented as a routing protocol that interconnects many areas, it is still an interior routing protocol. This characteristic is examined in much more depth in the next chapter, "Configuring OSPF in Multiple Areas."

To put all this in an understandable perspective, this chapter discusses OSPF operation in a single area. Later, the chapter progresses to more advanced topics as an introduction to Chapter 6.

5.3 OSPF Hierarchy

Previous chapters explained that a great part of OSPF's strength lies in its capability to support large Internetworks through its good scalability characteristics. One way to achieve this is by grouping routers into logical clouds called *areas*. In an OSPF network, an area often can be seen as an entity on its own in the larger picture of the entire Internetwork. Inter-area communication is kept to a minimum by exchanging only routing information that is necessary to stay connected. As a result, all computing takes place inside the area so that routers in one area cannot be overloaded with routing updates from other heavy loaded or malfunctioning routers in another area. This is an important design element of OSPF, because link state protocols are notorious for being CPU and memory intensive.

Taking the description of an OSPF area into account, there are three basic tasks that a router in an OSPF network could perform: operation in an area, inter-area connection, and connecting an entire autonomous system to, for example, an ISP. As you've learned, one of OSPF's key characteristics to accomplish this is its capability to assign specific functionality to a particular router. This functionality is defined by a set of tasks and responsibilities that depends on the router's position in the hierarchy of the network's OSPF design. Routers performing these roles have distinctive names in the OSPF lingo:

- *Internal router* (IR)   An IR functions only within an area. Its primary task is to maintain an accurate and up-to-date database that contains all of the area's subnets. It forwards data to other networks in the area, and routing or flooding to other areas always requires the intervention of an *Area border router* (ABR).

- *Backbone router* (BR)   One of OSPF's design rules is that every area in the network is to be interconnected through one single area, which is generally called *area 0* or the *backbone area*. Most backbone routers have an interface to the backbone area and one or more other areas. However, a router that has one or more interfaces that *only* connect it to the backbone is also called a backbone router. An important thing to remember here is that a backbone router is *not required* to have an ABR. Figure 5-1 shows the functionality and place of a BR in an OSPF network.

■ *Area border router* (ABR)   An ABR connects two or more OSPF areas, and therefore, multiple ABRs can exist in an OSPF network. To be able to perform this role, an ABR has multiple copies of a link state database. Each database holds a full topology of each area it is *connected to* and thus can be summarized. This information then is forwarded to the network's backbone for distribution. A key issue here is that an

Figure 5-1
OSPF router
definitions

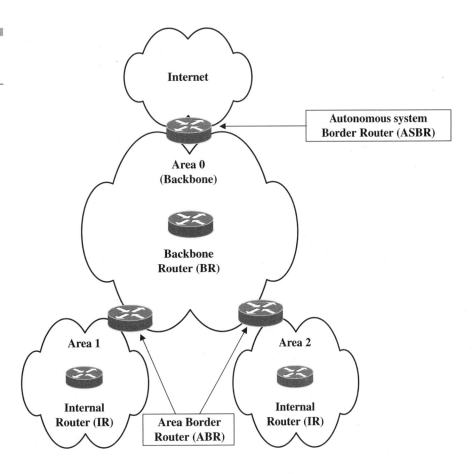

ABR is the place to configure summarization, because this is the place where the link state algorithm can maximize its capability to put the reduced routing updates to use. So when talking about OSPF's capability to minimize routing updates, think about the ABR's functionality in this concept.

■ *Autonomous system boundary router* (ASBR)   Remember that OSPF is an *interior routing protocol,* which means that if you have to connect to the world outside your OSPF autonomous system, or when you have to connect to another routing protocol, you need a router that can act as some sort of gateway between the two ASs. This is where the ASBR comes into play. Exchanging routing information with ASBRs of other ASs is the main purpose of an ASBR. This information consequently is distributed into the AS by the ASBR.

It is recommended that the positioning of an ASBR be well thought out in order for it to be used to keep the traffic overload minimized. Traffic that leaves the OSPF network for an external destination is likely to also leave the area it resides in. Therefore, positioning the ASBR in a location that all traffic leaving the area must cross makes good sense.

5.4 How OSPF Learns about Areas

This section explores how OSPF learns about the area it is in and how it builds the topology table. From this table, the routing table eventually is built, but that is discussed later.

These are the three steps an OSPF router needs to complete to be able to route traffic:

1. It must find its neighbor routers. To do this, it uses Hello packets. Usually, there are two special kinds of neighbors: the *designated router* (DR) and the *backup designated router* (BDR).

2. It learns about all the routes to other routers in the area and inserts them into the topology table.

3. It uses the *shortest path first* (SPF) algorithm to find the best routes and inserts them into the routing table.

5.4.1 Finding Neighbor Routers

Neighbors are the first step in discovering the network for the OSPF protocol. From these neighbors, adjacencies can be built, allowing the routers to exchange link state information and build their link state databases.

OSPF uses Hello packets to find neighbors and to see whether anything is changing with respect to them. Hello packets are multicast, which is a lot like a broadcast, but only devices running OSPF will accept such packets.

An OSPF Hello packet contains the following information:

- *Router ID*   This number can be an IP address or a manually entered number that uniquely identifies the router. It is a matter of choice whether the IP address or a number is used—it depends on the network designer. The router ID has a special function: It is used to break a tie if two routers are contesting over which should be the designated router.

- *Hello interval*   This number indicates how often a router will send a Hello packet. Hello packets are sent to see whether the neighbor routers are still alive and to inform them that it is alive itself. The default for this timer is 10 seconds and must be the same on all routers in the area; otherwise, they will not accept the neighbor.

- *Dead interval*   This interval is the amount of time a router will wait without receiving Hello packets before it considers its neighbor router to be dead. The default is four times the Hello interval, and this also must be the same for all routers in the area.

- *Area ID*   This is an identifier that tells other routers to which area it belongs. Routers will communicate only if they are in the same area. This number can be represented as a decimal number or as an address.

- *Router priority*   This number influences the decision of whether this router will become a *designated router* (DR). The default value is 1, and it can be set to a higher value in order for that router to always become the DR. If two routers have the same number, the protocol breaks the tie using the router ID number.

■ *DR and BDR*   If the router knows the IP address of the DR and BDR, it fills in this field with that information.

■ *Authentication password*   This is an optional feature to ensure that no foreign routers are allowed in the area. If this feature is enabled, both routers must exchange the password to authenticate. These passords can be exchanged at plain text or encrypted using the MD5 algorithm.

■ *Stub and Area flag*   This flag indicates that this area has only one router that connects the area to other areas. This is used to simplify the routing process.

■ *Neighbors*   If the router knows of any neighbors that it discovered through a neighbor-discovery process, it includes them in these fields.

So what happens when a router sends out a Hello packet? The routers have a table with all the neighbor routers that it knows of. The router goes through certain states that indicate how the communication is progressing:

1. When router A starts discovering the network, it is in the *down* state. It knows no neighbors and sends out a Hello packet to announce itself to other routers. Obviously, a lot of the fields in the Hello packet will be empty, because at this time, it does not have any information about its surroundings. See Figure 5-2.

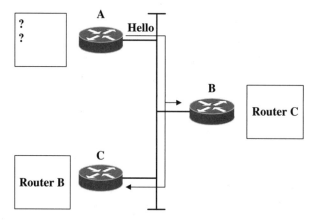

Figure 5-2
Router A sends a Hello packet.

2. All the routers that have seen the Hello packet create a new entry in the adjacency table. Then they send a Hello packet straight back to router A using a unicast. This Hello packet includes all the information the router knows of. Router A goes into *init* state. See Figure 5-3.

3. After router A receives all the Hello packets from the surrounding routers, it builds its own adjacency table. These adjacencies are set to the *two-way* state to indicate that the communication is up and running. See Figure 5-4.

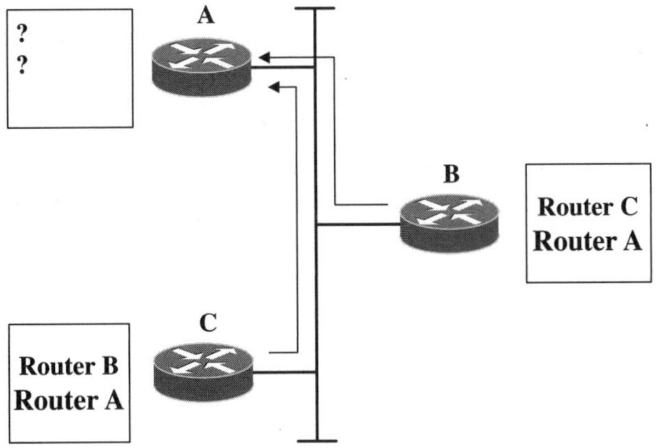

Figure 5-3
Router A gets a reply from routers B and C.

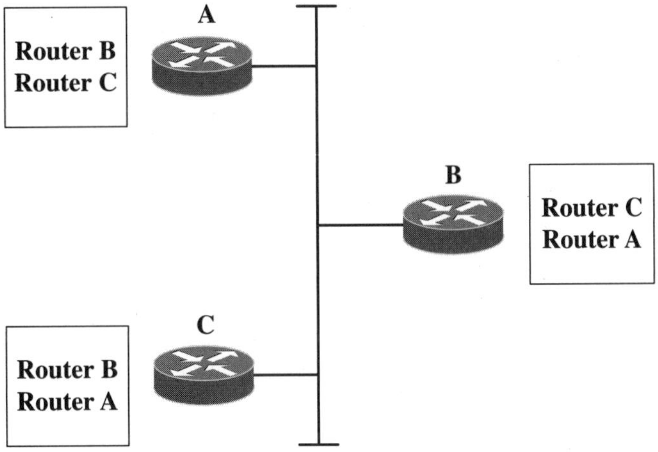

Figure 5-4
Router A has learned about neighbor routers, and two-way state has been achieved.

4. If no information about DRs and BDRs has been forthcoming from the returned Hello packets (for example, if all the routers are switched on at the same time), they will start to discuss who should be the DR and who should be the BDR.

5. The neighbors send Hello packets every few seconds, as indicated in the Hello Interval field in the Hello packet.

5.4.1.1 Special Cases   Two special cases change the way this system works:

1. If the routers are on a point-to-point link, there are obviously only two routers that talk to each other. In this case, step 4 is not necessary, no DR or BDR is elected, and the routers talk directly to one another.

2. If the network does not support multicast, it must be changed to accept multicast, or the adjacencies must be hand programmed to allow the routers to contact each other. If a meshed Frame Relay network is used, for example, multicast will not work. You then can choose to create multiple point-to-point broadcast subinterfaces for each router-router connection, or manually configure the routers to see the DR. Networks such as Frame Relay and X25 are called *non-broadcast multi-access* (NBMA) networks.

5.4.2 DR and BDR Election

Now that the routers can talk to each other to find out whether they are functioning properly, it is time to elect a DR and a BDR.

First the function of the DRs and BDRs will be examined. The DR acts as a central database for all link state information for the network for which it was chosen to be DR. All routers on the network then only send link state information to the DRs and BDRs, and only receive information from the DR.

Because all OSPF routers need to receive all the link state updates from all other routers, it is far more efficient to have one router act as a central point from which reliable information can be received and sent. It cuts down on the amount of traffic necessary to keep all the routers updated and makes it easier to ensure that all the routers have identical information about the network topology.

The BDR gets all the updates that the DR does, but it leaves the updating and synchronization of the link state information to the DR until it becomes unreachable.

- When there are no DRs or BDRs in a network, the routers examine the Priority field in the Hello packets, and the router with the highest number in this field becomes the DR. The next highest becomes the BDR. If the number in the Priority field is set to zero, then the router cannot become a DR or BDR.

- If there are two routers with the same highest number, the router ID number is checked, and the highest value in that field decides which router becomes the DR.

- If a router with a higher-priority value than the existing DR is inserted into the network, nothing changes. The new router can only be assigned as the BDR if the existing DR or BDR becomes unreachable.

- The DR is assumed to be unreachable by the BDR if it does not see the updates sent to the routers from the DR on a regular basis.

Figure 5-5 shows the result of a DR/BDR election.

5.4.3 Topology Discovery for the First Time

Now the routers have reached an important stage. They have learned the following:

- They know about all the other routers (neighbors) on their local networks (adjacency table).

- They know which router to send topology updates to, and from which router they will receive the updates (DR).

Now they must start building a topology or link state database of the whole area and learn about links to other areas.

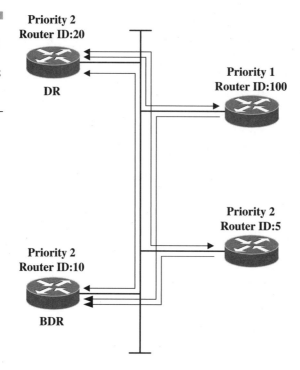

Figure 5-5
The result of DR/BDR
election. The arrows
show the logical links
formed through
adjacencies.

In the first instance, when the router has no link state database, the exchange protocol is used to get a complete picture from the DR —or, on a point-to-point link, from its neighbor.

This state is called the *exstart* state. When the router has received the whole link state database from the DR and sent its own connected network numbers to the DR, it is said to be in *full* state, and it has all the information needed to build its routing table.

The steps in transferring this information follow:

1. A router that decides it wants to receive link state information from another router sets up an adjacency. The router sends out a *database description packet* (DDP, also called DBD), informing the target router that it is the master and wants to send its link state database to the target.

2. The receiving router checks to see whether its own router ID has a higher value than that of the sending router. If this is the case, it refuses the transfer, appoints itself as master, and initiates a transfer of its own link state database to the original router. If it

has a lower value router ID, it accepts the offer. This method of using a master and slave system is necessary to ensure that the packets containing the database data can be sequenced to ensure safe delivery. Remember that the DR need not always be the master!

3. The master sends link state information to the slave router in DDPs and includes the sequence number. Each time the slave receives a DDP, it acknowledges the packet by returning an acknowledgement (LSAck packet) with the sequence number of the DDP it is acknowledging. This goes on until the whole database is transferred.

4. As the databases are being updated, the router might find that it lacks information on a certain route, or that it has better information on a route. It remembers these routes, and after the exchanges have taken place, it sends out link state request packets to get the exact information it needs.

5. When all of this has been done, the router is "full," and the forming of the adjacency is complete.

Figure 5-6 shows the topology database transfer sequence.

5.4.4 Filling the Routing Table

Now that all the routers on the network have complete link state databases, including all the possible routes to all routers in the area, they need to figure out the best routes to all the routers. Only that information is inserted in the routing table and used to route packets.

Link state protocols use the *shortest path first* (SPF) algorithm to calculate the best route to each network. This is done by building a picture of the network using the link state database data. The final picture looks like a tree, in which the router is the root. This makes sure that there is no routing loop possible.

As each "branch" is calculated, the router checks to see whether it is the shortest path. In the case of Cisco routers, it keeps a list of the six shortest paths to allow for load balancing.

To determine the shortest path, the router uses a metric called *cost*. Because the method for defining the cost of a route is not fixed

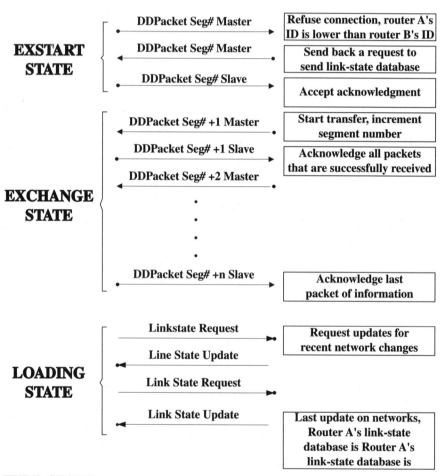

in OSPF, Cisco has decided to use the bandwidth parameter of the outgoing interface to calculate the metric.

The total metric of all the links that create a "branch" forms the metric used for the total "cost" for that particular route.

Each time the link state database changes because of a change in the network, the SPF algorithm is rerun to re-create the routing table. The larger the amount of links in an area, the more likely the chance of a change in the network somewhere, and the longer it will take to rerun the SPF algorithm. It is therefore very important not to create areas that are too large.

5.4.5 Maintaining the Link State Database

Now that the routers have a way to discover their neighbors and to create adjacencies, it is time to for them to maintain the routing information. In the case of multi-access broadcast networks, the routers are in a two-way state with all the neighbors, because they have discovered them using the Hello protocol. The routers only have the full state (adjacency) with the DRs and BDRs, however. Over this adjacency flows the updates telling the routers about changes in the network.

A few special cases exist, however:

- In a point-to-point link, there are only two routers, and they talk directly to each other. There is no need for a DR or BDR, so these routers directly forward any updates to each other.

- If there are no DRs or BDRs (possibly because all the routers have a priority value of 0), the routers make adjacencies with all routers on the local network. Obviously, this causes a great increase in update traffic compared to using the DRs and BDRs.

- If the routers are attached to a *non-broadcast multi-access* (NBMA) network, the adjacencies must have been programmed into the router. These routers form adjacencies based on the information programmed.

5.4.6 Flooding Protocol

Remember that in a link state network, all routers must know of all paths to all networks. It would create far too much traffic to have every router send its complete routing table to all its adjacent routers. So OPSF only sends changes it sees in the network to its adjacencies.

To make sure that all routers have the same topology information, the routers use the *flooding* protocol. This protocol sends *link state updates* (LSUs) to all adjacent routers as soon as the router wants to send link state information. The receiving routers pass the packet on to all of its adjacent routers, and so on, until the whole area knows about the change.

These mechanisms ensure that the information contained in the LSU packet is received properly:

- A router acknowledges the packet as soon as it is received. The acknowledgement is sent straight back to the sending router using a unicast, or directly if the network does not support multicasting. This ensures that all routers really receive the packet and that the sending router keeps on sending the update until an acknowledgement is received.

- A sequence number is set in each LSU packet. This enables routers to always use the most up-to-date version of the particular update if it receives multiple versions.

Figure 5-7 shows how a router treats the LSUs.

The next section looks at the sort of information contained in the LSU packets.

5.4.7 Link State Advertisements

The information in *link state updates* (LSUs) is split into six types and is called a *link state advertisement* (LSA). Each LSA sends a certain type of information:

1 Router LSA

2 Network LSA

Figure 5-7
A flow diagram of
the LSU process in
OSPF

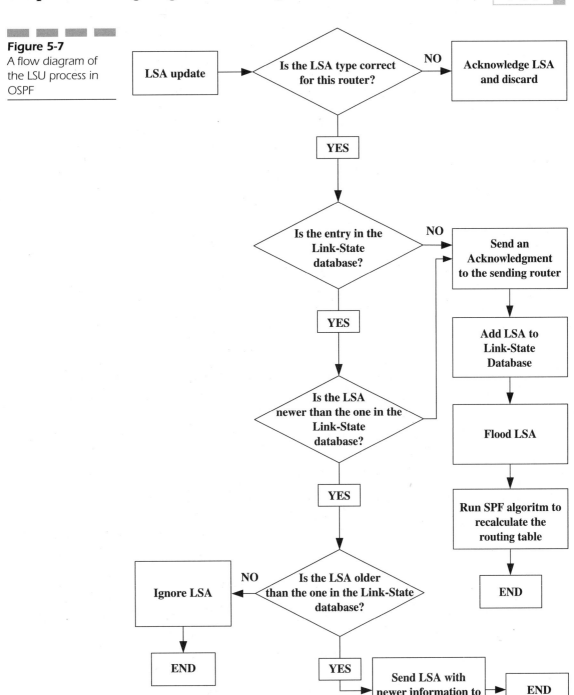

3 Summary LSA (ABRs)

4 Summary LSA (ASBRs)

5 *Autonomous System* (AS) external LSA

7 *Not-so-stubby area* (NSSA)

1. *Router LSA*   Router LSAs tell the rest of the area about the router. A router LSA contains information about all the connected interfaces of that particular router. It also has a flag that tells what kind of router it is in OSPF terms. The options follow:

   a. Endpoint to a virtual link adjacency (V type)
   b. *Autonomous System* (AS) boundary router (E type)
   c. Area border router (B type)

2. *Network LSA*   If a DR is on a network, it sends out network LSAs. In this LSA, it describes all the routers on the network that have an adjacency with the DR (usually, all of them). It also contains the network address and the DR's own IP address.

3. *Area border router* (ABR) *summary LSA*   Area border routers flood these LSAs to tell the routers in the area about the networks in other areas to which they are connected.

4. *Autonomous System border router* (ASBR) *summary LSA*   Much like the type-3 LSAs, these are flooded by ABRs to inform the areas about external routes.

5. *Autonomous System external LSA*   These LSAs are flooded through the area and contain the summaries of the external links. The ASBR is responsible for sending these LSAs through the area it is part of. The networks contained in the LSA are forwarded to other areas as type-4 LSAs by the ABRs.

6. Not used.

7. *Not-so-stubby area* (NSSA) *LSA*   This is generated by an ASBR in an NNSA and describes the external routes to the NSSA area. If the ASBR enables a special bit in the type-7 packet, it can be transformed into an AS external LSA (type 5) by the ABR for flooding through the other areas.

Figure 5-8 shows some examples of LSAs.

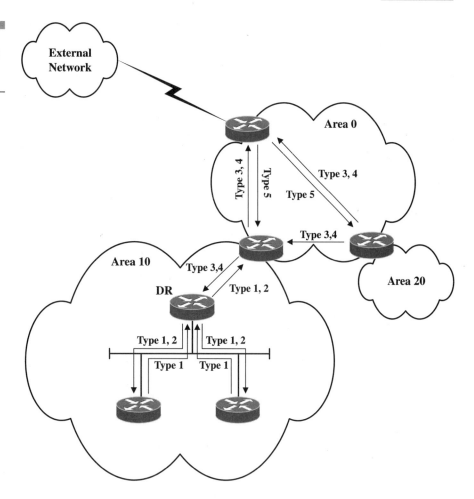

Figure 5-8
Various types of LSAs
and where they can
be found

5.5 OSPF Single Router Configuration

The following configuration example involves a single *internal router* (IR) within a single OSPF area. Here are the basic steps necessary to make an unconfigured router take part in an OSPF network:

1. Enable the OSPF routing protocol.

2. Assign a number to the OSPF process that is to be started.

3. Identify the area(s) the router or specific interfaces of the router are to connected with.

4. Identify the interfaces on which OSPF operation is required.

5. Assign a router ID for router identification in the network.

5.5.1 Step 1

Provided the OSPF protocol was not selected when the router SETUP was run, it has to be configured using the following command:

```
router(config)# router ospf process number
```

5.5.2 Step 2

The process number that has to be entered is for internal router use only for identifying every OSPF routing process that is running. Although it is perfectly possible to run multiple OSPF instances on one router, this is not a preferred situation because of the increased resource use it would cause. Although the process number doesn't have to be the same on all routers in the network, this is usually the chosen approach for reasons of clarity.

5.5.3 Steps 3 and 4

Now that the protocol is enabled on the router, it must be configured so that it knows in which areas the router has to take part. This is a mandatory step. This is the command to use:

```
router (config-router)# network network number wildcard
mask area area number
```

As with the network command in RIP or IGRP, this configures the OSPF process to take part in sending and receiving routing updates. The main difference with RIP and IGRP at this stage is the detail level. Recall that with these two protocols, configuring the protocol means that all interfaces would take part in the routing process. With OSPF, you can specify which IP address takes place in the OSPF process and which area it should connect to. Next, the interfaces that participate in the OSPF process are identified by OSPF using the *wildcard mask*. The interface IP address is compared with the address specified in the `network` command. This granularity makes it possible to configure what part of the address is to be used by OSPF. The entire class could be used, for example, or a specific interface address could be entered. Every interface that matches the configured network number takes part in the *area*—the last parameter issued in the network command.

5.5.4 Step 5

A router ID is required for each router to participate in an OSPF network. An IP address is used as the router ID, either manually defined or automatically set by the router. It is recommended that you manually enter this ID for reasons of clarity in the network documentation and in troubleshooting situations. When no ID is entered, the router selects the highest IP address that is configured on one of its interfaces. At some stage, this IP address could be changed, perhaps because of a design change. This could cause strange and hard-to-trace network behavior. Because there is no specific command to set the router ID manually, the following approach generally is used.

Instead of using the IP address of an existing, live interface, a loopback interface can be used for this purpose. Because this is not a physical interface, but instead is a virtual interface, it can never go down.

In Cisco's case, the OSPF process chooses the IP address with the highest numeric value assigned to any interface on the router. If the OSPF process finds a loopback interface, however, it gives that loopback interface's IP address precedence over any other IP address it finds. This is because a loopback interface cannot be influenced by physical problems—unlike an Ethernet or serial interface—and therefore ensures more stability in the routing process. When neither of these options is used and no router ID is set, the router selects the highest IP address configured on the router as its OSPF router ID.

To configure a loopback interface, use these commands:

```
router(config)# interface loopback interface number
router (config-if)# ip address ip address subnet-mask
```

5.6 Other OSPF Internal Router Configuration Options

Sometimes a situation can occur that makes it necessary to change the traffic pattern of a network. Such a situation could involve political or design decisions. OSPF provides support for such a change by making it possible to change the default cost that a router assigned to an interface. OSPF's calculation of the value for *cost* is based on the speed of the outgoing interface. The result of increasing this value is that the link in question has a better chance of being selected as the shortest path by the SPF algorithm.

To change the cost value on an interface, use the following command:

```
router(config-if)# ip ospf cost cost-value
```

Although the capability to change the cost value provides for greater configuration detail, the implications of such a change can affect the entire network's behavior. Therefore, great care should be taken before doing so. A general rule of thumb in such a situation is *never* to change default settings unless you can explain why the setting(s) should be changed. One such explanation could be that in order for the network to interoperate with other vendors' OSPF routers, the cost has to be changed.

Another situation in which a default setting can be subject to change is in the event of a nonpreferred router being chosen as the

DR or BDR. A router that is not preferred to become the DR or BDR could be one with insufficient CPU power or memory to fulfill this task. Remember that for a router to be eligible for election, its *priority* value must be set to a value between 1 and 255. A priority value of 0 means that a router cannot be elected to become a DR or BDR. The router with the highest value for priority configured wins the election and becomes the DR. The router with the second-highest value becomes the BDR. If no priority value is set on either router in the network, the default value of 1 is used. If that is the case, OSPF uses the router ID as the election discriminator.

To manually set the value for priority, use this command:

```
router(config-if)# ip ospf priority priority-value
```

Here are some other situations in which the priority must be changed:

- The selected router is an area border router, and its resources are not being used for the purpose of DR or BDR.
- All routers but the one selected router are connected to a stub area. (*Stub areas* are explained in the next chapter.)
- If there is a central router in an NBMA environment, it is most efficient to use this router as the DR, because it is the only one connected to all the other routers.

5.7 Verifying OSPF Operation on a Single Router

If part of your job is maintaining a network running OSPF, you need a basic set of IOS commands to accomplish this on an administration level:

```
show ip ospf
```
Gives a detailed overview of the OSPF process, such as the number of route recalculations that have occurred.

`show ip ospf interface`	Displays detailed OSPF configuration information for each interface.
`show ip ospf neighbor [detail]`	Gives detailed information on the relationship with the router's neighbors.
`show ip protocol`	Displays all configured settings for the IP on a router. Apart from showing all the interfaces, it also shows configuration details of IP routing protocols.
`show ip route`	Shows all the networks the router is aware of and the next hop on the preferred path toward them.
`show ospf database`	Displays the current contents of the router's link state database.

In order to make the most efficient use of the detailed output presented by the `show ospf` series of commands, a thorough understanding is required. The following sections give detailed descriptions of each command included in this summary.

5.7.1 show ip ospf

Syntax: `router#` **show ip ospf** *process-ID*
   Output example:

```
A#show ip ospf 1
 Routing Process "ospf 1" with ID 10.0.0.1
 Supports only single TOS(TOS0) routes
 SPF schedule delay 5 secs, Hold time between two SPFs 10
secs
 Number of DCbitless external LSA 0
 Number of DoNotAge external LSA 0
 Number of areas in this router is 1. 1 normal 0 stub 0 nssa
    Area BACKBONE(0)
```

```
          Number of interfaces in this area is 3
          Area has no authentication
          SPF algorithm executed 21 times
          Area ranges are
          Link State Update Interval is 00:30:00 and due in
   00:07:50
          Link State Age Interval is 00:20:00 and due in
   00:17:50
             Number of DCbitless LSA 2
             Number of indication LSA 0
             Number of DoNotAge LSA 0
```

Important Fields in the Output of This Command

Field	Description
SPF schedule delay	Indicates how long to wait before the SPF algorithm starts calculating after receiving an LSA update.
Hold time between two SPFs 10 secs	The minimum amount of time between calculating the SPF.
Number of DCbitless external LSA	Used with OSPF "demand circuits."
Number of DoNotAge external LSA	Used with OSPF "demand circuits."
Routing process "ospf 1" with ID 10.0.0.1	Displays the local process ID for OSPF and the router ID the router will advertise.
Supports only single TOS (TOS0) routes	OSPF is capable of carrying information about the type of service, or TOS, that the IP datagram had requested. Although this feature is supported by Cisco in compliance with RFC-1349, it is not implemented. Therefore, TOS always has a value of 0.
Summary link update interval is 0:30:00 and the update due in 0:07:50. (*)	This LSA would be transmitted into another area by an *area border router* (ABR). Because this router is an internal router, however, it is not capable of issuing this update.
External link update interval is 0:20:00 and the update due in 0:17:50. (*)	This LSA would be transmitted into another routing protocol, using redistribution, by an *Autonomous System boundary router* (ASBR). The update is external to the Autonomous System. Because this router is an internal router, however, it is not capable of issuing this update.

Field	Description
Area 1	Indicates the number of areas this router is a member of. This is an internal router; it is configured for a single area and therefore is a member of one area.
Number of interfaces in this area 3 Area has no authentication SPF algorithm executed 21 times Area ranges are	In one overview, you can see how many interfaces are in which area, whether MD5 encryption is used, the number of times the SPF was executed (an indication of network stability), and finally, the area ranges that show summarization, if configured.
Link state update interval is 00:30:00 and due in 00:18:54.	Indicates when the next update is and that the default was not altered. The LSA update timer defaults to 30 minutes, because this ensures the integrity of the link state database.
Link state age interval is 00:20:00 and due in 00:08:53.	Indicates the MAX-AGED update deletion interval and shows when the database will be purged next of out-of-date routes.

* Summary not included in the output example.

5.7.2 show ip ospf database

Syntax: router# **show ip database** *Output*

   This command displays the contents of the router's link state database and the different kinds of LSAs that populate the database. Because the router in the next example is an internal router, the LSAs displayed are the router and network updates. Many parameters can be issued with this command that enable you to examine the information it produces in great detail. The next example considers the general command.

   Output example:

```
A#show ip ospf database
        OSPF Router with ID (10.0.0.1) (Process ID 1)

        Router Link States (Area 0)

    Link ID    ADV Router    Age    Seq#              Checksum
    Link count
```

```
10.0.0.1    10.0.0.1    20    0x80000002 0xAA8D    1
10.0.0.2    10.0.0.2    22    0x80000002 0xF35B    1
10.0.0.4    10.0.0.4    26    0x80000002 0x86C8    1
10.0.0.9    10.0.0.9    25    0x80000002 0xE1C     1

            Net Link States (Area 0)

Link ID      ADV Router    Age    Seq#      Checksum
192.168.10.248    10.0.0.9    16    0x80000003    0x3048
```

Important Fields in the Output of This Command

Field	Description
OSPF router with ID (10.0.0.1) (Process ID 1)	The router ID and process ID of the router being viewed.
Router link states (Area 0)	Displays the router LSAs and shows the links connecting the router to neighbors discovered via the Hello protocol.
Link ID	The link ID equals the OSPF router ID.
ADV router	The advertising router's OSPF router ID. This ID is the same as the link ID when the router's LSAs are described. The reason for this is that the router is advertising these links in its router LSA to the area.
Age	Indicates the length of time since the last update, in seconds.
Seq#	Indicates the sequence number that is used to ensure that the LSA is truly an update that is more recent than anything currently in the link state database.
Checksum	This checksum is calculated on the entire LSA update and ensures the integrity of the update.
Link count	Shows the number of links the router has configured for OSPF. This field is shown only for the router LSA update.
Net link states (Area 0)	This information is taken from the network LSAs that have been received by the router.
Summary net link states (Area 0)	Taken from the summary LSAs that are passed between the area border routers. Because this router is an *internal router* (IR) in this area, this section would not be displayed in the output.

5.7.3 show ip ospf interface

Syntax: router# **show ip ospf interface** [*type-number*]

This command shows how OSPF has been configured. It provides detail to an interface level as well as its current functioning on each interface. Because of its high detail level, this command is extremely usable in various OSPF troubleshooting scenarios.

Output example:

```
A#show ip ospf interface
Ethernet0 is up, line protocol is up
  Internet Address 192.168.10.250/24, Area 0
  Process ID 1, Router ID 10.0.0.1, Network Type BROADCAST,
Cost: 10
  Transmit Delay is 1 sec, State DROTHER, Priority 1
  Designated Router (ID) 10.0.0.9, Interface address
192.168.10.248
  Backup Designated router (ID) 10.0.0.4, Interface address
192.168.10.253
  Timer intervals configured, Hello 10, Dead 40, Wait 40,
Retransmit 5
    Hello due in 00:00:09
  Neighbor Count is 4, Adjacent neighbor count is 2
    Adjacent with neighbor 10.0.0.4  (Backup Designated
Router)
    Adjacent with neighbor 10.0.0.9  (Designated Router)
  Suppress hello for 0 neighbor(s)
Loopback0 is up, line protocol is up
   OSPF not enabled on this interface
Serial0 is down, line protocol is down
  Internet Address 192.168.30.1/24, Area 0
  Process ID 1, Router ID 10.0.0.1, Network Type
POINT_TO_POINT, Cost: 781
  Transmit Delay is 1 sec, State DOWN,
  Timer intervals configured, Hello 10, Dead 40, Wait 40,
Retransmit 5
Serial1 is administratively down, line protocol is down
  Internet Address 192.168.20.1/24, Area 0
  Process ID 1, Router ID 10.0.0.1, Network Type
POINT_TO_POINT, Cost: 781
  Transmit Delay is 1 sec, State DOWN,
  Timer intervals configured, Hello 10, Dead 40, Wait 40,
Retransmit 5
```

Important Fields in the Output of This Command

Field	Description
Ethernet1 is up, line protocol is up	This single statement includes two statements. The first indicates whether the physical line is operational. The meaning of this depends on the type of interface. In this case, it indicates that a transceiver for Ethernet is present. The last part indicates that the data link layer is working.
Internet address 192.168.10.250/24	Shows the IP address and subnet mask as configured on the interface.
Area 0	Shows the OSPF area for which the interface is configured.
Process ID 1	The *Autonomous System* (AS) number, which really is the OSPF process ID.
Router ID 10.0.0.1/24	Shows the router ID that will be advertised in the LSA updates.
Network type BROADCAST	Displays the type of network the interface is connected to, which indicates how neighbors are found and adjacencies are formed.
Cost: 10	Shows the metric cost of the link that was dynamically chosen from Cisco defaults.
Transmit delay is 1 sec	The anticipated time taken to send an update to the neighbor (defaults to one second).
State DR	Indicates the state of the link in reference to establishing adjacencies. In troubleshooting situations, the information in this field is extremely useful. This field can display the following states: DOWN—I've heard from no one. ATTEMPT—I've sent a Hello on an NBMA but didn't hear anything back. INIT—I've heard a Hello, but I haven't achieved neighbor status yet. TWO-WAY—I have a full neighbor relationship; I've seen myself in my neighbor's Hello table.

Field	Description
	EXSTART—I'm starting up the link for exchanging DDPs.
	EXCHANGE—I'm sending DDPs to another router.
	LOADING—I'm building the LSA database from the DDPs.
	FULL—I have achieved an adjacency with my neighbor (which is now no longer a neighbor but an adjacent router).
	DR—This is the designated router for this LAN.
Priority 1	This value is sent in a field of the Hello protocol and is used to determine the election of the DR and the BDR. The value of 1 means the router is prepared to be elected. If every router has a priority value of 1, the router with the highest router ID is elected.
Designated router (ID) 10.0.0.9, interface address 192.168.10.248	The address of the DR that was elected. Note the difference between the ID and the interface ID. When troubleshooting a configuration error, this is a very useful field.
Backup designated router (ID) 10.0.0.4, interface address 192.168.10.253	The BDR's address with the ID and interface ID given. They both differ.
Timer intervals configured, Hello 10, Dead 40, Wait 40, Retransmit 5	These timers can be changed, and this is sometimes a necessity when connecting to other vendor's equipment that has different defaults from Cisco's. The values of these timers should be the same on all routers throughout the area. The defaults follow: Hello: 10 Dead: 40 Wait: 40 Retransmit: 5
Hello due in 00:00:09	Shows when the next Hello packet is due to be sent out of the interface.
Neighbor count is 4, adjacent neighbor count is 2	Indicates the number of routers that have neighbor relationships. The reason the number of routers with which adjacency is established is less than the neighbors is because there is a DR and a BDR, whose responsibility it is to maintain the adjacencies with all the routers on the LAN.

Field	Description
Adjacent with neighbor 10.0.0.4 (backup designated router) adjacent with neighbor 10.0.0.9 (designated router)	The adjacent router IDs: the BDR and DR.

5.7.4 show ip ospf neighbor

Syntax: router# **show ip ospf neighbor** [*type number*] [*neighbor-ID*] **[detail]**

This command shows OSPF neighbors. Every neighbor known to the router may be viewed, or a more detailed view can be shown. The neighbors can be viewed per interface, for example, or a specific neighbor can be examined in great detail. The general level of detail the output of this command delivers makes it very well suited for troubleshooting purposes.

Output example:

```
A#show ip ospf neighbor


Neighbor ID    Pri    State       Dead Time    Address
Interface
10.0.0.3    1    2WAY/DROTHER    00:00:32    192.168.10.252
Ethernet0
10.0.0.2    1    2WAY/DROTHER    00:00:35    192.168.10.251
Ethernet0
10.0.0.4    1    FULL/BDR     00:00:33    192.168.10.253
Ethernet0
10.0.0.9    1    FULL/DR      00:00:39    192.168.10.248
Ethernet0
```

Important Fields in the Output of This Command

Field	Description
ID	The router ID
Pri	Indicates the priority sent out with the Hello protocol to elect the DR and the BDR

Field	Description
State	Shows the state:
	2WAY—Neighbor relationship established.
	DR—Designated Router.
	BDR—Backup Designated Router.
	DROTHER—Not chosen—neither DR nor BDR. If the priority on the interface is set to zero, the state is always DROTHER, because it could never be elected as DR or BDR.
	FULL—Adjacency established.
Dead time	Indicates how long the router will wait without hearing the periodic Hello from its neighbor before it is declared dead. If this timer is not consistent on every router on the network, problems will occur.
Address	This is the interface address of the neighbor. Note that the router ID is not the same as the interface address. If the loopback address or the highest IP address on the router has been used, the address probably will differ.
Interface	The outgoing interface of the router—the interface on which the neighbor routers were heard.

5.7.5 show ip protocols

Syntax: `router#` **show ip protocols**

This command shows the configuration of the IP routing protocols on the router. It gives details on how the protocols are configured and how they interact with one another. If you need to get an understanding of how the network communicates about its router, or if you need an excellent troubleshooting tool, this command can be very helpful.

Output example:

```
A#show ip protocols
Routing Protocol is "ospf 1"
  Sending updates every 0 seconds
  Invalid after 0 seconds, hold down 0, flushed after 0
  Outgoing update filter list for all interfaces is not set
  Incoming update filter list for all interfaces is not set
  Redistributing: ospf 1
  Routing for Networks:
```

```
      192.168.0.0/16
  Routing Information Sources:
    Gateway     Distance    Last Update
    10.0.0.9      110      00:01:09
  Distance: (default is 110)
```

Important Fields in the Output of This Command

Field	Description
Routing protocol is "ospf 1"	Indicates that "this routing protocol is configured" on the router. If more routing protocols are configured, details of each are listed.
Sending updates every 0 seconds	Shows the frequency of the routing updates. Not relevant for a link state routing protocol that sends updates only when changes occur or at preset intervals.
Invalid after 0 seconds	Relevant for distance vector protocols. Indicates the period of time a route is considered valid from the time of the last update. The route is marked as unreachable if an update on the status of the route has not been received in this defined value.
Hold down 0	Only distance vector protocols use hold-down timers. If a distance vector protocol suspects that a route in its table is bad, it marks it down but does not accept another path with a less-favorable metric until the hold-down timer expires. This way, routing loops are avoided in the network. A link state protocol, in its turn, acts on the information when it hears a routing update.
Flushed after 0	The value indicated that this is a field used by distance vector protocols only. After marking a route as invalid, it flushes it from the routing table when the timer expires.
Outgoing update filter list for all interfaces is not set	Access lists may be set on an interface to filter networks from the routing update. This should be used with great care, because it affects connectivity.
Incoming update filter list for all interfaces is not set	The access list can filter outgoing or incoming routing updates.
Redistributing: ospf 1	If the routing protocol shares information with other configured routing protocols, it is displayed here. Because redistribution can be very complex and therefore sensitive for erroneous configuration, pay extra attention to this field. In this case, no redistribution is configured, making it seem as if OSPF is sharing information with itself.

Field	Description
Routing for networks: 192.168.0.0/16	Reflects the use of the network command when the router was configured. Remember OSPF's granularity; the entry shown here could be as specific as the interface address.
Routing information sources	Heading name for the gateway fields that represent the addresses of the routers that send updates to this router. In the routing table, these routers become the next logical hop.
Gateway 10.0.0.9	A subset of the routing information sources described earlier. Represents the address of the router that provides updates.
Distance 110	The administrative distance value given to the update's source. Indicates which source protocol to choose if more than one is available that provides a path to a remote network. (Don't confuse this with the metric, which indicates which path to choose when multiple paths are available.) Remember that the administrative distance precedes the routing metric.
Last update 00:01:09	Time since the last update was received from that source.
Distance: (default is 110)	The administrative distance—here, showing OSPF's default of 110. This value may be changed for the entire protocol or per source, as in the earlier gateway example. If the value had been changed, it would have been shown here.

5.7.6 show ip route

Syntax: **router#** `show ip route`

This command shows the IP routing table on a router. It delivers a view of the network, with the router itself as the viewpoint, and shows the sources from which the router learned its information. Again, this command is very suitable for getting a quick overview of how the network communicates in order to perform troubleshooting tasks.

Output example:

```
A#sh ip route
Codes: C - connected, S - static, I - IGRP, R - RIP, M -
mobile, B - BGP
```

```
        D - EIGRP, EX - EIGRP external, O - OSPF, IA - OSPF
inter area
        N1 - OSPF NSSA external type 1, N2 - OSPF NSSA
external type 2
        E1 - OSPF external type 1, E2 - OSPF external type 2,
E - EGP
 i - IS-IS, L1 - IS-IS level-1, L2 - IS-IS level-2, * -
candidate    default
        U - per-user static route, o - ODR

Gateway of last resort is not set

     172.168.0.0/24 is subnetted, 1 subnets
O       172.168.1.0 [110/20] via 192.168.10.248, 00:02:11,
Ethernet0
     10.0.0.0/32 is subnetted, 1 subnets
C       10.0.0.1 is directly connected, Loopback0
C    192.168.10.0/24 is directly connected, Ethernet0
```

Important Fields in the Output of This Command

Field	Description
O	Indicates the protocol from which the route was learned. Possible values follow:
	I—IGRP
	R—RIP
	O—OSPF
	C—Directly connected interface
	S—Static route
	E—EGP
	B—BGP
	i—IS-IS
172.168.20.0	Indicates the address of the remote network.
[110/20]	The first number indicates the administrative distance; the second indicates the route's metric.
via 192.168.10.248	Indicates the address of the next router to the remote network.
00:02:11	Specifies the last time the route was updated (hh:mm:ss).
Ethernet0	Specifies the interface through which the specified network can be reached.

5.8 Chapter Summary

This chapter discussed the basic communication between OSPF routers in a single area. It explored the stages in which a new router learns about its surroundings and eventually is able to take part in the routing process. Because OSPF is a link state protocol, it does not send out entire routing tables to neighboring routers; instead, it uses a sophisticated method of communication that only tells surrounding routers of changes in the network. Each router has a complete view of the whole network and uses the SPF algorithm to build the routing table from this information. Updates are sent in a safe and secure fashion through the use of authentication and packet acknowledgement. Designated routers are used to reduce traffic between routers by collecting updated link state information from adjacent routers and passing it on to all other adjacent routers. This makes it unnecessary for all routers to have to talk to one another.

 **5.9 Frequently Asked Questions (FAQ)**

Question: Which IP addresses are reserved for OSPF by the *Internet Assigned Numbers Authority* (IANA)? Which protocol number is reserved by the IANA?

Answer: Multicast address 224.0.0.5 is reserved for OSPF router communication, and 224.0.0.6 is reserved for designated router communication.

OSPF is assigned the protocol number 89. This number is an eight-bit number included in IP header and should not be confused with a port number.

For more information, refer to RFC 1700.

Question: Is it possible to route IPX traffic using OSPF?

Answer: OSPF does not route IPX; it only routes IP traffic. A possible other interior gateway protocol is Cisco's proprietary EIGRP (IPX-EIGRP).

Question: My router shows that it has a link with another router in "2way/DROTHER" when I do a `show ip ospf neighbor` command. What does this mean?

Answer: This means that the routers have exchanged Hello packets but that no adjacency is formed. `2way` indicates that the Hello protocol phase has been performed successfully, and the routers are neighbors capable of communicating, but no adjacency was formed. `DROTHER` means that during the DR and BDR election process, that router was not elected. This is one of the mechanisms OSPF uses to reduce LSA packet traffic, because the router will not send LSAs to the DROTHER router—only to the DR and BDR—and instead expects the DR to inform the DROTHER router about the update.

Question: Can I use host addresses on a loopback interface as a router ID?

Answer: Yes. OSPF can route host addresses (subnet mask 255.255.255.255). This enables you to Telnet to the OSPF router ID to log on to the router.

Question: I have an Ethernet with a network address of 192.168.10.128 255.255.255.192 (26-bit subnet mask). What does the statement look like that enables OSPF to route this network?

Answer: OSPF uses an inverse mask to signify the subnet mask of networks to be routed. A bit of 0 signifies the network portion of the address. So this example becomes

```
192.168.10.128  0.0.0.63
```

The octet in which the subnet split falls can easily be calculated by subtracting the subnet mask decimal value from 255 (255 - 192 = 63).

Question: How many OSPF routers can be in a backbone area without risking instability?

Answer: Cisco offers a conservative estimate of 40 routers. This can vary greatly, however, depending on the stability of the network. Keeping a close eye on convergence times, router CPU, memory load, and the amount of SPF recalculations is the best way to track when the area is reaching its limits.

Question: I have a secondary address configured on my OSPF router. Does OSPF advertise this address?

Answer: Yes, but only if the secondary address is in the same area as the primary. You cannot use it to create an ABR with only one physical Ethernet port.

Question: Does OSPF put a greater demand on the router CPU than RIP of IGRP?

Answer: In a stable network, OSPF uses fewer CPU resources. If the network is unstable, however, or if a link is flapping, the constant SPF recalculations can make OSPF much more CPU intensive.

Question: Will a Cisco router running OSPF be able to communicate with another brand of router running OSPF?

Answer: Yes. OSPF is an open standard, but beware that not all manufacturers use the same default values for the timers. These values must be the same in order for OSPF to work properly.

5.10 Case Study

Consider the network communication scheme illustrated in Figure 5-9; it shows the DR, the BDR, and the other routers on the multi-access segment.

1. What OSPF decision could have caused router R2 to become the BDR?

   ▪ R2's priority was lower than R1's but higher than the other routers.

   ▪ In the case of two routers having the same priority, R2's router ID was lower than R1's but higher than the other routers.

2. Related to the DR, what is the function of R2 in the network?

   (To provide immediate backup if the DR fails. It receives and processes the same information as the DR, but only the DR updates the adjacent routers.)

Figure 5-9
Case study example

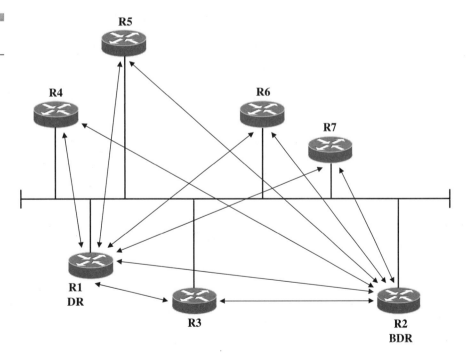

3. R6 has its priority value set to 0. Can this router become a DR? Why?

   (No. A priority of 0 is a way to configure a router so that it never becomes a DR or BDR.)

4. What OSPF state does R5 have with R1 and R2?

   (An adjacency is formed among the DR, BDR, and all other routers. Adjacent routers are in FULL state in respect to each other, as opposed to just being neighbors in a two-way state.)

5. R1 sends out LSAs of type 2 on the network. What are these type-2 LSAs, and what kind of information do they contain?

   (These are network LSAs and describe the network and the IP address of the DR.)

6. Which of the routers in the diagram have an adjacency with the DR?

   (All the routers have an adjacency with the DR. The adjacency enables the DR to send and receive LSAs to and from the other routers.)

5.11 Questions

1. How often does an OSPF router send Hello packets?

2. List the different LSA types.

3. What mechanism is used to elect a designated router in a broad-cast network?

4. How and why are adjacencies formed between routers?

5. What does it mean when a router has its priority set to 0?

6. What are the contents of the topological database?

7. What types of packets have been transferred between two routers prior to becoming adjacent?

8. Why is RIP v1 unsuitable in large networks? Give three reasons.

9. What is the purpose of the SPF algorithm?

10. How many OSPF processes can be run on a Cisco router?

11. Why is it advisable to configure a loopback interface with an IP address when using OSPF?

12. How does a Cisco router running OSPF usually choose its router ID?

13. Suppose that you have an Ethernet interface in area 0, configured with an IP address: 192.168.10.10 255.255.255.128. The entire network range on the interface must be used for the OSPF process. List the commands used to accomplish this.

14. Which command would you use to identify the DR and BDR on a network?

15. What is the definition of a *neighbor* in OSPF?

16. In the output of the `show ip ospf database` command, there is a field that shows the `SPF DELAY`. What does this mean?

17. How would you define an internal router?

18. Name two commands that can be used to verify OSPF operation.

19. How would you define a summary LSA?

20. Which state indicates that the link state databases have been synchronized?

5.12 Answers

1. The default is 10 seconds.

2. Type 1: Router link

Type 2: Network link

Type 3: Summary link from ABR, internal AS

Type 4: Summary link from ABR, external networks

Type 5: Summary link from ASBR, external networks

Type 7: Summary link from ASBR in NSSA area

3. 1. Hello packets are exchanged between all routers to form neighbors.

 2. The highest-priority router becomes the DR, and the router ID is used as the tiebreaker.

4. An adjacency is formed when neighbors have exchanged their complete topological databases. LSA updates are only flooded over adjacencies, not to neighbors. For this reason, routers only form adjacencies with DRs and BDRs to minimize update traffic load.

5. It cannot be elected to become the DR or BDR for that network.

6. It contains a map of the routes within the area. Also all the paths to all other areas and external routes are stored, if they have been flooded into the area by an ABR.

7. ■ Hello packets

 ■ Database description packets

 ■ *Link state request* (LSR) packets

 ■ LSU packets (reply to LSR packets containing the LSA updates)

 ■ LS acknowledgement packets (reply to receiving the requested information)

8. ■ It has a maximum hop count of 15.

 ■ It sends a routing table every 30 seconds.

 ■ Convergence time is increased due to poison-reverse and hold-down timers.

9. This algorithm finds the best paths to the destination networks in the topological database without creating loops. The result is put in the routing table. If there are multiple equal-cost paths, OSPF can load balance between them.

10. Running one process is the common approach. It is possible to run multiple instances of the OSPF protocol, but multiple topological tables will be kept and the SPF algorithm must be run for all instances.

11. The loopback interface IP address will be used as the router ID. Because the loopback interface is not vulnerable to failure, the router ID will not change after a router reload.

12. If there is no loopback interface, it uses the highest IP address that is configured on the router. Otherwise, it uses the highest configured loopback address.

13. `Router ospf 10`

    `Network 192.168.10.128 0.0.0.127 area 0`

14. `show ip ospf neighbor`

    or

    `show ip ospf interface`

15. A neighbor is part of the same network and can send and receive Hello packets.

16. This command indicates how long the router will wait between receiving an LSA update and running the SPF algorithm.

17. An internal router is a router that has all its interfaces connected in one single area.

18. ■ `show ip OSPF <process ID>`

    ■ `show ip OSPF border-routers`

    ■ `show ip OSPF interface <interface ID>`

    ■ `show ip OSPF neighbor`

    ■ `show ip OSPF database <network, summary, asbr-summary, external, database-summary>`

    ■ `show ip OSPF virtual-links`

19. A summary LSA is a type-3 or type-4 LSA sent into an area by the ABR that summarizes links to networks in other areas and to external routes.

20. FULL state

CHAPTER 6

Configuring OSPF in Multiple Areas

6.1 Objectives Covered in This Chapter

To better understand what is necessary to build a scalable network, the following objectives will be covered.

Table 6-1

BSCN objective

BSCN Objective
Understand the issues involved when configuring OSPF for operation in multiple areas
Understand differences between area types, router roles and LSA types
Understand configuration of Stubby, Totally Stubby and Not-So-Stubby Areas
Understand OSPF verification in a multi area network

6.2 Chapter Introduction

Chapter 5 explained how OSPF works in a single area and introduced a few multiple-area issues. This chapter goes into more depth on how OSPF works in multiple areas.

As the number of routers in a single OSPF area grows, it becomes necessary to limit the amount of LSAs produced by the routers to keep convergence and stability within reasonable bounds. This is done by splitting the single area into multiple areas and, in doing so, restricting the LSAs to their own area. This chapter discusses different types of areas and how the information flows between them.

The main reasons for creating multiple areas follow:

1. To reduce the amount of LSAs being sent between the routers
2. To reduce the size of the link state database
3. To reduce the number of reruns of the SPF algorithm
4. To reduce the size of the routing tables through the use of summary routes between areas

6.3 Multiple Areas

When creating multiple areas in OSPF, a hierarchical network is created in which different areas form boundaries with other areas (see Figure 6-1). Within each boundary, the routers share the same link state database, and the SPF algorithm is run based on this area-specific data. Special routers on the area borders receive information about the world outside the area and pass it on into the area so the routers can learn about routes outside the area. The way this data is passed on and the type of data forwarded depends on the type of area the routers are in. This is discussed in detail later in this chapter.

Figure 6-1
A basic OSPF
network with areas

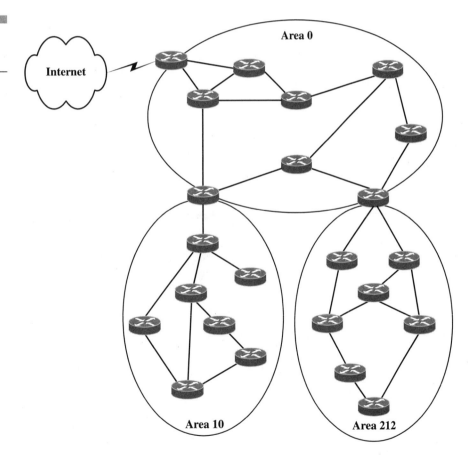

Each area is assigned a unique number, the *area ID,* identifying it for the other areas. The numbers can be arbitrary numbers or IP addresses. Because areas often are designed along with the IP address space design, it can be helpful to use the IP network address assigned to the area as its area ID. The highest area in the hierarchy is a special case and must always have the number 0. This is because the area 0 must be directly attached to all the other areas (see Figure 6-2). It also must summarize all the routing information from all the areas and pass it on to the others. For this reason, the area 0 must not be broken into multiple parts (see Figure 6-3). Areas may not have direct links to each other, called *back doors,* or the hierarchy would be broken (see Figure 6-4).

Three main types of informational traffic must be dealt with in the *Autonomous System* (AS):

- *Intra-area*   Traffic that stays within an area and describes the area's information. See Chapter 5.

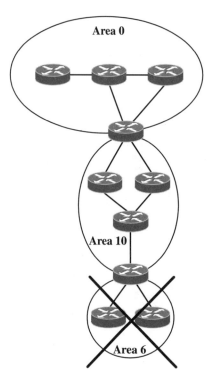

Figure 6-2
All areas must be connected to the central area.

Figure 6-3
Area 0 must
not be split.

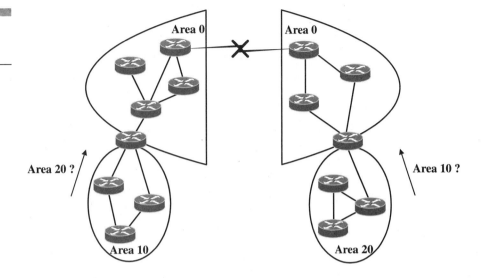

Figure 6-4
No back doors may
exist between areas.

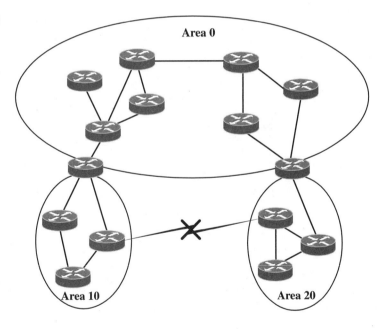

- *Inter-area* Traffic that moves among the areas and has
  information about the other areas for the area in question.
  There is a special type of inter-area information:

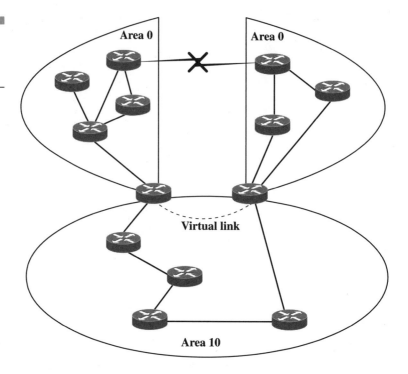

- *Virtual links*   To avoid partitioning of area 0, a virtual link can be made through another area (see Figure 6-5). The virtual link is terminated in both parts of area 0 and traverses the other area without interacting with the routers in the non-area 0. In this way, area 0 still can act as a single contiguous area. See "Configuring OSPF," later in this chapter, for command-specific information.

- *External*   Traffic that moves between the OSPF AS and a different AS

To be able to form this hierarchical network and differentiate between the three types of traffic, OSPF offers Router and Area packet types, which work together to form the AS.

6.3.1 LSA Packet Types

Table 6-2 gives an overview of the LSA types that are used by OSPF to propagate routing information.

Table 6-2	LSA type number	Name	Description
OSPF LSA types	1	Router LSA	Tells the other routers in an area about itself.
	2	Network LSA	Tells the other router in an area about the networks, and which routers are connected to them.
	3	ABR Summary LSA	This LSA is sent by ABRs, and contains summaries of the areas to which the ABR routers are attached.
	4	ASBR Summary LSA	This LSA is also sent by the ABR routers to announce routes to the outside world.
	5	AS External LSA	This LSA contains information about the routes learned by the ASBR about the network outside the AS. The ABRs convert this packet to a type 4 when crossing an area border.
	6	MOSPF LSA	Not implemented by Cisco
	7	NSSA LSA	Quite a recent addition to Cisco IOS, it allows an ASBR to connect a stubby area to an external network. When this happens, the stubby area becomes a NSSA. Routes learned by the ASBR can be kept within the NSSA area, or forwarded as type 5 LSAs by the ABR router.

6.3.2 Router Types

Table 6-3 gives and overview of the different functions that OSPF routers can have in a multi-area Internetnetwork.

6.3.3 Area Types

Table 6-4 gives an overview of OSPF area types.

Table 6-3

OSPF Router types

OSPF Router type	Description
Internal Routers	These routers are part of the same area. All the internal routers in one area should have the same information in their Link-State databases.
Backbone Routers	These are much like internal routers, but are part of Area 0.
Area Border Routers (ABR)	These are backbone routers that join an area to the area 0. The ABR routers must summarize the route information from the connected area, and pass it on to the area 0. They also send the summary data of the other areas, received through area 0, into the connected area.
Autonomous System Boundary Routers (ASBR)	These are routers that join an area to a network out side the AS.

Table 6-4

OSPF area types

OSPF area type	Description
Standard area	This area is as was described in Chapter 5. All other areas are based on the default OSPF area, but restrict certain types of traffic, or offer extra services.
Area 0 (Backbone area)	This area links all the other areas, and exchanges route summaries and data from one area to another.
Stub Area	This is an area that receives updates about all the networks in the AS, but not about the external links that the AS might have (type 4 and 5 LSAs). The routers use a default route of 0.0.0.0 to reach the external networks, through the ABR. To become a stub area, the following criteria must be met:

■ The routers must be programmed to become a stub router, advertise this in the Hello packets, and only create adjacencies with other stub routers.

■ Virtual links can not exist in stub areas, as these have connections in other areas.

■ No ASBR routers can exist in a stub area. This is because the type 4 and 5 LSAs that the ASBR needs are not propagated within the area.

■ Because there can only be one default route, stubby areas can only use one of the ABRs to connect to the external links.

OSPF area type	Description
	The Stub area is created to reduce the size of the link-state database by replacing the external routes with a single default route of 0.0.0.0 to the ABR. The ABR in turn does know to which ASBR to forward the data to.
Totally stubby area	This is a stub area, with the exception that it also does not accept routes to networks in other areas, (type 3, 4 and 5 LSAs). The same criteria must be met as for the stub area. In other words, the routers in a totally stubby area only know of the networks in their own area, and rely on the ABR to forward data to other areas, and external networks. This method further reduces the load on the routers.
Not-So-Stubby-Areas (NSSA)	This is a type of area that is like a stub area, but it solves the issue of not being able to connect to remote networks from the stub area. As you have read, the stub site uses a default route to connect to all external sites. It does not allow an ASBR in its area, as the type 4 and 5 LSAs are not permitted in the area. To solve this, an ASBR can be programmed to send out type 7 LSAs, which are accepted, in this special type of stub area. The type 7 LSAs are flooded through the NSSA area, so all the routers know about the external connection. The NSSA ASBR has the option to allow the ABR to propagate the type 7 LSAs into the rest of the network as type 5 LSAs, but this is disallowed by default. The alternatives to using a NSSA are:

- To allow type 5 LSAs, and thereby making the area a standard area, but needing more powerful routers

- Using another routing protocol throughout what would be the NSSA, and regarding it as an external link, from the point of view of the area 0 |

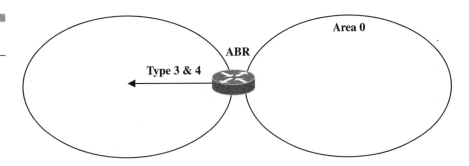

Figure 6-6
OSPF Standard Area

Figure 6-7
OSPF Stubby Area

Figure 6-8
OSPF Totally
Stubby Area

Figure 6-9
OSPF Not So
Stubby Area

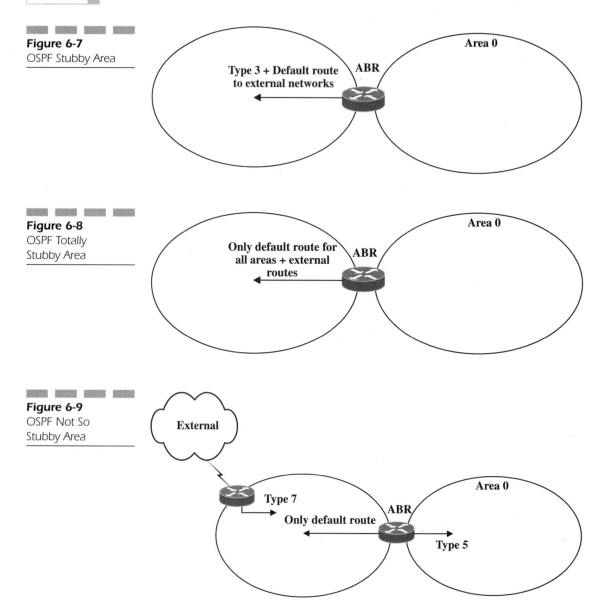

6.4 Route Summarization

In contrast to RIP and IGRP, OSPF was designed with VLSM and CIDR in mind. When combined with stubby, totally stubby, and NSSA areas, OSPF can reduce the amount of routing update traffic and the

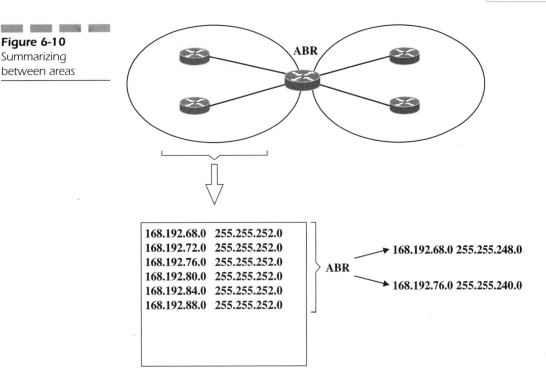

Figure 6-10
Summarizing
between areas

size of the link state database considerably (see Figure 6-10). If an Internetwork has been designed well, it is possible to assign a contiguous range of IP addresses to an area and let the ABR advertise this range only to area 0 in a single advertisement (and vice versa).

Summarizing also can increase the stability of the routing process, because the routers in one area do not need to know about everything that goes on in another area. If a network fails in a summarized area, the summary stays the same and the routers in the other areas do not have to rerun the SPF algorithm.

If two areas are connected through two or more ABRs, care should be taken when summarizing. Because the ABR does not advertise the exact metric to each network, it is impossible for the routers to find the optimal path to one of the networks in the summary.

What if there are multiple routes from one area to another? How does the router determine the best route?

This is done using the route cost, which is determined in the following manner:

Interarea summarized routes:

A total cost of an Inter-area route is the sum of the cost of the summary route, plus the cost of the route to the ABR advertising the route.

External routes:

External routes come in two types, E1 and E2. These routes are advertised by the ASBR, and it can be configured to send either the E1 type or the E2 type.

- E1 routes have a cost that is the sum of the cost of the external route, and the cost of the areas crossed within the Internet network. This is a useful method to use if there are multiple ASBR routers, as the router trying to find the best external route will also take into consideration the cost of crossing the Internet network.

- E2 routes do not contain the cost of crossing the Internet network. They simply state the external cost. This can be used when there is only one ASBR. This type is default, and preferred by a router finding a best cost route if multiple types exist.

6.5 NBMA Networks

Networks based on Frame Relay, ATM, or X25 are *non-broadcast multi-access* (NMBA) networks. The issue is that OSPF regards these networks as broadcast networks and therefore assumes that the DRs and BDRs can reach all the other routers on the network. These networks are usually partially meshed, however, so some routers will not have a direct connection to the others.

The traditional way of solving this problem is to assign a router that has full access to all the routers in the NBMA cloud and to use the priority command to make sure it becomes the DR. Because these networks do not support broadcasts, the neighbors also must be statically defined in the DRs and BDRs by using the neighbor command. This method works but is not very flexible, is not easy to manage, and lacks the redundancy of a broadcast network (see Figure 6-11).

Figure 6-11
An NBMA network
example

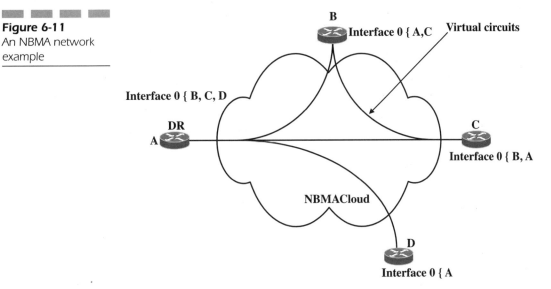

B
Interface 0 { A,C   Virtual circuits

Interface 0 { B, C, D

DR
A

C
Interface 0 { B, A

NBMACloud

D
Interface 0 { A

Figure 6-12
Point-to-point
subinterfaces over
an NBMA network

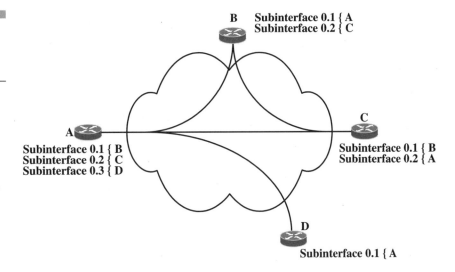

B   Subinterface 0.1 { A
Subinterface 0.2 { C

C
Subinterface 0.1 { B
Subinterface 0.2 { A

A
Subinterface 0.1 { B
Subinterface 0.2 { C
Subinterface 0.3 { D

D
Subinterface 0.1 { A

Cisco offers the possibility of configuring subinterfaces. These
interfaces define multiple point-to-point links over a single physical
interface (see Figure 6-12). In this way, the NBMA cloud will be
regarded as multiple point-to-point interfaces by OSPF, where only
two routers exist and no DR and BDR election is necessary.

6.6 Configuring OSPF

This section discusses some of the configuration options available on Cisco IOS.

6.6.1 Configuring OSPF ABRs and ASBRs

Making a router an ABR or ASBR does not require the use of any special commands; the router takes up this role by virtue of the areas to which it is connected (see Figure 6-13). The basic steps to configure OSPF on a router follow:

1. Enable OSPF:

   ```
   router(config)#router ospf process-ID
   ```

2. Configure each IP network on the router that is to take part in the OSPF network:

   Identify the area each network belongs to. When you have to configure multiple OSPF areas, make sure you associate the correct network address with the area ID of the area it has to become part of.

Figure 6-13
Two areas connected
by an ABR

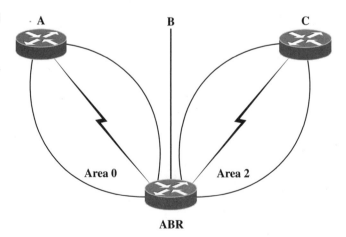

```
router(config-router)#network address
wildcard-mask area area-ID
```

3. If the router has one or more interfaces connected to a non-OSPF network, you have to perform additional configuration, because the router now has to take up the role of the ASBR.

For a detailed discussion on exchanging or redistributing non-OSPF route information with other OSPF routers, see Chapter 12, "Optimizing Route Update Operation."

6.6.2 Configuring Route Summarization

With OSPF, summarization is off by default. To configure route summarization on an ABR, follow these steps:

1. Configure the OSPF protocol as shown in the previous example.
2. Have the ABR summarize routes for a specific area before injecting them into another area:

```
router(config-router)#area area-ID range address
mask
```

where *area-ID* is the identifier of the area about which routes are to be summarized, *address* is the summary address designated for a range of addresses, and *mask* represents the IP subnet mask used for the summary route.

To configure router summarization on an ASBR to summarize external routes (see Figure 6-14), use these steps:

1. Configure the OSPF protocol as shown in the ABR example.
2. Configure the ASBR to summarize external routes before injecting them into the OSPF domain:

```
router(config-router)#summary-address address mask
```

where *address* is the summary address that is designated for a range of addresses, and *mask* is the IP subnet mask used for the summary route.

Figure 6-14
A route
summarization
configuration
example with
two areas

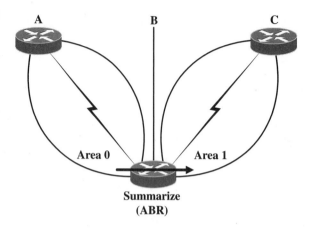

6.6.3 Configuring Stub and Totally Stubby Areas

An area can be configured as stub or totally stubby (see Figure 6-15) with these steps:

1. Configure the OSPF protocol as shown in the ABR example.

2. Define an area as stub/totally stubby by adding the following command to every router within the area:

   ```
   router(config-router)#area area-ID stub [no summary]
   ```

   where *area-ID* is the identifier for the stub/totally stubby area, which can be a decimal value or an IP address, and **no-summary** is an option to create a totally stubby area. Adding **no-summary** prevents an ABR from sending any summary link advertisements to the stub area. It can be configured only on ABRs that are attached to totally stubby areas.

3. This step is optional for ABRs only and defines the cost of the default route that is injected in the stub/totally stubby area. Use the following command:

   ```
   router(config-router)#area area-ID default-cost cost
   ```

   where *area-ID* is the identifier for the stub area, which can be a decimal value or an IP address, and *cost* is the cost for the

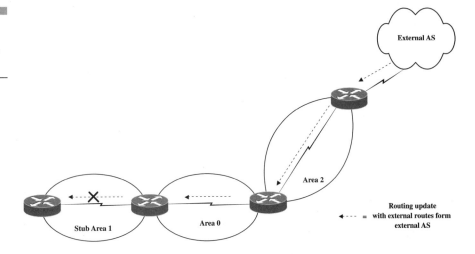

Figure 6-15
A configuration
example of an OSPF
stub area

default summary route used for a stub/totally stubby area. The value can be a 24-bit number, with a default cost value of 1.

Consider the preceding example. To configure the area as totally stubby, the keyword `no-summary` is added to the `area-stub` command on the router. This causes inter-area summary routes to also be blocked from the stub area. In this situation, every router inside the area chooses the closest ABR as the gateway to the world outside the area. The result is that only two types of routes appear in the router's routing table: intra-area routes (designated with an O in the routing table) and the default route. Because the area now is configured to be totally stubby, no inter-area routes (designated with `IA` in the routing table) are included.

6.6.4 Configuring a Not-So-Stubby Area (NSSA)

Follow these steps to configure an OSPF NSSA (see Figure 6-16):

1. Configure OSPF (as described in the ABR configuration example) on the ABR connected to the NSSA.
2. Configure the area as NSSA using this command:

```
router(config-router)#area area-ID nssa
```

Figure 6-16
Overview of
an NSSA

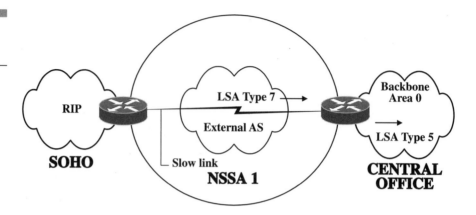

This works only if every router in the same area agrees that the area is an NSSA; this is necessary in order for the routers to be able to communicate with each other.

3. There's an option that enables control over summarization or filtering during the translation. The following example shows how router *x* summarizes routes using this command:

```
router(config-router)#summary-address address
mask prefix mask [not-advertise]
```

6.6.5 Configuring Virtual Links

A virtual link can be configured (see Figure 6-17) using the following steps:

1. Configure the OSPF protocol as shown in the ABR example (6.6.1)
2. Create the virtual link on each router that is to be part of it. These routers follow:

   - The ABR that connects the remote area to the transit area
   - The ABR that connects the transit area to the backbone area

   Use this command:

```
router(config-router)#area area-ID virtual-link
router-ID
```

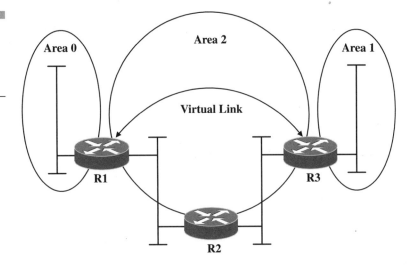

Figure 6-17
A virtual link
connecting area
1 to area 0 through
area 2

where *area-ID* is the area ID of the transit area for the virtual link (decimal or dotted decimal format, which has no default value) and *router-ID* is the router ID of the virtual link neighbor.

6.7 Chapter Summary

This chapter discussed the hierarchical method OSPF uses to subdivide large Internetworks into manageable parts. OSPF provides more scalability and stability, and provides a large reduction in bandwidth use compared to distance vector protocols. OSPF is an open standard, making it suitable for use in multivendor networks that require advanced features such as VLSM, fast convergence, and scalability.

The next chapter focuses on EIGRP—a hybrid protocol that leans very heavily on Cisco's distance vector IGRP protocol. Most of the disadvantages of IGRP have been solved, however, without the necessity of creating a hierarchical area-oriented Internetwork, such as when using OSPF. EIGRP is a Cisco proprietary protocol, however, and therefore has limitations for companies that have invested in non-Cisco hardware.

6.8 Frequently Asked Questions (FAQ)

Question: How do I set up the central router in an NBMA hub-and-spoke environment?

Answer: In the NBMA environment, no broadcasts are available. In the hub-and-spoke environment, each spoke is a point-to-point interface. Because this links only two routers, DR and BDR election is not necessary.

In some cases, it might be necessary to use the following IOS command to tell the router that the subinterface is a point-to-point interface:

```
ip ospf network point-to-point
```

Question: What is a stub area?

Answer: A stub area is an area that is defined not to learn about routes external to the autonomous system. Instead of learning about the external routes, the area's ABR injects a default route into the area.

The area 0 cannot be a stub area.

Virtual links cannot be configured across stub areas.

Stub areas cannot contain an ASBR. (See "Configuring a Not-So-Stubby Area (NSSA)," earlier in this chapter, for more information.)

Question: If an ABR summarizes a contiguous range of subnets in one summary, and a link to one of the subnets fails, will OSPF continue to advertise the summary even though there is now a hole in the range of subnets?

Answer: Only if all the subnets contained in a summary fail will the ABR stop sending the summary update for that range. Traffic destined for the failed subnet will traverse the areas until it reaches the ABR of the area in which the subnet is situated; traffic then will be dropped.

Question: On a Frame Relay subinterface, does OSPF use the CIR value of the PVC to determine the metrics for the route?

Answer: Not by default. OSPF uses the bandwidth of the major interface, not the subinterface. This gives OSPF an indication of the bandwidth that is really available on the subinterface. Use the `bandwidth` command on the subinterface.

Question: Is snapshot routing available for OSPF networks?

Answer: No. Snapshot routing works only with distance vector routing protocols. Link state protocols rely on regular routing updates to keep their topology table up to date.

Question: Will OSPF load balance over two serial connections that connect one area to another?

Answer: OSPF will load balance if it sees that both links are of equal cost. To verify whether this is the case, use the `show ip route` command.

Question: When creating a virtual link to avoid partitioning of area 0, is it possible to let it run through more than one area?

Answer: This is not possible. However, it is possible to define two or more virtual links—each running through different areas.

Question: When configuring `redistribute static` for injecting subnetted static routes into the OSPF process, the routes are not distributed. Why?

Answer: By default, OSPF redistributes only nonsubnetted routes. Use `redistribute static subnets` instead to make OSPF redistribute the subnets.

Question: When I do `show ip route` on an OSPF router, one of the entries is like this:

```
O E2 12.0.0.0/8 [110/20] via 192.168.10.249,
00:07:19, Ethernet0
```

What does the `E2` signify?

Answer: The E2 means that the route is a type-2 external route. This is the default for a route learned from an ASBR. Type-2 routes have a metric defined by the ASBR and are not incremented with the cost of the route through the OSPF AS. Type-1 routes signify routes that have a route of the sum of the external cost and the internal AS cost.

Question: Sometimes I see the backbone area advertised as area 0.0.0.0, and sometimes as area 0. Are these the same?

Answer: Yes. The decimal number is simply another way of writing the four-octet area number. They are interchangeable.

6.9 Case Study

Drake, Linsson & Meyers is a company providing financial constancy services. It has three locations that are interconnected by a Metropolitan Area Network running Cisco hardware. Its network designers opted for OSPF as their protocol of choice and divided the network into three OSPF areas.

Consider the multi-area OSPF network shown in Figure 6-18.

1. Why do you think the network designers configured a virtual route between router 1 and router 2?

   (To comply with the OSPF design rule that all areas must be attached directly to area 0. If this connection is not possible in a physical way, the virtual link is the only alternative.)

2. Is the solution that the virtual route provides advisable? Why?

   (No. It is only a method to temporarily solve a connectivity issue, or to provide backup to an existing physical connection to an area 0. In the long term, it is better to concentrate on a good design than to use such methods.)

   After a merger, the network suddenly had to be redesigned to offer interconnection between both companies. Time was of the

Figure 6-18
Case study example

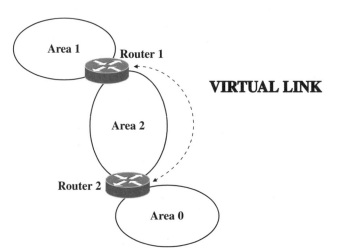

Figure 6-19
Case study example

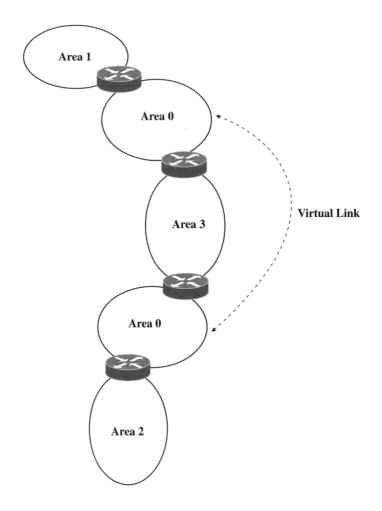

essence in designing a connection between both OSPF networks.
Figure 6-19 shows the new network as it appeared in the
redesign proposal.

3. Is the proposed configuration a valid one? Why?

(Yes, this proposition is valid. All areas have a connection to area
0, and through the use of a virtual link, area 0 is not
partitioned.)

4. Why do you think the network designers came to this decision?

(If the companies could not find a quick method to merge the two area 0s, the virtual link is a good solution. However, it is important to realize that the bandwidth demands on area 3 will be increased dramatically until a permanent solution is found for joining the two area 0s.)

6.10 Questions

1. What is the purpose of a virtual link in OSPF?

2. What are the function and location of area 0?

3. In which area must an ABR reside?

4. If the networks have converged and there are no changes, why do the routers still send out LSAs, and how often do they do it?

5. What is an ABR, and what type of LSAs does it send out?

6. What is the difference between a stub area and a totally stubby area?

7. Which command would you use to see whether a network is in the same area or another? Which field gives you this information in the output?

8. With which command can you define a totally stubby area?

9. Where should summarization be configured?

10. What is the difference between an ABR and ASBR?

11. Which command is used to assign a fixed cost to routes advertised to a stub area? On which router is this command issued?

12. What type of LSAs can be found in an NSSA area?

13. Give two examples of NBMA network types.

14. What Cisco IOS command is used to define an NSSA router?

15. Does snapshot routing work in OSPF networks?

16. What is the definition of an external link?

17. Give three reasons for summarizing routes in OSPF.

18. Does an internal OSPF router automatically summarize network addresses?

19. Are type-7 LSAs flooded outside the NSSA area?

20. What alternative is there to connecting a stub area to an external route without creating an NSSA area?

6.11 Answers

1. In OSPF, area 0 must not be partitioned. Also, all areas must be directly connected to area 0. If this is not possible, the virtual link can be used as a tunnel to extend area 0 through another area.

2. Area 0, or the backbone area, is the central area. All other areas are directly connected to it. Routing information is passed into the backbone from the other areas' ABRs. This routing information then is forwarded to all other areas. The backbone also provides the links between different areas.

3. Area 0, as well as the area it is connecting to area 0. It has two topological databases—one for each area it is connected to.

4. To be sure that the integrity of the topological database stays intact, the routers send out LSAs every 30 minutes.

5. ABR stands for *area border router,* and it sends out type-3 and type-4 LSAs.

6. A stub area will not flood type-5 packets through the area and uses a default route to send data for other areas to the ABR. A totally stubby area will not flood type-4 and type-5 packets through the area and uses a default route to send all data with a destination outside the area to the ABR.

7. `show IP route`

   Check the second field: `IA` indicates another area, and nothing indicates the same area.

8. As a subcommand of the

   `router ospf <process ID> ;`

   `Area <area ID> stub no-summary`

9. It should be configured on the area boundaries.

10. The ABR joins an area to area 0. The ASBR joins external networks to an area.

11. `Area <area id> default-cost <cost>`

    On the ABR

12. Type 1, 2, and 7

13. ■ Frame Relay

 ■ X.25

 ■ ATM

14. `Area <area ID> nssa`

15. No. Snapshot routing only works with distance vector network protocols.

16. A route that has a destination outside the OSPF AS. Its last hop in the OSPF AS is always an ASBR.

17. ■ It lessens the CPU load on the routers through fewer SPF recalculations.

 ■ It lessens the memory usage due to a smaller topology database.

 ■ Network failures in one area do not affect the topology databases in other areas.

18. No. Summarization must be explicitly switched on.

19. No. However, if configured on the NSSA ASBR, the ABRs in the NSSA area can transform the type-7 LSAs into type-5 LSAs.

20. Use a non-OSPF routing protocol between the OSPF stub area and the external network, and redistribute the external routes into the stubby area.

CHAPTER 7

Configuring Enhanced IGRP (EIGRP)

7.1 Objectives Covered in This Chapter

To better understand what is necessary to build a scalable network, the following objectives will be covered, as outlined in Table 7-1.

Table 7-1

BSCN objectives

BSCN Objective
Describe Enhanced IGRP features
Describe operation of Enhanced IGRP
Describe how Enhanced IGRP can be configured for usage in a scalable Internetwork
Verify Enhanced IGRP operation in a scalable Internetwork

7.2 Chapter Introduction

The *Enhanced Interior Gateway Protocol* (EIGRP) is the successor to Cisco's proprietary IGRP. The two work together seamlessly, even though EIGRP has many advantages over IGRP. EIGRP has been designed to offer the following benefits when compared to other protocols:

■ Rapid Convergence.

■ Reduced bandwidth usage.

■ Support for multiple network-layer protocols.

The following list shows in short how EIGRP achieves these goals.

■ *Neighbor discovery*   EIGRP checks its neighbors on a frequent basis, using small hello packets.

■ *Multiple sessions*   A single router can run multiple instances of EIGRP, and it can pass information from one instance to another.

- *Incremental routing updates* EIGRP does not unnecessarily flood its neighbors with routing information. Also, EIGRP will only send information to the neighbors that need it, and not flood information such as link-state protocols do.

- *Classless routing* It is a huge advantage over IGRP, EIGRP supports classless routing.

- *Equal cost load balancing* EIGRP can use multiple circuits to send traffic.

- *Diffusing-Update Algorithm (DUAL)* The core of EIGRP, this algorithm makes the decisions on which routes to use and which not to use. It finds loop-free routes and uses distance information similar to IGRP to find the least-cost path. The next hop for DUAL is called a successor, and DUAL keeps a list of "feasible successors" to speed convergence in the case of topology changes in the network.

- *Reliable Transport Protocol (RTP)* This guarantees the transport of important data, such as routing table updates.

- *Protocol-dependant modules* EIGRP uses modules to learn about network-level protocols such as IPX, AppleTalk, and IP. These modules all inject their information into the DUAL mechanism that makes the decisions and outputs its findings back to the software module. For each protocol, separate tables are maintained for neighbors, topology, and routing.

EIGRP is sometimes called a hybrid routing protocol, and sometimes it is called a distance vector protocol. It is basically a distance vector protocol that has been constructed in such a way that it has many of the advantages of link-state protocols. From Cisco's point of view, however, it is an *advanced* distance vector protocol.

When comparing the features to other distance vector (RIP/IGRP) and link state (OSPF) protocols, one finds the following comparisons, as shown in Table 7-2.

The ease of implementation and flexibility do have a downside. OSPF requires a reasonably rigid network structure and encourages a structured network design, whereas EIGRP is easier to implement

Table 7-2

Comparing EIGRP to other routing protocols

	RIP/IGRP	OSPF	EIGRP
Convergence	Slow	Fast	Fast
Configuration	Easy	Difficult	Easy
Design complexity	Low	High	Medium
Incremental updates	No	Yes	Yes
Classless routing support	No	Yes	Yes
Compatible with IGRP	-/-	No	Yes
100% loop-free	No	Yes	Yes
Hop count limitation	RIP (16)	No	No

in an ad hoc fashion. Every protocol has limits, however, and EIGRP will eventually fail if the design and hierarchy are not given sufficient attention.

So how does EIGRP manage to do all these wonderful things? Read on!

7.3 EIGRP hello Protocol

EIGRP starts by finding neighbors. Neighbors are routers that can be reached using EIGRP's hello protocol. This protocol uses a multicast address of 2214.0.0.10.

When a router has receives a reply to a hello packet, it checks the autonomous system number and the metric calculation values. If these match, then the information contained in the reply is entered into the Neighbor Table. By doing this, the routers form an adjacency. See Figure 7-1 for an overview of the adjacency building process.

The neighbor table contains the following information about the neighbor:

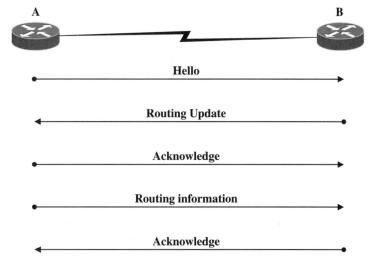

Figure 7-1
The information flow for the EIGRP initial hello process

- The IP address and interface through which the router can be reached.
- *The hold time*   This is the amount of time to wait before assuming that the other router is dead.
- *The up time*   This is the amount of time that the adjacency has been in place between the two routers.
- *Smooth Round Trip Timer* (SRTT)   This number indicates an average of how long the round trip takes for a packet between the routers.
- *RTO*   This is the retransmit interval for the connection.
- *Q*   This shows how many packets are waiting in queue to be sent to the other router. High values indicate congestion problems.

To check the neighbor table, use the following command:

```
Show ip eigrp neighbors
```

The output is as follows:

```
A#show ip eigrp neighbors
IP-EIGRP neighbors for process 10
```

H Address	Interface	Hold (sec)	Update	SRTT (ms)	RTO	Q Cnt	Seq Num
0 192.168.0.10	Se1	9	14:05:34	6	200	0	6

When the adjacency has been formed and the neighbor has been added to the neighbor table, the routers exchange routing information which is stored in the topology table, ready for the DUAL process (the dual process is covered in the next chapter).

EIGRP also uses the Hello protocol to keep an eye on its neighbors. If no Hello packets are received from a neighboring router for a certain period of time (the 'hold time'), then the neighbor is declared dead, and the routes learned from that neighboring router are removed from the topology table.

The default timer for sending hello packets is 5 seconds, but on slower links such as multipoint links with a bandwidth of less than T1 speed, the timer is 60 seconds.

The default values of the hello timer can be adjusted per interface using the following command:

```
Ip eigrp hello-interval <seconds>
```

The hold timer, which is typically 3 times the value of the hello interval timer, tells the router how long to wait without receiving any sign from the neighboring router before declaring the neighbor dead.

This timer, as seen in the 'show ip eigrp neighbors' output, will be reset by either a Hello packet from the neighboring router, or any other EIGRP update packet. On older versions of Cisco's IOS, the hold timer will only be reset by the receipt of a Hello packet.

The value of the hold timer can be changed using the following interface command:

```
IP eigrp hold-time <seconds>
```

It is not strictly necessary for these timers to be exactly the same on both neighbor routers, but as you can imagine, if one router has a hello interval that is longer than the other router's hold time, then the neighbor connection could easily suffer stability problems.

This method of using the Hello protocol to build adjacencies gives EIGRP a link-state-like advantage over distance vector protocols. It enables EIGRP to react very quickly to link failures.

To enable EIGRP on a router and start the hello process, the following commands are necessary:

```
Router(config) #router eigrp AS-number
Router(config) #network ip network address
```

The first statement enables EIGRP in the router with an autonomous system number. All routers that wish to form adjacencies need to share this common number.

The network statement tells EIGRP which networks to include in the routing process. Multiple network addresses can be entered, as separate network commands.

The next step that the router will take upon having EIGRP enabled, and finding adjacencies is the DUAL process. This is the core of EIGRP, and is described in the next chapter.

7.4 EIGRP Reliable Transport Protocol

EIGRP Reliable Transport Protocol or RTP is used by the router to guarantee ordered delivery of critical EIGRP packets to its neighbors. As EIGRPs routing mechanism relies on the building of a loop-free routing table from correct information in the topology table, it is logical that EIGRP puts a great deal of effort into making sure that the routing information that fills the topology table is correct and up-to-date. This greatly enhances the stability of the routing protocol, especially when the network is under stress from congestion or unstable circuits.

Only packets that need the reliability and therefore explicit acknowledgment are sent using RTP.

Packets sent using RTP are

- Query
- Update
- Reply

Packets that do not need RTP are

- Hello
- Ack

The process of RTP keeps a list of reliably sent packets, numbering each one to ensure ordered delivery. If an acknowledgement packet is not received, then the information is retransmitted.

In the case of multi-access networks, RTP can use multicast as a method to send data to its neighbors. Herein lies a potential problem, as RTP will wait for acknowledgment of the receipt of a packet before sending the next one. In a multicast environment, it would have to wait for all the acknowledgments from the routers before the next packets could be sent. RTP solves this problem by retransmitting the data as a unicast packet to the slow router, and carrying on with the multicast to the faster routers. This avoids delays in the transmission of routing information.

RTP will try 16 times to retransmit a packet to a neighbor. If after this period still no acknowledgement has been received the adjacency is removed.

7.5 EIGRP DUAL

Now that the router knows about its surroundings and has filled its topology table with routes learned from its neighbors, it must decide which routes to use for routing. The routes it chooses to use for routing are entered into the third database, the routing table. The mechanism used to choose the best routes is called the *EIGRP Diffusing Update Algorithm* (EIGRP DUAL).

What does DUAL do?

- It keeps track of the routes advertised by the neighbors.

- It selects a *loop-free* path to a destination network, the next hop being the successor. Any routes that also lead to the same destination network can become feasible successors.

- If successor connection is lost, use feasible successor immediately. If no feasible successor is known, then query all neighbors for a possible route.

- DUAL only involves the routers in its recomputations that actually are affected by a topology change. This saves bandwidth and processor time.

To get a good idea of how DUAL manages to do this, we will look at the variables used in the DUAL decision process. The distances used by EIGRP are composite metrics. They are calculated by each router, taking into account the following variables:

- *Bandwidth* The smallest bandwidth between router and destination

- *Delay* The total delay from router to destination

- *Reliability* The worst reliability between router and destination. Each neighbor connection is valued-based on the amount of keepalive packets lost.

- *Load* The highest load on any link between the router and destination

- *Maximum transmit unit* (MTU) The smallest MTU between the router and destination

This set of variables is compatible with those of IGRP, making the two easy to combine.

7.5.1 Reported Distance (RD)

The *reported distance* (RD) is the metric (distance) that is advertised to the router by its upstream neighbors. Upstream means a router that is nearer the destination network.

In Figure 7-2, routers B and D report the distance they have calculated to router A. The distance reported is the total of all the distances to a remote network. In this case, we use 192.168.10.0 as the remote network. In the figure, this becomes the following, as shown in Table 7-3.

In other words, router A has a copy of all its neighbors' routing tables, as the metrics therein are the RDs for router A.

7.5.2 Feasible Distance

When the router has received the reported distances to the remote network from a neighbor, it adds the distance from itself to that reporting router and calls that the *feasible distance* (FD). The route with the shortest FD is used to populate the routing table and will therefore become the route used to send data.

Figure 7-2
EIGRP and distances

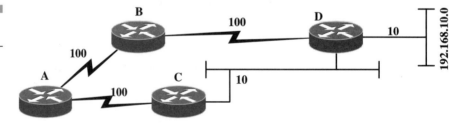

Table 7-3

Reported distances example

Neighbor Router	Total Distance	RD
B	100 + 10	110
C	10 + 10	20

Neighbor Router	Total Distance	FD
B	100 + 100 + 10	210
C	100 + 10 + 10	120

Table 7-4

Reported distances example

In Table 7-4, you can see that it is faster for router A to choose the link over router C to router D to get to network 192.168.10.0. The numbers represent the metrics for the links. The router will calculate the feasible distances for network 192.168.10.0 as shown in the table.

Here the route with lowest FD is promoted from the topology table to the routing table and is therefore used to send data. If multiple links are used, load-balancing multiple routes can be copied from the topology table to the routing table. The neighbor router whose route is being used to reach the destination network is called a *successor*.

7.5.3 Loop Avoidance and Feasibility Conditions

So, the router has now chosen a route or routes to use for routing. However, it still has a list of routes that have a higher feasible distance to the destination network in the topology table.

The EIGRP router marks these routes as feasible successors if it is sure that they are not part of a routing loop. In the case of an outage where the route to the destination network is lost, EIGRP can immediately start using one of its prepared and tested feasible successor routes. This gives EIGRP very fast convergence as the router does not need to calculate anything or communicate with its neighbors to find the new route.

As mentioned, EIGRP does check the alternative routes to see if they are loop-free. This test is quite simple and is done by comparing the FD of the route in use with the RD of the alternative path. If the RD is smaller than the FD, then a loop is not possible. This is called

Figure 7-3
Feasible distances

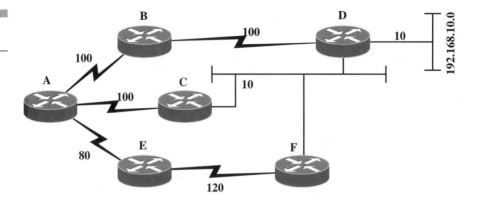

the *feasibility condition*. All neighbor routers advertising routes that pass this test are marked as feasible successors and can be used at a moment's notice. In Figure 7-3, you can see a more complicated setup, where routers E and F have been added.

Here the route A-E-F-D does not pass the feasibility condition as can be calculated (see Table 7-5).

So, here we see that even though the distances to the remote network via router E and via router B are the same, router A will not enable router E's route to be a feasible successor because it might also be a loop.

If the routes via router B and C are lost, leaving only the route via E, then the router must rerun the DUAL calculation, which will then find the route over router E to be the only one and therefore the best.

Table 7-5

Calculating the
feasibility condition

Router	RD	FD	Feasible Condition
B	110	220	Feasible successor
C	20	120	Successor
E	140	220	Failed 140 (RD) >120 (FD of C)

7.5.4 Examples of DUAL

As we have now seen, DUAL can, in some cases, recalculate the routing table without querying its neighbors. This is called passive mode, and is the fastest method for DUAL to find a new route.

If there is no feasible successor for a lost route, then DUAL must query its neighbors for a possible new route. This is called active mode, and due to the necessity of sending out query packets, etc., it is a lot slower than passive mode.

Let's have a look at an example of a passive change to the routing table:

Looking at Figure 7-3 and Table 7-5, we see a stable network with a route from router A to network 192.168.10.0 having router C as successor, router B as feasible successor, and router C as unused.

If now the route over router C fails, router A will check the topology table to see if there are any feasible successors.

In this case there is one, the route over router B. Dual keeps the route in passive state, and promotes the feasible successor to successor, putting it in the routing table and using it.

Next it will recalculate the feasibility condition, to see if there are any new feasible successors.

In this case the previously unused route over router E is promoted to feasible successor, because the reported distance of router E is less than feasible distance reported by the new successor, router B.

Next we will look at an example of an active change to the routing table:

Figure 7-4 shows a network, Table 7-6 shows the topology table of router A and Table 7-7 shows the topology table of router E.

If router C reports that the route to network 192.168.10.0 has failed to router A, then EIGRP will remove the route from the routing table and DUAL will check the topology table for feasible successors, and, in this case, not find one. Now the following happens:

1. The route is put into active state in the topology table, signifying that the route is down, and a new one needs to be found.

2. Router A will send out a query to all neighbors, except C, as this router reported the loss of connectivity.

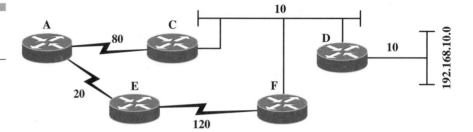

Figure 7-4
Active DUAL
computations

Table 7-6

Topology table of
router A

Router	RD	FD	Feasible condition
C	20	100	Successor
E	140	160	Failed 140 (RD) >100 (FD of C)

Table 7-7

Topology table of
router E

Router	RD	FD	Feasible condition
A	100	120	Successor
F	20	200	Feasible successor (20<120)

3. Router E receives the query, and realizes that the route over router A to the destination network is down. This route is removed from the routing table and the topology table and Router E checks the topology table for a feasible successor. The route via router F is found and promoted to Successor.

4. Router E sends a reply to router A, indicating that a successor has been found.

5. Router A waits until all the replies have been received from all its neighbors (only router E in this case), fills the topology table with them, and calculates which route is the successor and any possible feasible successors. The route via router E is the only one in this case, so in this case it becomes successor, placed in the routing table, and the route is moved from active state back to passive state.

7.5.5 Finding Information About the DUAL Process

To troubleshoot the DUAL process, the following commands can be used.

The `show ip eigrp topology` command can give insights into the DUAL process and highlight problems. The routing table can show which protocol is advertising the routes and quickly show you which decisions the router has made. Here are some partial outputs from a router. First look at the following topology table, generated from what the router sees of the surrounding world:

```
A#show ip eigrp topology
IP-EIGRP Topology Table for process 10

Codes: P - Passive, A - Active, U - Update, Q - Query, R -
Reply,
       r - Reply status

P 192.168.10.0/24, 2 successors, FD is 10665472
        via 192.168.20.30 (10665472/10639872), Ethernet0
        via 192.168.20.20 (10665472/10639872), Ethernet0
 .
 .
 .
```

The value before the slash between the brackets is the FD for that route, and the value behind the slash is the RD.

This route has a special case of two successors, meaning that two neighbors have supplied a route that has met the feasibility condition. Using more than one successor is called *load-balancing* and will be discussed in Section 7.5.6. This case can only happen by default if the FDs are exactly the same size. If there had been any difference, the lower one would become the only successor and the other possibly the feasible successor.

The P designation means that the topology information is passive. This means that no queries are outstanding for this route. The A means active, signifying that the router is recalculating the topology information using new updates requested from the neighboring routers. Obviously, this is a less than optimal state, and if many routes are like this, then it can mean that the network is experiencing stability problems.

The router can also send warning messages when a neighboring router does not reply to a request for information. This is called a *stuck-in-active state*. This can occur occasionally when a network experiences high loads, but if it becomes a chronic message, then it should be seen as a warning that the network could be becoming seriously unstable.

Now we look at the routing table, which is the list of routes that the router has chosen to use, using the DUAL algorithm:

```
A#show ip route
Codes: C - connected, S - static, I - IGRP, R - RIP, M -
    mobile, B - BGP
    D - EIGRP, EX - EIGRP external, O - OSPF, IA - OSPF
    inter area
    N1 - OSPF NSSA external type 1, N2 - OSPF NSSA
    external type 2
    E1 - OSPF external type 1, E2 - OSPF external type 2,
    E - EGP
    i - IS-IS, L1 - IS-IS level-1, L2 - IS-IS level-2, *
    - candidate defaultU - per-user static route, o - ODR

D    192.168.10.0/24 [90/10665472] via 192.168.20.20,
     00:01:24, Ethernet0
                     [90/10665472] via 192.168.20.30,
                     00:01:25, Ethernet0
C    192.168.20.0/24 is directly connected, Ethernet0
.
.
```

Here you can see that both the routes in the topology table have been promoted to the routing table. This is because EIGRP automatically does equal-cost load-balancing, which will be discussed in the next section. The D signifies that the route was learned through EIGRP.

7.5.6 EIGRP Load Balancing

We can tweak EIGRP to use more than one link to route traffic over. Normally, EIGRP will only use two links to split the traffic load if both links have exactly the same metric. This can be seen in the examples in Section 7.5.3. However, we can tell EIGRP to enable routes with different metrics to be used for sending data. The advantage here is of having more bandwidth to the destination network, but the disadvantage is that slower routes might cause data packets to arrive on the destination network out of sequence.

To enable the unequal-cost load-balancing, use the following command in the router eigrp configuration:

```
router(config-router)#variance 2
```

Here the multiplier has been set to 2. The router takes the smallest FD from the topology table, multiplies it by the variance multiplier (2 in this case), and enables all other routers with an FD smaller than that number to be promoted to the routing table.

The default value of the variance multiplier is 1, which explains why routes with identical FDs are automatically used for equal-cost load-balancing. Look at Figure 7-5 as an example of EIGRP variance.

In this figure, the route over router B is best, with an FD of 15. The route over router C has an FD of 35. If we set a variance of 2, then the router will enable all routes with an FD of 30 or less to carry data

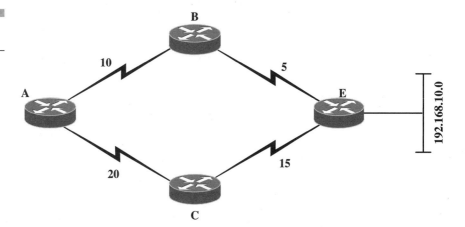

Figure 7-5
EIGRP variance

to the destination network, which is not enough to let route A-C-D join in. Clearly, we will need to set a variance of 3 to allow this network to use both routes.

7.6 EIGRP Summarization

EIGRP has a flexible mechanism for summarizing IP information. Whereas OSPF only summarizes on border routers, EIGRP can be left to automatically summarize or it can be manually configured to summarize on each interface.

EIGRPs automatic summarization always tries to advertise the smallest amount of subnets. If the Internetwork is non-contiguous, then this can cause problems, as a router might advertise a subnet in its update that is actually somewhere else in the Internetwork.

Obviously, having a non-contiguous IP addressing scheme is a bad thing, but sometimes it is unavoidable due to company politics, history, complexity, or simply due to IP re-addressing work.

In Figure 7-6, the routers both advertise the Class C network and not the individual 27-bit subnets. The router in the middle does not know how to get to the individual subnets.

In this case, auto summarization should be switched off. This is done for the routing process as a whole:

```
router(config)#router eigrp process-ID
router(config-router)#no auto-summary
```

Figure 7-6
EIGRP auto summary

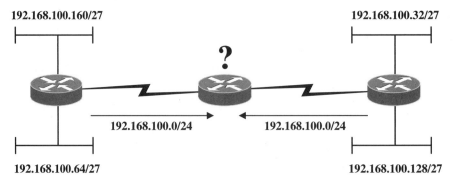

Do not forget that disabling auto summarization forces the router to advertise every subnet in the routing process. This can place a heavy burden on small-bandwidth circuits. EIGRP will use up to 50 percent of the bandwidth of a circuit by default.

In some cases the network operator might not want automatic summarization to be switched on, but having the burden of many updates running over the Internetwork is also not an option. In this case manual summarization can be used. The following section explains.

Summarizing manually is done as follows:

```
router(config)#interface serial 0
router(config-if)#ip summary-address eigrp 10 192.168.100.0
255.255.255.0
```

As you can see, the summarization is performed on the interface configuration and is linked to the routing process ID. In this case, the process ID is 10. The IP network address shows the address that will be advertised out of the serial 0 interface. Finally, the subnet address shows that the address will be advertised as a 24-bit address, which is also commonly called a Class C address.

7.7 EIGRP in an NBMA Environment

In comparison to Multiaccess (ie. LANs), and Point-to-point (i.e., PPP) connections, *Non-Broadcast Multi Access* (NBMA) networks can require some extra attention. EIGRP has two issues to watch out for when configuring for such networks.

On slow NBMA networks, such as many Frame Relay networks, EIGRP will send out hello packets to the neighbors every 60 seconds, instead of the default five seconds (see Figure 7-6). By slow, we mean any link with a speed of less than a T1. Also, the hold timer becomes 180 seconds, instead of 15. EIGRP learns about the bandwidth of a circuit by looking at what was configured in the interface bandwidth command. See the summary at the end of the chapter for the syntax of changing this parameter.

Figure 7-7
EIGRP and NBMA

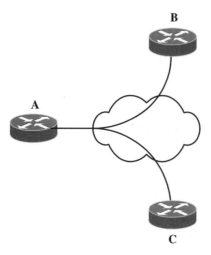

These values can be adjusted to suit your own purposes, but this is rarely necessary in a well-designed network. To do so, use the following command on the interfaces:

```
router(config-if)#ip hello-interval eigrp 10 30
```

This configures the router to send out its hello packets destined for neighbors in AS 10 every 30 seconds. It will also be necessary to change the timeout value, which is usually three times the hello interval. For this, use the following command:

```
router(config-if)#ip hold-time eigrp 10 90
```

This tells the router to assume that a neighboring router is dead if no updates are received from it during 90 seconds. It is also important to change these values on all the other routers that are on the receiving end of such changes.

EIGRP also by default has Split Horizon switched on for all interfaces. In an NBMA environment, however, it can be necessary to switch it off to enable the updates to reach all the routers.

Earlier, in Figure 7-7, if router B sends an update over the NBMA network to router A and then uses Split Horizon, router A will not send back information about that route out of its interface. Router C will therefore never learn about this route.

If Split Horizon is switched off, then router A will send the update from B back out the interface, thus informing router C of the destination networks advertised by router B.

The command for switching off `eigrp split horizon` on an interface is the following:

```
router(config-if)# no ip split-horizon eigrp 10
```

Here Split Horizon is switched off for updates from AS 10.

Apart from creating an expensive, fully meshed NBMA, these problems can be avoided by using a subinterface for every virtual link across the NBMA network. Each subinterface can be provided with the information about that circuit, and EIGRP will treat the subinterfaces as separate links.

7.8 EIGRP Bandwidth Usage

EIGRP will by default not use more than 50% of the bandwidth stated in the interface 'bandwidth' command. However this command is often used to influence the routing decisions, as changing the bandwidth changes the metric over that interface.

In this case the administrator can assign a different EIGRP bandwidth usage percentage to an interface.

This is done as follows:

```
Router (config) #interface serial 0
Router (config-if) #bandwidth 128
Router (config-if) #ip bandwidth-percent eigrp 10 25
```

In this example we have set the bandwidth of the serial 0 interface to 128 Kbit using the bandwidth command. This has nothing to do with the actual bandwidth of the interface, it is simply a value used by the router to calculate the metric and determine the maximum bandwidth it can use to send EIGRP data over.

Say that the physical speed of the interface is 64Kbit. In that case EIGRP would assume in the default situation that it can use 50% of the programmed 128Kbit bandwidth, which is 64Kbit. In other words EIGRP could use the whole physical bandwidth for itself!

To counteract this, we use the `ip bandwidth-percent eigrp <AS><percentage>`. We have entered 10 as the EIGRP autonomous system number, and allow 25% of the programmed bandwidth to be used. This results in EIGRP using a maximum bandwidth of 32Kbit for its own updates.

Another use of the bandwidth command is to tell the router how much bandwidth is available over Point-to-Point interfaces. By default the router sets point-to-point (sub)interfaces to 1544Kbit. It is wise to use the bandwidth command to reflect the real bandwidth of the interface. This can also be done on point-to-point Frame-Relay subinterfaces. In this case set the bandwidth to the CIR value assigned to the PVC.

In the case of a multipoint network interface, all the neighbors will be accessed through the same interface, and therefore they must share the bandwidth. When deciding how much bandwidth EIGRP can use, use the speed of the slowest circuit multiplied by the amount of neighbors to find the correct bandwidth value.

7.9 Features Added to Recent Cisco IOS Versions

Along with the more recent versions of Cisco's IOS (12.0 and later), a number of new commands have been added to enhance and simplify the configuration of EIGRP on a router.

These enhancements will be discussed in this chapter, but it should be noticed that these features might be built upon further in the future.

The areas in which Cisco has added new features are the following:

- Classless networking
- Neighbor control
- Stub routers

7.9.1 Classless Network Enhancements

In the previous versions of EIGRP, the network statement in the router EIGRP command will tell the router which attached networks are parts of the EIGRP routing process. If an interface which does fall within the given network statement range should not be included in the EIGRP process, then the only option is to define the interface as a passive interface. This stops the interface from sending EIGRP updates.

However now Cisco has enhanced the command to include a wildcard mask, so that it becomes possible to define exactly which addresses will, and which will not participate in the routing process. In Figure 7-8 you can see that the two network commands have a wildcard added to them. The first enables the EIGRP process to include the whole 10.10.0.0 network. The second statement enables the 192.168.0.0 /18 network, because of the 0.0.63.255 wildcard mask. In this case it means that the 192.168.10.0/24 and 192.168.20.0 /24 networks will participate, but the 192.168.180.0 /24 network will not participate in the EIGRP routing process.

Figure 7-8
Using wildcards
in the network
command

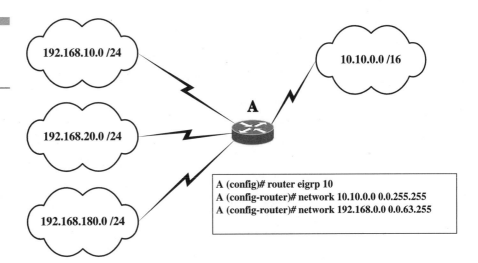

```
A (config)# router eigrp 10
A (config-router)# network 10.10.0.0 0.0.255.255
A (config-router)# network 192.168.0.0 0.0.63.255
```

7.9.2 Neighbor Control

Cisco has now added a command to enable explicit defining of neighbors on an interface level. Up to now, EIGRP relied on broadcast / multicast to dynamically discover neighbors as discussed earlier in the chapter.

This mechanism has two advantages;

You can define neighbors over non broadcast / multicast networks, and over multiaccess networks the explicit defining of neighbors can add to the security.

The following two commands are used:

```
A (config-router)# no eigrp neighbor auto-discovery
<Interface>
```

This command disables the automatic discovery of neighbors on the specified interface.

```
A (config-router)# eigrp neighbor <IP address>
```

This command tells EIGRP explicitly what the IP address of a neighboring router is.

7.9.3 Stub Routers

EIGRP now allows the creation of stub routers. This is a great advantage to large hierarchically designed networks, which can use the stub to reduce update traffic and the possibility of update storms if the network experiences instability.

The stub router is designed to be a router that does not pass routing information on to other routers. It is furthest down the hierarchy, which is called the Access layer. This layer connects LANs to the distribution layer, and basically it does not need to know much, as on one side it has connected LANs, and on the other side it has the corporate network.

If part of the distribution network goes down, then by nature of the EIGRP process, the routers that have lost connectivity will ask all neighboring routers if they know of a feasible route to the unreachable network. It can be easily understood that asking a stub router if it knows of a new route to a network is useless, as the stub router is there only to connect the LANs. If the stub routers also have multiple connection into the distribution layer, then the possibility exists that the stub routers will send out their own queries, back into the distribution network, asking whether the network is available. This can lead to unnecessary update storms.

This is where the new 'stub' command comes into play.

This command is set on the router that is to be a stub router, after which it will inform all the routers it is connected to that it is a stub router, and that it does not want to receive any queries. By not receiving queries, it is blissfully unaware of what is going on in the distribution layer, and relies on it to deliver data into the Internetwork. See Figure 7-9.

What you can see in the example is that the connection between router A and B has failed. Router B will generate a query, if it has not found a feasible successor in its topology table.

This update is sent to all routers except the configured stub router (E). Router C, which has only a LAN connection, is also sent the query, and it in turn, sends a query to router D.

These two queries are useless as we know that router C will never have a connection to router A. In this case a lot of bandwidth can be saved, and possibly also an update storm by also making router C a stub router.

Figure 7-9
An example of a stub
and non-stub router

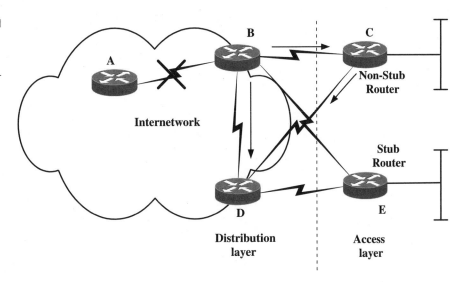

To do this the following command is used:

```
A (config-router)#stub
[connected][static][summary][receive-only]
```

This command, which is used on the remote router, will instruct the router to advertise itself as a stub router. The four values which can be used with the command indicate which type of updates it expects to receive.

7.10 EIGRP Scalability

As we have seen in the previous paragraphs, EIGRP is a very flexible and scalable routing protocol, combining features from distance-vector and link-state protocols to form a hybrid protocol.

However, when implementing an EIGRP network it is important to keep a close eye one the growth of EIGROP queries. This is the most important factor in maintaining a stable EIGRP network, and is often underestimated when the growth of an Internetwork is fast.

As an EIGRP network grows, the following factors must be monitored and dealt with if necessary:

- *Query overload* As the network increases in size, the amount of queries will increase. The mechanisms described earlier, such as summarization and hierarchical network design, can keep the query traffic within limits. If this is not done, then eventually the routers will bog down in the DUAL process and query processing.

- *Redundancy* Redundancy is essential for a network to maintain a good level of service, as outages cannot be avoided, but the network can be designed to cope with them. However, if too much (badly designed) redundancy is introduced, then the burden of dealing with the many extra routes can bring an Internetwork to its knees. For this reason it is important not to add routes for safety's sake, but to come to a good understanding of where and why an extra circuit will be most effective in maintaining a stable network.

- H*op count* Even though EIGRP is a hybrid protocol, hop count does play a role in large, complicated non-summarized networks.

Imagine a large Internetwork where a link goes down. The amount of effort required to converge the network will be large, if the network architecture is flat. This can become so bad that update storms erupt and the network becomes unusable for extended periods.

- *Summarization* Summarization has a direct effect on the speed at which an Internetwork converges. Logically due to summarization the topology and routing table are reduced in size, and the amount of queries after a circuit failure are reduced. This has many positive effects, in reducing the amount of memory, processing power, and bandwidth required by the EIGRP process. However, summarization requires a well designed network to be of any effect.

7.10.1 Query Problems

An error often found in conjunction with EIGRP is the 'stuck in active' state. This means that the router has sent out a query to its neighbors for a route to a network which it has lost. As we have learned in the previous paragraphs, the offending route is set to active state in the topology table. We also know that the router will wait for all queries to be answered before rerunning the DUAL mechanism. If one or more routers do not answer to the query, the router reports the 'stuck in active' state.

This is a serious message that something is wrong.
Possible causes are:

- The neighboring router is too busy to answer to the query. Check the processor usage using the `show proc cpu` command. This offers a number of averages of CPU usage so the operator can determine if a router is becoming overloaded. An average maximum cpu load of 60% allows the router to cope with bursts of activity.

- The neighboring router can be having memory problems, and cannot allocate resources to reply to the query. Use the command `show memory summary` to check the memory usage and possible leaks reducing the amount of usable memory.

- Packet loss or unidirectional links can be a cause, in which case the neighboring router does respond, but the originating router never receives the reply.

Resolving these issues can be complicated, as it can be difficult to find the cause. Reducing the query range through the use of route summarization, distribution lists and stub routers will help in reducing or eliminating such problems. Realize however that all of these mechanisms reduce the amount of information going to each router, and so every time the decision must be made if a router can make the correct routing decisions based on the information it receives.

This is best achieved by introducing hierarchy into the network, where the knowledgeable and powerful routers are placed at the core, and the routing information is filtered down the hierarchy to the access layer.

7.11 Overview of Useful Commands

Table 7-8 provides an overview of the commands used in configuring and troubleshooting EIGRP.

7.12 Chapter Summary

In this chapter, we have looked at the workings of Cisco's EIGRP. With this insight, it should be possible to understand, configure, and troubleshoot EIGRP on an Internetwork.

EIGRP is one of the easiest-to-implement interior gateway protocols, as it supports many powerful features, it is well supported by Cisco, and has an enormous install base. However, it is a proprietary protocol and, as such, you should remember that you will be confined to using Cisco routers for this protocol.

Also, as EIGRP is very easy to setup, it is possible to create a badly scalable network that works fine for a long period. Then when EIGRP cannot keep the network converged, it can bring on enormous costs to rectify the problems that have evolved. OSPF's stricter design rules make such disasters less likely, at the price of much less flexibility.

Table 7-8

Command overview

Command	Description
auto-summary	Enabled by default, this command enables automatic route summarizations at network boundaries
bandwidth *kilobits*	This specifies the value for the bandwidth parameter on an interface. Bandwidth is expressed in kilobytes per second. It has influence on EIGRP's metric calculation and the maximum bandwidth use for EIGRP messages. It does not represent any physical bandwidth.
delay *tens-of-milliseconds*	Specifies the value for the delay parameter on an interface. Delay is expressed in tens of milliseconds.
ip bandwidth-percent eigrp *process-ID seconds*	Specifies the value for the percentage of bandwidth used by EIGRP. The default value is 50%.
ip hello-interval eigrp *process-ID seconds*	Sets the timer for sending hello protocol updates over a specific interface
ip hold-time eigrp *process-ID seconds*	Sets the timer for EIGRP to assume a neighbor router is down. Typically, it is three times the hello-interval.
ip split-horizon eigrp *process-ID*	Enabled by default, this command stops EIGRP from sending updates out the interface from which they were learned.
ip summary-address eigrp *process-ID address mask*	Configures a router to send a summary EIGRP advertisement. Set per interface.
metric weights *tos k1 k2 k3 k4 k5*	Specifies the values that are given to the band width, load, delay, and reliability parameters of IGRP and EIGRP
network *network-number*	Specifies the network address of one or more interfaces on which EIGRP processes should be enabled. Set in the router EIGRP configuration.
passive-interface *type number*	Disables the broadcast transmission or the multi casting of routing updates on an interface
router eigrp *process-ID*	Enables an EIGRP routing process
show ip eigrp neighbors *[type number]*	Displays the contents of the EIGRP neighbor table
show ip eigrp topology [process-ID|[ip address]mask]]	Displays the contents of the EIGRP topology table

Table 7-8

continued

Command	Description
`timers active-time {minutes|disabled}`	Changes or disables the active time (the default is three minutes)
`traffic-share {balanced|min}`	Specifies which way EIGRP should balance traffic if multiple routes are available. Balanced shares traffic by metric; min shares traffic among the best routes. This is configured in the router eigrp configuration.
`variance multiplier`	Specifies a route multiplier by which a route metric can vary from the lowest-cost metric and still be included in an unequal-cost, load-balancing group.

7.13 Frequently Asked Questions (FAQ)

Question: I get many DUAL-3-SIA messages on the log of my router. What should I do?

Answer: SIA stands for *Stuck in Active*. As you have read in this chapter, Active is the state in which EIGRP is actively looking for a new path to a destination network. If, through network or router problems, a query is not answered, it can lead to SIA messages being reported. Using the command *eigrp log-neighbor-changes* can help in finding the source of the troubles.

Question: I get the message `neighbor not on common subnet` on two routers that communicate over my LAN. What should I do?

Answer: If you are using secondary IP addresses on the LAN interfaces, check if both routers' primary IP addresses are part of the same subnet. When EIGRP sends hello packets using the primary address only, it expects the results to come from the same subnet.

Question: Does EIGRP support all the functions of IGRP?

Answer: Yes, it supports IGRP and adds many features like DUAL, variable length subnet masks, CIDR, and reduced bandwidth usage for routing updates.

7.14 Case study

1. Which four configuration commands are necessary on Router C to run EIGRP and advertise all the networks?

   ```
   router eigrp 100
   Network 10.0.0.0
   Network 192.168.20.0
   Network 192.168.10.0
   ```

2. Disable automatic summarization and enable manual summarization of the whole 192.168.0.0/16 network to router B on router C.

   ```
   router eigrp 100
   No auto-summary
   Interface serial 0
   Ip summary-address eigrp 100 192.168.0.0 255.255.0.0
   ```

3. Assuming the link B-C has a metric of 100 and the link B-A has a metric of 75, how would you configure router B to use both serial links to send data to network 192.168.10.0?

   ```
   router eigrp 100
   Variance 2
   ```

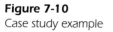

Figure 7-10
Case study example

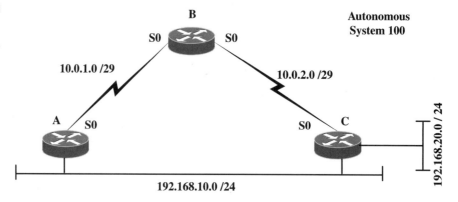

7.15 Questions

1. What are the technologies used by the EIGRP protocol?
   a. DUAL
   b. Area 0
   c. RTP
   d. MTU
   e. All of the above
   f. a, b, c
   g. a, c

2. What does DUAL stand for?
   a. Dual Update Algorithm
   b. Diffused Update Algorithm
   c. Double Update Algorithm
   d. Dual Unreachables Always Linked

3. EIGRP sends updates over fast links every ___ seconds.
   a. 6
   b. 50
   c. 15
   d. 5

4. RTP guarantees _____.
   a. nothing
   b. the best load-balancing over multiple links
   c. that packets for routing updates get to the neighbor
   d. the topology table stays intact

5. How many routable protocols can EIGRP route independently?
   a. 1
   b. 2
   c. 3
   d. 4

6. EIGRP supports VLSM but not CIDR.
   a. True
   b. False

7. By default, how many update packets must stay unanswered before EIGRP assumes the neighbor is dead?

   a. 1
   b. 2
   c. 3
   d. 4

8. Which command shows the neighbors that EIGRP has found?

   a. show eigrp neighbors
   b. show ip eigrp neighbors
   c. show router eigrp Process-id
   d. show ip eigrp networks

9. What is the *reported distance* (RD)?

   a. The distance from a router to its successor
   b. The distance from a router to a destination network
   c. The distance from a successor to a feasible successor
   d. The distance from a successor to a destination network

10. Which is the highest value in the case of a feasible successor?

    a. The feasible distance
    b. The reported distance
    c. The feasibility condition

11. The topology table shows

    a. What the router learned from its neighbors
    b. Which routers it knows of
    c. Which networks it will route data to

12. In a routing table, which letter shows that the route was learned through EIGRP?

    a. I
    b. E
    c. D
    d. EX

13. Which command is used to tell the router to load-balance over unequal paths?

   a. `eigrp load-balance` *destination-network*
   b. `variance` *multiplier*
   c. `load-balance` *process-id*
   d. `variance` *destination-network*

14. Which command stops EIGRP from automatically summarizing network addresses?

   a. `no auto-summary`
   b. `ip summary-address eigrp` *process-id network address*
   c. `no auto-summary eigrp` *process-id*
   d. `no auto-summary interface` *interface-id*

15. Switching off automatic summarization can reduce the burden on the router significantly.

   a. True
   b. False

16. EIGRP uses different timers for the hello protocol on slow NBMA networks than on fast ones.

   a. True
   b. False

17. EIGRP will automatically load-balance over two identical links.

   a. True
   b. False

18. If a route is lost, EIGRP must always ask its neighbors for an alternative route.

   a. True
   b. False

19. How much bandwidth will EIGRP use as a maximum by default?

   a. 5 percent
   b. 20 kbps
   c. 15 percent
   d. 50 percent

20. Which alternatives are there to disabling Split Horizon on NBMA networks?

    a. Configure the subinterfaces

    b. Use an access list to block the updates

    c. Make the NBMA network fully meshed

    d. a, b

    e. b, c

    f. a, c

7.16 Answers

1. g
2. b
3. d
4. c
5. c
6. b
7. c
8. b
9. d
10. a
11. a
12. c and d
13. b
14. a
15. b
16. a
17. a
18. b
19. d
20. f

CHAPTER 8

Basic Border Gateway Protocol

8.1 Objectives Covered in This Chapter

Table 8-1	**BSCN Objective**
BSCN objectives	Understand when to use and when not to use BGP
	Understand BGP terminology
	Understand BGP operation
	Understand the differences between Internal BGP (IBGP) and External BGP (EBGP)
	Understand basic BGP configuration
	Understand BGP operation verification

8.2 Chapter Introduction

In the following two chapters, we will explore BGP version 4, which is the standard at this moment because it is the first to support *Classless Inter-Domain Routing* (CIDR) and other essential standards. Although the routing protocols that have been discussed earlier are designed to perform routing functions within *autonomous systems* (ASs), BGP is designed to perform routing between and through ASs. Take, for example, two *Internet service providers* (ISPs) that each run their own routing protocols within their AS. They will need to exchange information with each other to enable Internet traffic to pass into or through their AS.

In the case of the Internet, a huge amount of ASs are in use, each interacting with others and each having rules on the traffic that may or may not pass through its boundaries. For this reason, BGP v4 is designed to be extremely scalable, supporting thousands of ASs. The price to pay is slower convergence, but this is of lesser concern because it does not affect the overall stability. In this chapter, we will discuss the basics of BGP, and in Chapter 9, "Scaling Border Gateway Protocol," we will cover the scalability issues when using BGP in large Internetworks.

8.3 BGP Operation

For BGP to work, the BGP routers open a TCP connection on port 179 with their neighbors. At first, BGP exchanges its entire routing table with its neighbors, after which it will only send updates when the routing information changes. The only other traffic consists of KEEPALIVE packets to ensure that the other router is still available. BGP does not send regularly scheduled updates, as most other routing protocols do. BGP comes in two forms: *Internal BGP* (IBGP), which is used for all BGP activity within an AS, and *External BGP* (EBGP), which is used for all BGP routing between ASs.

During the beginning of the BGP connection setup, the AS number of a BGP router is sent to the neighbor using the OPEN message. The routers then deduce whether the router is in the same AS as itself or in another one.

By default, EBGP expects to be directly connected to its neighbor in the neighboring AS, whereas IBGP can have multiple hops between its neighbors. Traffic between the IBGP routers is routed by the AS's IGP, such as OSPF, EIGRP, RIP and so on. Figure 8-1 provides a basic overview.

Figure 8-1
EBGP and IBGP routers

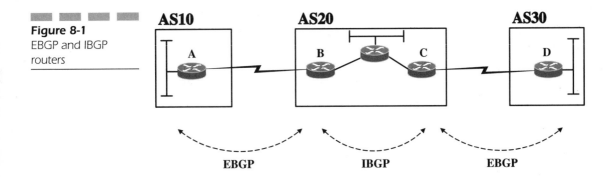

In the figure you can see that EBGP operates between autonomous systems, and IBGP operates within autonomous systems. In the figure, the IBGP running in AS20 relies on an IGP to route its traffic from router B to C and visa versa. This concept is essential to remember.

This seems a lot like the routing protocols we have already examined. Where is the difference? Well, it is mainly in the scale. BGP is the highest level routing protocol on the Internet. The BGP routers on the Internet know paths to all known IP addresses in the world, using CIDR to reduce the massive amount of routing entries.

BGP is not interested in routing within ASs. That is a job it leaves to the IGPs. BGP only performs the routing between the ASs, which send each other information about the reachable networks within the AS and surrounding ones. As soon as a data packet has reached a BGP router that is part of an AS in which the destination network resides, BGP will hand over the routing to the IGP, which can route the packet through the AS.

For its own purposes, BGP needs to send its own (IBGP) routing information to other BGP routers within an AS. This is sent as host-to-host traffic within an AS, assuming that the IGP will ensure that all the BGP routers are reachable within the AS. It must be well understood that all the BGP routers in one AS share the same routing information and propagate the same policies towards the outside world.

To enable the BGP process on router A, the following basic configuration is necessary (see Figure 8-2):

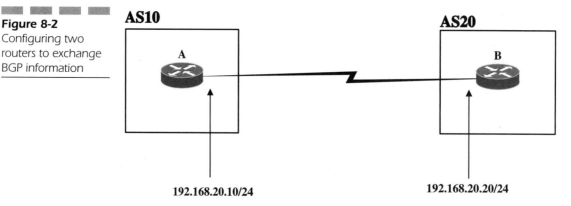

Figure 8-2
Configuring two routers to exchange BGP information

AS10

A

192.168.20.10/24

AS20

B

192.168.20.20/24

```
A#configure terminal
A(config)#router BGP 10
A(config-router)#neighbor 192.168.20.20 remote-as 20
```

On router B the following commands enable the BGP process:

```
B#configure terminal
B(config)#router BGP 20
B(config-router)#neighbor 192.168.20.10 remote-as 10
```

Checking the neighbor status in BGP is done in the following example:

```
A#show ip BGP neighbors
BGP neighbor is 192.168.20.20,  remote AS 20, external link
  Index 1, Offset 0, Mask 0x2
  BGP version 4, remote router ID 10.0.0.4
  BGP state = Established, table version = 1, up for
02:17:48
  Last read 00:00:48, hold time is 180, keepalive interval
is 60 seconds
  Minimum time between advertisement runs is 30 seconds
  Received 140 messages, 0 notifications, 0 in queue
  Sent 140 messages, 0 notifications, 0 in queue
  Connections established 1; dropped 0
  Last reset never
  No. of prefix received 0
Connection state is ESTAB, I/O status: 1, unread input
bytes: 0
Local host: 192.168.20.10, Local port: 11000
Foreign host: 192.168.20.20, Foreign port: 179

Enqueued packets for retransmit: 0, input: 0  mis-ordered: 0
(0 bytes)

Event Timers (current time is 0x7F30B0):
Timer           Starts      Wakeups             Next
Retrans            142            1             0x0
TimeWait             0            0             0x0
AckHold            140          137             0x0
SendWnd              0            0             0x0
KeepAlive            0            0             0x0
GiveUp               0            0             0x0
PmtuAger             0            0             0x0
DeadWait             0            0             0x0
```

```
iss: 2822377729   snduna: 2822380400   sndnxt: 2822380400
sndwnd:   15187
irs: 2807761949   rcvnxt: 2807764620   rcvwnd:       15187
delrcvwnd:    1197

SRTT: 300 ms, RTTO: 607 ms, RTV: 3 ms, KRTT: 0 ms
minRTT: 8 ms, maxRTT: 300 ms, ACK hold: 300 ms
Flags: higher precedence, nagle


Datagrams (max data segment is 1460 bytes):
Rcvd: 143 (out of order: 0), with data: 140, total data
bytes: 2670
Sent: 280 (retransmit: 1), with data: 140, total data
bytes: 2670
```

You might ask yourself when to use BGP. Isn't it a lot of hassle for a service which can possibly be dealt with using static routes and access lists?

This is very true. In many cases it is unwise to use BGP, as it asks for high standards of network management, and adds to the network complexity.

You can consider using BGP is any of the following conditions occur:

- Your Internet network is that of an ISP, and you connect to multiple ASs, or is a transit AS for other ASs.

- Your Internet network is a corporate network and you have multiple connections to ISPs or your AS forms a transit AS for other ASs.

- You need to implement rules on which traffic enters and leaves your AS.

You should not implement BGP if the following conditions apply:

- Your organization does not have a full understanding of BGP and the consequences of running it.

- Your AS only has one connection to an ISP. The use of static routes can be advisable in this case.

- The routers do not have the power or memory available to support BGP.

- The link(s) to other ASs are solely bandwidth.

These questions should be asked before implementing BGP. The following sections will explain the operation of BGP, and go into the commands and policy manipulation options available using BGP.

8.3.1 BGP Routing

Much like a distance vector routing protocol, BGP maintains a routing table, transmits updates, and makes routing decisions based on route metrics. An important concept that is often misunderstood is that BGP can route to networks, which can be seen in the routing table. However, BGP bases its routing decisions by regarding ASs as its hops, ignoring the actual content of the ASs. BGP assumes that the routing will be performed by an IGP inside an AS. The task of BGP is to provide paths through ASs to the destination AS, applying the filtering rules set up by the individual operators of the ASs. It must also be understood that BGP performs all its routing updates over TCP/IP, so it can communicate using other routing protocols within an AS (IGPs).

BGP stores information about paths to networks and maintains a loop-free list of paths to other ASs. Between the ASs, it is possible to enforce policies on the routing information that is shared. In this way, ISPs can form relationships with other ISPs and use BGP to enable or disable traffic based on the source of the destination addresses.

BGP uses a number of methods to determine the best route to its neighboring ASs. These methods will be explained as well as the way BGP routers communicate and advertise their policies.

In short BGP works in the following manner:

- EBGP performs policy based routing between ASs.
- IBGP maintains reliable connectivity between BGP routers within a single AS.
- BGP updates are transmitted reliably, using TCP port 179.
- BGP uses incremental, triggered updates and periodic keepalives.

- BGP uses advanced metrics to determine best paths.
- BGP guarantees loop-free inter-AS routes.
- Can scale to massive networks.
- BGP routes *between* ASs, routing with an AS is left to the IGP (EIGRP, OSPF, RIP etc.)

8.4 BGP Peers, BGP Messages, and the Finite State Machine

Routers must communicate with each other to convey their state, routing updates, and so on. Internally, the router must maintain the TCP/IP connection to the other routers and build up or break down the neighbor (peer) connections based on various states in which the router finds itself. This is discussed in the "BGP's Finite State Machine" section. First, we will focus on the messages that are sent by a BGP router to another when the TCP/IP connection is in place.

BGP routers talk to each other using four possible types of messages:

- OPEN
- UPDATE
- NOTIFICATION
- KEEPALIVE

8.4.1 OPEN Message

When an EBGP router finds a new neighbor, it opens a TCP connection on port 179, and the routers exchange OPEN messages. The goal of the OPEN message is to discuss basic communication parameters before any routing information is exchanged.

Within the OPEN messages, the following information is included:

- *BGP version*   This identifies the BGP version that will be used. For example, BGP version 4 was the first to use CIDR. Therefore, if one of the two BGP routers is running BGP version 3, the other must adapt its messaging to not include CIDR information. The routers will both default to the highest version of BGP that both routers can support.

- *AS*   This indicates the AS number of which the BGP router is a part.

- *Hold time*   This is the amount of time that elapses before a BGP router assumes that the other is inoperative. The timer is reset by an UPDATE or KEEPALIVE message. If this value is set to zero, the timer will never end and the routers will assume that they are always reachable. The router requesting the lowest value for the hold time will be used.

- *Router ID*   Much as in the OSPF world, each router uses the highest IP address it has on an interface to identify itself. If loopback addresses exist, then the highest of them will be used instead of a physical interface IP address.

- *Optional parameters*   These are added to the OPEN message as necessary for authentication purposes, for example.

8.4.2 The Update Message

When EBGP routers transfer routing information, it is done by using UPDATE messages. Each message contains information about the route that is called *path attributes*.

If BGP needs to change a route, either because it has become unreachable or if a better path has become available, it first sends an UPDATE message removing the old route(s) and then an UPDATE message containing information for each new route. Each time a BGP router changes the routing table, it increments a counter. This counter is a measure for the stability of the BGP routing process on that router. The attributes contained in the UPDATE message are an important part of the BGP communication process and will be discussed later. First, we will continue to build the picture of what goes on globally within the BGP process.

8.4.3 The Notification Message

If BGP finds an error in a message, it will send a notification message and return the link state between the BGP routers to an idle state. The network administrator must check the notification message to find out what has gone wrong in the communication, set the problem right, and then reset the connection. Table 8-1 displays errors and error codes to watch for.

8.4.4 The KEEPALIVE Message

If no changes or updates are necessary, the BGP routers will send KEEPALIVE messages. These are basically stripped UPDATE messages and, being very small, do not use much bandwidth.

8.4.5 BGP Finite State Machine

When BGP communicates with a neighbor, it does so using a TCP/IP connection. The communication take place in various states, and these states are triggered by BGP events. Only when the BGP-to-BGP communication process has reached the "established" state can the routers start exchanging routing information, as described in the next chapter.

First, we will show the states a BGP router can be in during the communication setup between routers. To move from one state to another, the router analyzes what is happening to itself and makes decisions on which state to move to, based on what is going on. These events are described in Table 8-2. Tables 8-3 through 8-8 describe the actions the router takes based on the state it is in and the event that it has noticed. The BGP states are as follows:

1   Idle

2   Connect

3   Active

4   Opensent

5   Openconfirm

6   Established

Table 8-1

Errors and error codes

Error Code/Subcode	Error	Error Subcode
1.1	Message header error	Connection not synchronized
1.2		Bad message length
1.3		Bad message type
2.1	OPEN message error	Unsupported version number
2.2		Bad peer AS
2.3		Bad BGP identifier
2.4		Unsupported optional parameter
2.5		Authentication failure
2.6		Unacceptable hold time
3.1	UPDATE message error	Malformed attribute list
3.2		Unrecognized well-known attribute
3.3		Missing well-known attribute
3.4		Attribute flags error
3.5		Attribute length error
3.6		Invalid origin attribute
3.7		AS routing loop
3.8		Invalid NEXT_HOP attribute
3.9		Optional attribute error
3.10		Invalid network field
3.11		Malformed AS_path
4	Hold timer expired	
5	Finite state machine error	
6	Cease	

Table 8-2

Event messages

	Event
1	BGP start
2	BGP stop
3	BGP transport connection open
4	BGP transport connection closed
5	BGP transport connection failed
6	BGP transport fatal error
7	Connect retry timer error
8	Hold timer expired
9	KEEPALIVE timer expired
10	Receive OPEN message
11	Receive KEEPALIVE message
12	Receive UPDATE message
13	Receive NOTIFICATION message

Table 8-3

A BGP router in an idle state

Event	Action by Router	Message Sent	Next State
BGP starts	Initializes resources, starts the connect retry timer, and initiates the TCP/IP connection	None	2
All others	None	None	1

The Event messages sent to BGP routers that are used by the routers to communicate their states are shown in Table 8-2.

How a BGP router runs through these states is described in Tables 8-3 through 8-8.

Table 8-4

A BGP router in
a connect state

Event	Action by Router	Message Sent	Next State
BGP starts	None	None	2
BGP transport connection open	Completes TCP/IP setup	OPEN	4
BGP transport connection failed	Restarts connect retry timer	None	3
Connect retry timer error	Restarts connect retry timer and initiates TCP/IP connection	None	2
All others	Release resources	None	1

Table 8-5

A BGP router in
an active state

Event	Action by Router	Message Sent	Next State
BGP starts	None	None	3
BGP transport connection open	Completes TCP/IP setup	OPEN	4
BGP transport connection failed	Closes TCP/IP connection and restarts connect retry timer	None	3
Connect retry timer error	Restarts connect retry timer and initiates TCP/IP connection	None	2
All others	Release resources	None	1

Table 8-6

A BGP router in an
open sent state

Event	Action by Router	Message Sent	Next State
BGP starts	None	None	4
BGP transport connection closed	Closes TCP/IP connection and restarts connect retry timer	None	3
BGP transport fatal error	Releases resources	None	1

continues

Table 8-6

Continued

Event	Action by Router	Message Sent	Next State
Receival of OPEN message	OPEN message OK	KEEPALIVE	5
Receival of OPEN message	OPEN message not OK	NOTIFICATION	1
All others	Closes TCP/IP connection and releases resources	NOTIFICATION	1

Table 8-7

A BGP router in an open confirm state

Event	Action by Router	Message Sent	Next State
BGP starts	None	None	5
BGP transport connection closed	Releases resources	None	1
BGP transport fatal error	Releases resources	None	1
KEEPALIVE timer expired	Restarts KEEPALIVE timer	KEEPALIVE	5
Receival of KEEPALIVE message	Completes connection setup and restarts hold timer	NOTIFICATION	6
Receival of notification message	Closes TCP/IP connection and releases resources	Undefined	1
All others	Closes TCP/IP connection and releases resources	NOTIFICATION	1

Table 8-8

A BGP router in an established state

Event	Action by Router	Message Sent	Next State
BGP starts	None	None	6
BGP transport connection closed	Releases resources	None	1
BGP transport fatal error	Releases resources	None	1

Event	Action by Router	Message Sent	Next State
KEEPALIVE timer expired	Restarts KEEPALIVE timer	KEEPALIVE	6
Receival of KEEPALIVE message	Restarts hold timer	NOTIFICATION	6
Receival of UPDATE message	Update message OK	Update	6
Receival of UPDATE message	Update message not OK	NOTIFICATION	1
Receival of NOTIFICATION message	Closes TCP/IP connection and releases resources	Undefined	1
All others	Closes TCP/IP connection and releases resources	NOTIFICATION	1

8.5 Policy-Based Routing Using the UPDATE Message Attributes

Path attributes give the administrator the chance to implement policies into the traffic routing, but it can also create complicated problems for which BGP is famous. Also, as BGP evolves, new attributes might be implemented that older versions do not understand. For this reason, path attributes come in four flavors: well-known mandatory, well-known discretionary, optional transitive, and optional nontransitive. All of them are detailed here:

- *Well-known mandatory* An attribute of this type must be known to the BGP implementation. It must also be a part of the UPDATE message. If this is not the case, an error message will be generated and the BGP link is closed.

- *Well-known discretionary* An attribute of this type must also be known to the BGP implementation, but it need not necessarily be included in an UPDATE message

■ *Optional transitive*   An attribute of this type need not be known by the BGP implementation because it could be a vendor-specific attribute. This leaves some area of flexibility in the BGP implementations. The transitive part means that if the BGP implementation receiving an UPDATE message containing this attribute does not understand the attribute, it should pass it on anyway.

■ *Optional non-transitive*   This attribute, like optional transitive, need not be recognized by the receiving BGP router. If the router does not understand the attribute, it should not forward it, but silently discard it.

The attributes used at this time by Cisco are listed in Table 8-9. We will discuss the first seven types of BGP attributes and how they are used. We will also discuss Cisco's weight attribute, as it is used quite extensively in Cisco's BGP implementation.

Table 8-9

Cisco path attributes

Attribute Type Number	Name	Attribute Type
1	ORIGIN	Well-known mandatory
2	AS_path	Well-known mandatory
3	NEXT_HOP	Well-known mandatory
4	MULTI_EXIT_DISC	Optional non-transitive
5	LOCAL_PREF	Well-known discretionary
6	ATOMIC_AGGREGATE	Well-known discretionary
7	AGGREGATOR	Optional transitive
8	COMMUNITY	Optional transitive (Cisco proprietary)
9	ORIGINATOR_ID	Optional non-transitive (Cisco proprietary)
10	Cluster List	Optional non-transitive (Cisco proprietary)
N/A	Weight	Router local attribute (Cisco proprietary)

8.5.1 ORIGIN

The ORIGIN attribute tells a BGP router which type of routing protocol created this routing information. BGP uses this to discriminate between multiple routes and prefers the routes originated by the lowest value in the ORIGIN attribute. In other words, IGP is best, then EGP, and then INCOMPLETE. ORIGIN can have three values, namely 0,1,2, as detailed here:

0 IGP: The network information was originally learned within the AS. It has the highest priority when BGP must choose a route.

1 EGP: The information was originally learned from an EGP outside the AS.

2 INCOMPLETE: The information was not learned through an IGP or an EGP. This can be the case when redistribution is used to inject routes into BGP.

The ORIGIN's attribute can be checked using the show ip bgp command. In the path column, the letter i stands for type 0, e for type 1, and ? for type 3. In the following example, check for type i and ?:

```
A#sh ip bgp
BGP table version is 11, local router ID is 10.0.0.1
Status codes: s suppressed, d damped, h history, * valid, >
best, i - internal
Origin codes: i - IGP, e - EGP, ? - incomplete

    Network          Next Hop          Metric LocPrf Weight
Path
*> 192.168.30.0     192.168.20.20         0              0
20 i
*> 192.168.50.0     192.168.20.20     2195456            0
20 ?
```

8.5.2 AS_PATH

The AS_PATH attribute describes which ASs need to be traversed to reach the advertised network. This attribute can come in a sorted fashion, the nearest AS first in the list, and the farthest last. It can also come in an unsorted fashion. The first is called AS_SEQUENCE and the second, AS_SET.

When a BGP router sends an update to another AS (EBGP), it will add its own AS number to the beginning of the AS_PATH list. If the update is an internal update (IBGP), then there is no crossing of AS boundaries, and the AS_PATH list remains unchanged.

The AS_PATH attribute is used to avoid loops in BGP routing. If a BGP router receives an update that contains its own AS in the AS_PATH list, this means that that update has already passed through the AS. Therefore, it will refuse the update. Figure 8-3 shows how the AS_PATH develops from the destination network to a remote router.

8.5.3 NEXT_HOP

This NEXT_HOP attribute tells the BGP router the IP address of the next hop of the advertised route. BGP uses some smart tricks to

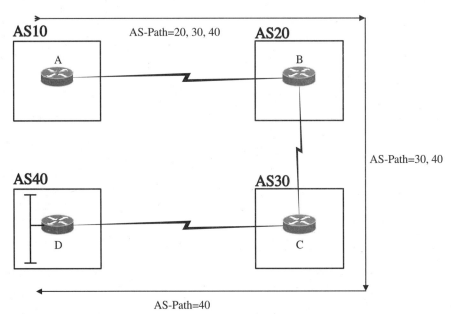

Figure 8-3
AS-PATH over multiple autonomous systems

cut down on the amount of hops necessary over BGP routers to reach a destination network.

Inside an AS, the NEXT_HOP address is not altered. As we know, the AS contains an IGP that takes care of the routing. So, there is no need for the BGP routers to form NEXT_HOP paths within the AS.

EBGP alters the NEXT_HOP. The router can never send an advertisement to another BGP router and use that router's interface address as the next hop. Also, a router receiving an advertisement can never use it if it has a NEXT_HOP with its own IP address.

If a number of routers exist on a shared media, such as Ethernet, then the NEXT_HOP IP address is not altered (see Figure 8-4). The value remains that of the router originally advertising the route.

In Figure 8-4, router A talks BGP to router B, which in turn talks EIGRP to router C. Routing updates from router C are redistributed to BGP by router B. All three routers are on the same Ethernet segment, sharing the same IP subnet. Router B will advertise the route to 10.10.20.0 /24, and using BGP's NEXT_HOP attribute, it will tell router A to pass packets for this network directly to router C. Using the `show ip route` command, this can be checked as follows:

Figure 8-4
NEXT_HOP attributes over shared media

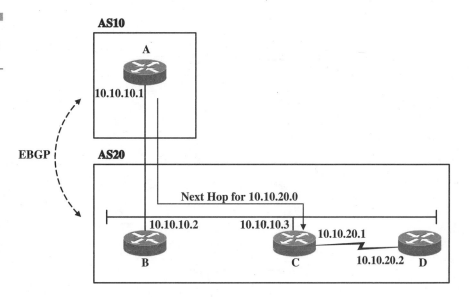

```
A#sh ip route
Codes: C - connected, S - static, I - IGRP, R - RIP, M -
mobile, B - BGP
        D - EIGRP, EX - EIGRP external, O - OSPF, IA - OSPF
inter area
        E1 - OSPF external type 1, E2 - OSPF external type 2,
E - EGP
        i - IS-IS, L1 - IS-IS level-1, L2 - IS-IS level-2, *
- candidate default
        U - per-user static route

Gateway of last resort is not set

C       10.10.10.0/24 is directly connected, Ethernet0
B    10.10.20.0/24 [20/409600] via 10.10.10.3, 00:29:55
```

As useful as the NEXT_HOP attribute is for avoiding needless extra hops over shared media, it can cause some problems in a non-fully meshed, *non-broadcast multiple access* (NBMA) media. As shown in Figure 8-5, router A does not have direct access to router C. The trick used by BGP in the shared media environment would

Figure 8-5

A NEXT_HOP attribute over NBMA media

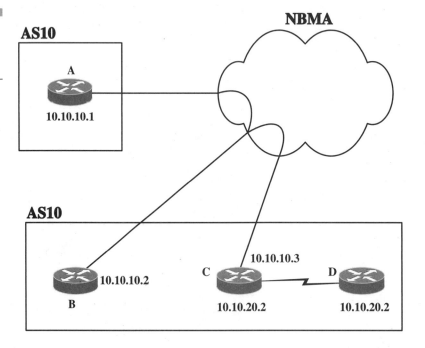

cause router A to try to send packets directly to router C, resulting in the packets getting lost.

In this case, we need to tell router B to advertise the routes learned from router C with itself as the next hop. The command for this is

```
B#conf t
B(config)#router bgp 20
B(config-router)#neighbor 10.10.10.1 remote-as 10
B(config-router)#neighbor 10.10.10.1 next-hop-self
```

If we check the routing table on router A, we will see the difference in comparison to the table found in the shared media example:

```
A#sh ip route
Codes: C - connected, S - static, I - IGRP, R - RIP, M -
mobile, B - BGP
       D - EIGRP, EX - EIGRP external, O - OSPF, IA - OSPF
       inter area
       E1 - OSPF external type 1, E2 - OSPF external type 2,
       E - EGP
       i - IS-IS, L1 - IS-IS level-1, L2 - IS-IS level-2, *
       - candidate default
       U - per-user static route

Gateway of last resort is not set

C       10.10.10.0/24 is directly connected, Ethernet0
B     10.10.20.0/24 [20/409600] via 10.10.10.2, 00:35:40
```

8.5.4 MULTI_EXIT_DISC (MED)

MULTI_EXIT_DISC (MED) is an attribute that determines which multiple connections between two ASs are preferred. The value, which is called a *metric*, is learned from a neighboring AS, and it is only propagated throughout the AS. It is not passed to other ASs. The lower the MED's metric value, the higher the preference to use that link to the neighboring AS. If a router does not assign a MED value to a route, it defaults to 0.

When an AS creates a MED value to advertise to an external AS, the metric in the MED is linked to the metric of the AS's IGP. In this

Figure 8-6
MED used to indicate
a preferred route to
AS 20

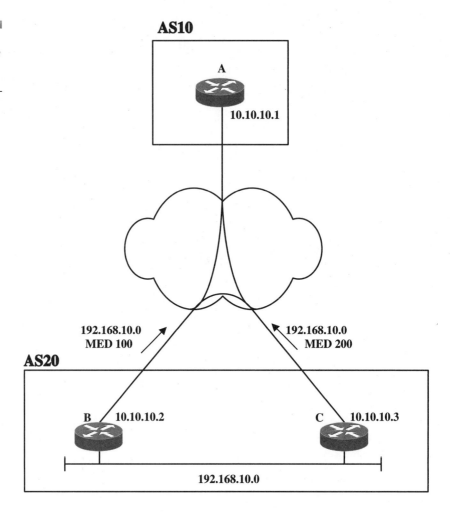

way, the external AS can form an idea as to which link the AS will
use to reach a certain network most efficiently. Figure 8-6 displays
an example where router A chooses to send data for 192.168.10.0/24
to router B due to the lower MED value.

To configure the MED, use the following commands on router B
and router C:

```
B#conf t
B(config)#router bgp 20
```

```
B(config-router)#neighbor 10.10.10.1 remote-as 10
B(config-router)#neighbor 10.10.10.1 route-map SETMED out

B(config-router)#route-map SETMED permit 10
B(config-router)#set metric 100

C#conf t
C(config)#router bgp 20
C(config-router)#neighbor 10.10.10.1 remote-as 10
C(config-router)#neighbor 10.10.10.1 route-map SETMED out

C(config)#route-map SETMED permit 10
C(config)#set metric 200
```

Do not worry too much about the exact syntax of the route-map commands. They will be explained in Chapter 12. For now, it is important to realize that when using the route-map command, the MED value is inserted into the outgoing BGP update to router A.

By default, the Cisco router only compares MED values originating from a single AS, such as in the previous case. However, if it is necessary to compare the MED values received from multiple autonomous systems that are advertising the same network, use the following command:

```
A#conf t
A(config)#router bgp 10
A(config-router)#neighbor 10.10.10.2 remote-as 20
A(config-router)#neighbor 10.10.10.3 remote-as 20
A(config-router)#neighbor 10.10.20.1 remote-as 30
bgp always-compare-med
```

8.5.5 LOCAL_PREF

LOCAL_PREF (local_preference) is an attribute that a router attaches to routes learned through EBGP. This attribute is passed through the AS and is used by the routers to decide which is the preferred exit point out of the AS to the advertised network. So, if one network is advertised over two links into a single AS, the link with the highest local preference will be the one that carries the traffic to the destination. Local preferences are not passed on to other autonomous systems; they stay within the one AS.

Figure 8-7
Using the
LOCAL_PREF attribute

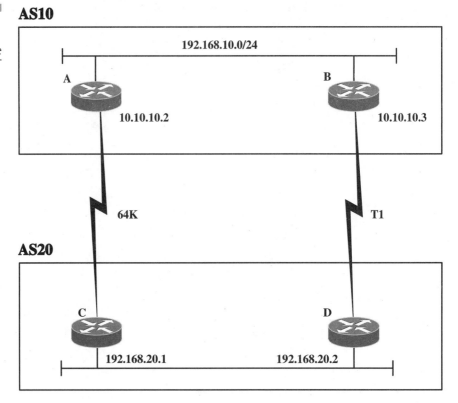

The router can be told about this attribute using one of two methods. For the first method, take the example in Figure 8-7. AS 20's network operator wants to use the T1 link to access AS 10. To do this, we tell router C to assign a lower local preference value to the incoming updates than router D:

```
C#conf t
C(config)#router bgp 20
C(config-router)#neighbor 10.10.10.1 remote-as 10
C(config-router)#neighbor 192.168.20.2 remote-as 20
C(config-router)#bgp default local-preference 100

D#conf t
D(config)#router bgp 20
D(config-router)#neighbor 10.10.10.2 remote-as 10
D(config-router)#neighbor 192.168.20.1 remote-as 20
D(config-router)#bgp default local-preference 200
```

The route to the Ethernet segment in AS 10, 192.168.10.0/24, will be advertised throughout AS 20 with a local preference of 200 by router D and with a preference of 100 by router C. Therefore, the preferred route to use will be the T1 link over router D.

The second method uses route maps to define the assigning of the local preference value more precisely. Because this can seem rather complicated the first time, each new command will be followed by some explanation. For this example, we will tell router D to assign a local preference of 200 to all routes coming from remote AS 10:

```
D#conf t
D(config)#router bgp 20
D(config-router)#neighbor 192.168.20.2 remote-as 20
D(config-router)#neighbor 10.10.10.1 remote-as 10
D(config-router)#neighbor 10.10.10.1 route-map LOCPREF in
```

In the previous code, we tell the router that incoming data from the specified neighbor should be processed by the route-map process called LOCPREF, which is an arbitrary name.

```
D(config)#route-map LOCPREF permit 10
```

This defines the route map called LOCPREF. The integer at the end is an arbitrary number that defaults to 10. If the LOCPREF route maps have multiple parts, then the lowest number will be processed first.

```
D(config-route-map)# match as-path 5
```

This filter drops all routes except those that match as-path access list 5. This access list is defined later.

```
D(config-route-map)# set local-preference 100
```

In the previous line, we assign a local preference of 100 to the matching updates.

```
D(config)#route-map LOCPREF permit 20
```

This route map with number 20 will be processed after the number 10 route map. It enables all routes to pass. This is necessary as route map 10 drops all non-updates not coming from AS 10.

```
D(config-router)#ip as-path access-list 5 permit _10
```

Now we assign access list number 5 to filter as-path information to only permit as-path strings that start with the number 10. Ten is the number of the AS that is sending the updates with which we want to modify the local preference.

8.5.6 ATOMIC_AGGREGATE

A BGP router may find that it can group multiple destinations into one update. However, because this can lead to problems regarding the exact path to the different destinations, the update must have the ATOMIC_AGGREGATE attribute set to warn other routers that the information about the route might not be complete.

Updates with the ATOMIC_AGGREGATE attribute set cannot be made more specific by another router. This attribute, once set, is passed to all other routers and outside the AS. When looking at the routing information of a specific route, this informational attribute can be seen.

It is also possible to have the BGP router summarize routes manually.

This is done using the BGP configuration command:

```
A(config-router)#aggregate-address <ip-address><mask>
[summary-only][as-set]
```

The IP address and mask is the address of the summary.

The `summary-only` subcommand indicates to the router only to advertise the summary, and not any of the more specific routes. By default BGP will advertise both the summary and the specific routes.

The `as-set` subcommand indicates that the router will include all the AS numbers of the specific routes in the summarized route. By default the router will set the atomic aggregate, as described previously.

8.5.7 AGGREGATOR

A router that is aggregating a number of routes into one can insert the optional attribute known as AGGREGATOR. It consists of the router's ID (IP address) and its AS. This indicates which router is responsible for the aggregation to the other routers and network engineers debugging the internetwork.

8.5.8 Weight

This Cisco proprietary weight attribute is local to the router on which it is used. It tells the router which path is best if it learns of multiple paths to a destination. The attribute is purely local to the router and is therefore not sent to others. A higher value of the weight attribute signifies a better route (see Figure 8-8).

Three ways exist for setting the weight attribute in the router:

■ Assign a default weight to the updates from a certain router using the neighbor weight command. On router C, we will assign the updates from router B to get a weight of 500 and the updates from router A to get a weight of 1000:

```
C#conf t
C(config)#router bgp 30
C(config-router)#neighbor 192.168.20.2 remote-as 20
C(config-router)#neighbor 192.168.20.2 weight 500
C(config-router)#neighbor 192.168.10.2 remote-as 10
C(config-router)#neighbor 192.168.10.2 weight 500
```

■ We can also use an as-path access list to configure weights from specific neighbors and autonomous systems:

```
C#conf t
C(config)#router bgp 30
C(config-router)#neighbor 192.168.20.2 remote-as 20
C(config-router)#neighbor 192.168.20.2 filter-list 10
```

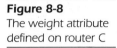

Figure 8-8

The weight attribute defined on router C

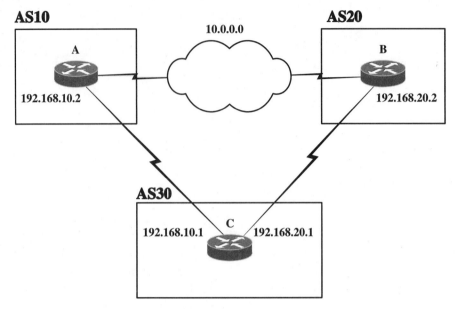

```
weight 500
C(config-router)#neighbor 192.168.10.2 remote-as 10
C(config-router)#neighbor 192.168.10.2 filter-list 11
weight 1000

C(config)#ip as-path access-list 10 permit ^20$
C(config)#ip as-path access-list 11 permit ^10$
```

Here the weight is only added to the update from the specified neighbor if it passes the *ip as-path* command. This command checks if the as-path contains the string supplied at the end of the command, such as ^20$. Here we have used the ^ and $ symbols to signify that the AS number must be the beginning and the end of the as-path string. In other words, it must be the only number in the as-path string. More on this will be covered in Chapter 12.

▪ We can also use route maps, which are the most flexible means of implementing attribute changes:

```
C#conf t
C(config)#router bgp 30
C(config-router)#neighbor 192.168.20.2 remote-as 20
```

```
C(config-router)#neighbor 192.168.20.2 route-map WEIGHT in
C(config-router)#neighbor 192.168.10.2 remote-as 10
C(config-router)#neighbor 192.168.10.2 route-map WEIGHT in

C(config)#ip as-path access-list 6 permit ^20$
C(config)#ip as-path access-list 5 permit ^10$

C(config)#route-map WEIGHT permit 10
C(config-route-map)#match as-path 6
C(config-route-map)#set weight 1000

C(config)#route-map WEIGHT permit 20
C(config-route-map)#match as-path 5
C(config-route-map)#set weight 500
```

In this way, we use the route map only to change the weight, but it can also be used to change other attributes if deemed necessary.

8.5.9 Route Selection

You have seen the most commonly used attributes and that BGP uses them to define the best route. Now it is time to learn how BGP looks at all the attributes to choose the best route out of multiple instances. It is useful when troubleshooting to understand how the router judges the available routes.

The following 10 steps describe the decision process when a BGP router is presented with a new route:

1. If the next_hop is inaccessible, the route is discarded.
2. In a Cisco router, the route with the greatest weight is selected.
3. If the weights are identical, use the largest local_ preference.
4. If the local_ preferences are identical, then give a preference on the routes learned locally by the router.
5. If the origin attributes are the same, use the route with the shortest AS_path attribute.
6. If the AS_paths are the same, choose the route with the lowest ORIGIN attribute value.

7. If the ORIGIN attribute values are the same, choose the route with the lowest MED attribute value.

8. If the routes have the same MED, the external route is chosen over the internal route.

9. If the routes are all external or internal, calculate the distances over the IGP routing protocol to each BGP next_hop and use the shortest one.

10. If the internal path lengths are the same, use the next_hop's BGP router ID as a tie breaker. The lowest router ID wins.

8.6 IBGP Issues

IBGP relationships are formed when one AS has multiple BGP routers within the AS. The tasks that a router has in regard to the local AS include the following:

- It must discover routes from the IGP in the AS. The IGP can be EIGRP, RIP, IGRP, OSPF, and so on.

- It must find routes from the other BGP routers in the AS to find networks that are attached to other BGP routers.

To perform these tasks, the IBGP router must have a connection to all other IBGP routers in the area because it will not forward routing information it has learned inside the AS to other routers in the AS. In short, we say that logically the IBGP routers must be fully meshed (see Figure 8-9). This can lead to scalability problems, but solutions to this can be developed and will be discussed later.

Often IBGP routers use a loopback address to serve as the IP address when communicating. This is because using a loopback address forms a more robust connection. Within the AS, BGP uses the IGP to route the TCP sessions it has to other BGP routers. If a link were to fail to one of the BGP routers and that link's IP address was used to form the TCP link, then the neighbor would assume the router to be inoperative. If a loopback address were to be used, an alternative route to the router could be found and used. Using loop-

Figure 8-9
IBGP fully meshed

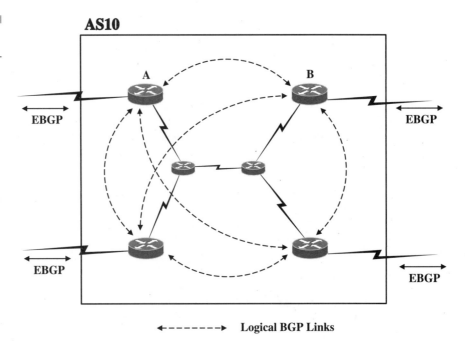

back addresses for EBGP routers is not usually done because they typically have a single connection with each other.

To specify that a router must use its loopback address when sending messages to other BGP routers, add the following command to the router BGP command:

```
#neighbor [ip address] update-source loopback 0
```

In Figure 8-10, the routers in A have lost their connections because the physical interface IP address used for the BGP connection is unreachable due to the serial link being down. In B, loopback addresses are used, and the routers can look for an alternative path to find each other.

When EBGP routing information passes through an AS from one AS to another, the IBGP routers must synchronize the route information that they advertise with the IGP in their local AS to enable the local AS's IGP time to converge.

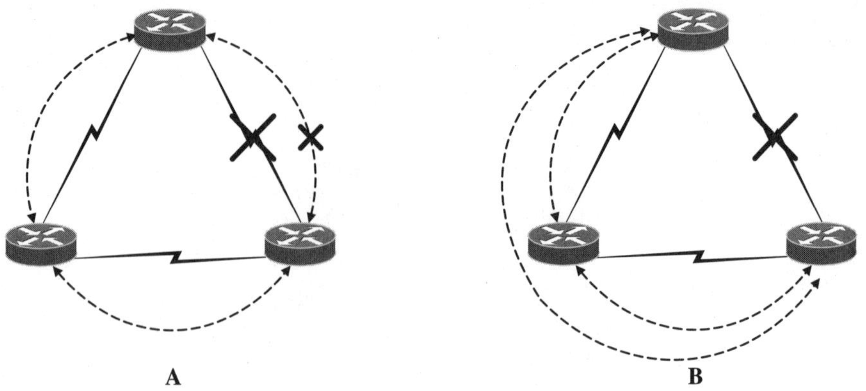

Figure 8-10
IBGP using loopback
addresses

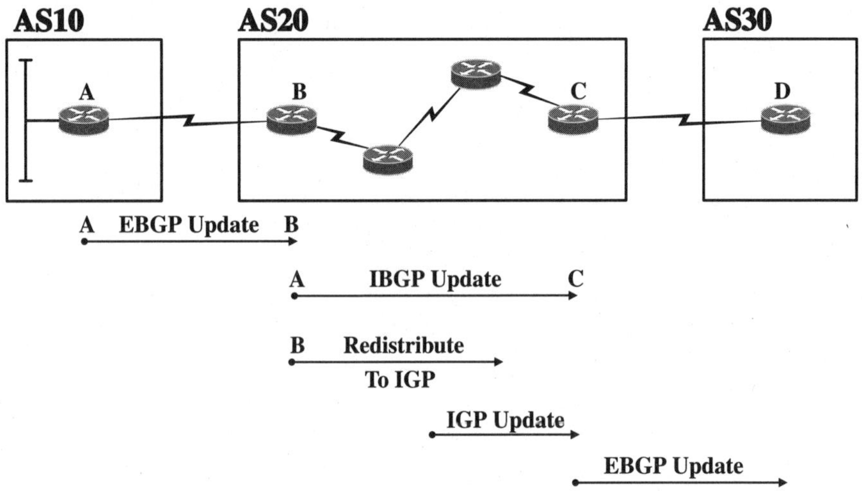

Figure 8-11
EBGP
synchronization

For example, in Figure 8-11, router B learns about a remote network from router A. This information is passed on to router C, which
could pass the information to router D. However, if the IGP of AS 20
has not converged yet, then any packets sent by router D to router C
with the new network as a destination would be dropped by the IGP.
So, by default, router C will wait until it hears of the new network
advertised by the IGP before it passes the route on to router D. This
avoids unnecessary traffic and drops. To avoid the routers synchro-
nizing, add the following command to the router BGP command:

```
#no synchronization
```

8.7 EBGP Issues

Although the next chapter will be dedicated to the intricacies of EBGP, one useful trick can help resolve any issues regarding EBGP. Up to now, we have always assumed that EBGP has a direct connection to its neighbor, as it is used to connect autonomous systems. In some cases, however, it can be useful to enable EBGP to build a connection over an intermediate router. This special case is called *BGP multihop* and only applies to EBGP.

For example, if two autonomous systems are connected, but one router is unable to run BGP either because it does not have the correct hardware or software, then a neighboring router can fulfill the function. The non-BGP router just forwards the traffic between the BGP routers. Figure 8-12 provides an example where router B does not run BGP.

The configurations are as follows:

```
A#conf t
A(config)#router bgp 10
A(config-router)#neighbor 192.168.20.2 remote-as 20
A(config-router)#neighbor 192.168.20.2 ebgp-multihop 2

C#conf t
C(config)#router bgp 20
C(config-router)#neighbor 192.168.10.1 remote-as 10
C(config-router)#neighbor 192.168.10.1 ebgp-multihop 2
```

In the `neighbor...ebgp-multihop` command, the optional number 2 signifies the maximum amount of hops that can be covered to reach the remote EBGP neighbor.

To ensure that BGP policies are set correctly after a configuration change, it is necessary to reset the BGP process after each configuration change.

This is done using the following command;

```
A#clear ip bgp <* | ip address> [soft[in | out]]
```

The BGP table can be cleared for all routes using the *, or for just one or more networks by indicating the IP network address range.

Figure 8-12
EBGP multihop

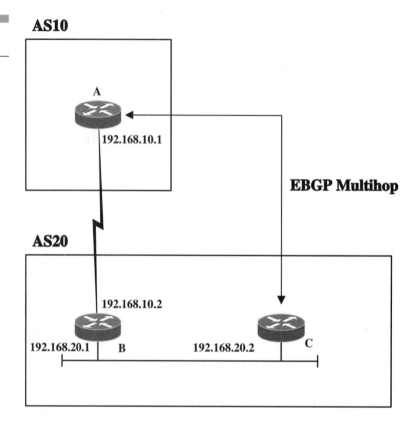

The command will reset the BGP sessions, and reload all the routing updates from the surrounding BGP routers.

If you simply want to reload the routing information, without resetting the peer connections, then add the 'soft' keyword to the command. It is also possible to tell the router to perform the 'soft' reset for only inbound or only outbound updates.

8.8 Chapter Summary

In this chapter, we covered the basic principles behind BGP. BGP can run in two modes: *Internal BGP* (IBGP) and *External BGP* (EBGP). IBGP takes care of the communication between BGP routers within an AS. In this way, BGP can route traffic through an AS or decide which EBGP router is best for sending traffic into a neighboring AS. IBGP uses the IGP within the AS to provide reliable routing between the IBGP routers. IBGP uses TCP/IP for all its communication and usually uses a loopback interface defined on each BGP router as source and destination IP addresses when communicating. IBGP must be logically fully meshed because IBGP routers never pass BGP routing information to other IBGP routers.

EBGP is the mode that BGP uses when it communicates between two different autonomous systems. EBGP routers are normally connected over point-to-point links, and so an EBGP router expects a peer router to be on the same subnet as itself. When this is not possible, a router utilizes a process known as BGP multihop. EBGP also uses attributes in its routing updates to advertise its policies and preferences.

In the next chapter, some more complicated issues will be discussed, mostly for using BGP in large Internetworks. The chapter will rely heavily on the knowledge gained in this chapter.

8.9 Frequently Asked Questions (FAQ)

Question: Which *Request for Comments* (RFCs) can I read about BGP in general?

Answer: RFC1771, A *Border Gateway Protocol 4* (BGP-4); RFC1772, Application of the Border Gateway Protocol; RFC1773, Experience with the BGP-4 protocol; and RFC1774 BGP-4, Protocol Analysis

 # 8.10 Case Study

1. Configure basic BGP on router D to interact with EBGP routers A, B, and C.

```
Router bgp 30
Neighbor 10.1.1.1. remote-as 10
Neighbor 10.1.2.1. remote-as 10
Neighbor 10.1.4.1. remote-as 20
```

2. Configure router B with bgp, and advertise a MED attribute with a metric of 100 to router D.

```
Configure terminal
Router bgp 10
Neighbor 192.168.10.1 remote-as 10
Neighbor 10.1.3.2 remote-as 20
Neighbor 10.1.2.1 remote-as 30
Neighbor 10.1.2.1 remote-map case out
Remote-map case permit 10
Set metric 100
```

3. If routers A, B and C were all to advertise route 192.168.10. 0/24 to router D, and use the MED attribute, which extra command is necessary on Router D to allow it to choose a path over router C?

```
Bgp always-compare-med
```

Figure 8-13
Case study example

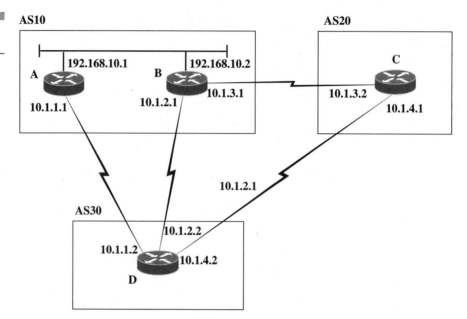

8.11 Questions

1. BGP routers communicate using

   a. TCP/IP
   b. NetBIOS
   c. CDP

2. Which port number does BGP use when communicating with a neighbor?

   a. 187
   b. 53
   c. 179
   d. 178

3. BGP automatically learns routes from other routing protocols.

   a. True
   b. False

4. BGP routers with different AS numbers communicate using

   a. EBGP
   b. IBGP
   c. EIGRP
   d. IGP

5. Which types of messages does BGP exchange?

   a. UPDATE
   b. OPEN
   c. NOTIFICATION
   d. KEEPALIVE
   e. All of the above
   f. a, c

6. All BGP routers in an AS must be logical neighbors.

   a. True
   b. False

7. All routers in an AS must have BGP enabled.

   a. True
   b. False

8. Which command enables BGP on a router?

  a. `enable ip-bgp <AS>`

  b. `router bgp <AS>`

  c. `neighbor <ip address> remote-as <AS>`

9. Which command shows the connection state in which the surrounding BGP routers are located?

  a. `show ip bgp neighbors`

  b. `show bgp neighbors`

  c. `show bgp state neighbors`

10. When BGP starts up a connection with a neighbor router, which message type is used?

  a. KEEPALIVE

  b. UPDATE

  c. NOTIFICATION

  d. OPEN

11. Which message type is sent after detecting an error in BGP communication?

  a. KEEPALIVE

  b. UPDATE

  c. NOTIFICATION

  d. OPEN

12. Which possible connection state does not occur in BGP?

  a. Connect

  b. Established

  c. Closed

  d. Open confirm

  e. Open sent

  f. Idle

  g. Active

13. At which state of connection can BGP start sending and receiving routing information?

   a. Connect

   b. Established

   c. Closed

   d. Open confirm

   e. Open sent

   f. Idle

   g. Active

14. BGP attributes are sent using which BGP message type?

   a. KEEPALIVE

   b. UPDATE

   c. NOTIFICATION

   d. OPEN

15. The origin attribute tells the BGP router:

   a. In which AS the advertised network originates.

   b. What type of router is sending the update.

   c. In which way the network was discovered by BGP.

16. The first item in the AS-Path string is always the AS of the receiving BGP router.

   a. True

   b. False

17. The next-hop attribute is always equal to the IP address of the BGP router that sent the update.

   a. True

   b. False

18. IBGP routers in the same AS all have TCP/IP connectivity with each other.

   a. True

   b. False

19. Weight can be only be configured on a Cisco router using route maps.

    a. True

    b. False

20. Using loopback interfaces as source and destination, for EBGP over a serial link can increase stability.

    a. True

    b. False

8.12 Answers

1. a
2. c
3. b
4. a
5. e
6. a
7. b
8. b
9. a
10. d
11. c
12. c
13. b
14. b
15. c
16. b
17. b
18. a
19. b
20. b

CHAPTER 9

Scaling Border Gateway Protocol

9.1 Objectives Covered in This Chapter

9.2 Chapter Introduction

Whereas the previous chapter discussed the tools that a *Border Gateway Protocol* (BGP) uses to communicate, here we will have a look at solving *Internal BGP* (IBGP) scalability problems, various methods for controlling policies, grouping large numbers of BGP routers to make administration easier, and other issues that companies bump into when deploying BGP.

9.3 Improving IBGP Scalability

As discussed in Chapter 8, "Basic Border Gateway Protocol," all the BGP routers in an *autonomous system* (AS) must be able to communicate with each another. An IBGP router will not pass routing information from one BGP router to another. This situation can become difficult when many BGP routers exist in an AS, as can be the case when many *Internet service providers* (ISPs) connect to many other autonomous systems. To combat this problem, route reflectors can be used.

Figure 9-1
BGP without route
reflectors

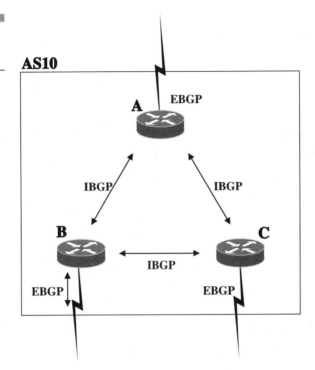

AS10

Route reflectors reduce BGP traffic within an AS by limiting the amount of necessary neighbor connections. This is done by enabling an IBGP router to advertise another neighbor's advertisement. In this way, a certain hierarchy can be introduced where BGP routers talk to a single router that passes information to other routers. This specific router is known as the route reflector. An AS can have multiple route reflectors, each managing their own group of routers and talking to each other.

For the basic situation, see Figure 9-1. Here only straightforward IBGP is spoken between the routers, and each router has a TCP/IP connection to each other router. Note that the intra-AS physical connections are not drawn because the communication only requires TCP connectivity, which could be performed over many IGP routers in the AS.

In Figure 9-2, router B and C do not communicate with each other directly. They use router A to forward the messages. As you can see, this reduces the amount of IBGP TCP/IP connections from 3 to 2.

Figure 9-2
A simple BGP
route reflector

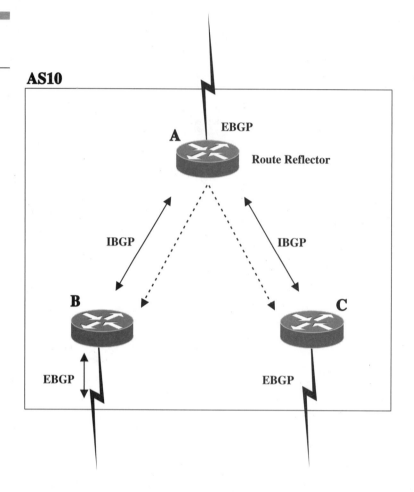

This might not seem like a huge savings, but when this technique is used on ASs with up to 100 IBGP routers, the savings in bandwidth as well as router processor and memory requirements can be huge.

How do we configure a route reflector? In the following example, router A is the reflector:

```
A#conf t
A(config)#router bgp 10
A(config-router)#neighbor 192.168.10.10 remote-as 10
A(config-router)#neighbor 192.168.10.10 route-reflector-client
A(config-router)#neighbor 192.168.20.10 remote-as 10
A(config-router)#neighbor 192.168.20.10 route-reflector-client
```

Router B does not need the reference to router C anymore. It will receive all updates via router A. Here is the configuration of router B:

```
B#conf t
B(config)#router bgp 10
B(config-router)#neighbor 192.168.10.20 remote-as 10
```

Now let's check the network attached to router C, 192.168.60.0, from router B's perspective. For this, we use the command show ip bgp <ip network address>:

```
B#sh ip bgp 192.168.60.0
BGP routing table entry for 192.168.60.0/24, version 8
Paths: (1 available, best #1)
   Local
      192.168.20.10 (metric 10476) from 192.168.20.20
(10.0.0.2)
         Origin IGP, metric 0, localpref 100, valid, internal,
best
         Originator : 10.0.0.2, Cluster list: 10.0.0.1
```

We can see that router C (router id 10.0.0.2) originated the route (refer to Chapter 8), and we can see which route reflectors the routing information has passed through, signified by the *cluster list* of router IDs. In this case, there is only one reflector, so only one ID appears in the list.

This is a small example where we have only created a single group of routers that use a route reflector. This group of routers is called a *cluster*, and this concept becomes more important as we increase the amount of route reflectors within the AS. We will also have to start to use mechanisms to avoid loops because we have lost the benefit of having all the routers talking to each other in a fully meshed manner.

Here are a few points to remember:

- A router that has route reflecting configured is called the route reflector.

- A router that communicates with other routers through a route reflector is called a route reflector client.

- A group of reflector clients and a route reflector are called a cluster. Multiple clusters can exist within an AS. Only route reflectors will communicate IBGP outside the cluster, as routing loops are otherwise unavoidable.

■ A cluster can have multiple route reflectors, in which case a cluster ID must be assigned to each route reflector router in that cluster to avoid routing loops within the cluster. When there is only one route reflector per cluster, the router ID is used as a cluster ID. The router ID is usually the IP address of a loopback interface.

Let's examine Figure 9-3. Here is what we can ascertain from it:

■ The arrows signify logical BGP connections, not necessarily physical ones.

■ Routers A, B, and C are route reflectors.

■ Router D is an IBGP router with a basic configuration.

■ A and B are part of the same cluster and provide a backup of BGP routing services to router F in case routers A or B fail.

■ Routers A and B need to have a cluster ID configured because they are in the same cluster.

Figure 9-3
BGP route reflectors and clusters

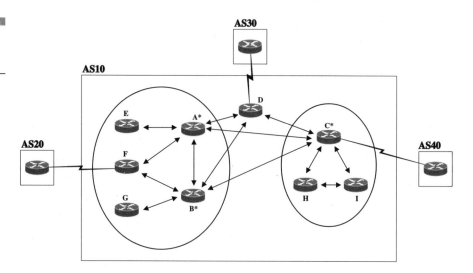

- Routers A, B, C, and D are fully meshed and all communicate using the normal IBGP rules.
- EBGP connectivity can be made through a route reflector or a route reflector client.

To avoid cluttering up Figure 9-3, check the following list for the routers' IP addresses:

IP address router A : 192.168.10.10

IP address router B : 192.168.20.10

IP address router C : 192.168.30.10

IP address router D : 192.168.40.10

IP address router E : 192.168.50.10

IP address router F : 192.168.60.10

IP address router G : 192.168.70.10

IP address router H : 192.168.80.10

IP address router I : 192.168.90.10

Here is the configuration of router A. Router B's configuration is comparable.

```
A#conf t
A(config)#router bgp 10
A(config-router)#neighbor 192.168.40.10 remote-as 10
A(config-router)#neighbor 192.168.20.10 remote-as 10
A(config-router)#neighbor 192.168.30.10 remote-as 10
A(config-router)#neighbor 192.168.50.10 remote-as 10
A(config-router)#neighbor 192.168.50.10 route-reflector-client
A(config-router)#neighbor 192.168.60.10 remote-as 10
A(config-router)#neighbor 192.168.60.10 route-reflector-client
A(config-router)#neighbor 192.168.70.10 remote-as 10
A(config-router)#neighbor 192.168.70.10 route-reflector-client
A(config-router)#bgp cluster-id 100
```

You might have asked yourself why there is an arrow between router H and I in Figure 9-3. Because router C is a route reflector, it should not be necessary to have router H and I communicate, as router C is passing all the information.

Situations occur when you will want a fully meshed cluster. This is when you are going to perform peering within the cluster to ease the amount of configuration work. This will be discussed later in the chapter.

So what's the use of configuring route reflectors and then enabling fully meshed communication again? Well, we have only enabled the full mesh within this cluster, and traffic to other clusters within the AS will still only take one route via the reflector (router C).

To make all of this work, we must learn one new command. The command, `no bgp-client-to-client reflection`, is used to tell router C not to reflect routes between reflector clients (routers H and I). Routers H and I need to have each other added to their router BGP configurations so that they will make a normal IBGP connection with each other:

```
C#conf t
C(config)#router bgp 10
C(config-router)#no bgp client-to-client reflection
C(config-router)#neighbor 192.168.10.10 remote-as 10
C(config-router)#neighbor 192.168.40.10 remote-as 10
C(config-router)#neighbor 192.168.100.10 remote-as 40
C(config-router)#neighbor 192.168.80.10 remote-as 10
C(config-router)#neighbor 192.168.80.10 route-reflector-client
C(config-router)#neighbor 192.168.90.10 remote-as 10
C(config-router)#neighbor 192.168.90.10 route-reflector-client
```

9.4 Policy Control Using BGP

Because BGP is usually found routing between ASs, it is important to have the right tools to control the distribution of networks advertised by BGP. Policies that are decided upon between ISPs need to be enforced using BGP between the ISP's routers.

Cisco has done a lot to give administrators as much freedom as possible to define and control the routing information. From IOS version 10.0, distribute lists were available, adding features in version 11.0 and 11.2. In version 12.0 of the Cisco IOS, prefix lists were added, having some significant advantages for distribute lists. These will be discussed in the following section.

9.4.1 The Distribute List

Basically, the *distribute list* is an access list that is applied to the IP network addresses that are sent or received by the BGP routing process from or to a neighbor or group of neighbors. The distribute list is applied in the router BGP configuration as follows:

```
A#conf t
A(config)#router bgp 10
A(config-router)#neighbor 192.168.10.10 remote-as 10
A(config-router)#neighbor 192.168.10.10 distribute-list 10 in
```

This example applies standard access list number 10 to all updates arriving from neighbor 192.168.10.10. Here are some points to keep in mind:

- The access list can be a standard or extended access list (numbers 1 through 199), or it can be applied to a named access list.

- The filter can be applied to incoming or outgoing advertisements using the in or out statement.

- The IP address can be replaced by a peer group name. Refer to Chapter 8 for information on peer groups.

This mechanism can get a bit complicated, especially when extended access lists are used. See Chapter 11 for more information on access lists.

Most extended access lists use a source and a destination address to determine if the rule will apply or not. In the case of distribute lists, the access lists use the first set of bits to match the network address and the second to match the subnet mask. For example, if we want to permit network 10.10.0.0 255.255.0.0, then we have to make the BGP process look at the IP address and the subnet mask. So, we get the following:

```
A(config)#access-list 101 permit ip 10.10.0.0 0.0.255.255
host 255.255.0.0
```

The `10.10.0.0 0.0.255.255` tells the router only to accept IP addresses with 10.10.x.x. The host `255.255.0.0` tells the router to accept only a subnet mask of exactly 16 bits.

9.4.2 Prefix Lists

Prefix lists were introduced in Cisco IOS 12.0 and are used to get around the difficulties of maintaining long distribute lists. They also perform better with large lists when compared to distribute lists. The user interface of a prefix list is also more understandable because of the way the matches are made, as opposed to trying to fit it into the extended access list form.

So, how do these lists work? First, we set up a list of prefixes that we want to match in a certain situation. Similar to the access list, the prefix list follows the following rules:

- An empty prefix list always enables all traffic to pass.
- The prefix list is always followed by an implicit deny.
- Prefix lists use sequence numbers to define which rule is used to match first. Giving the rules with the highest number of matches and the lowest sequence numbers will increase the efficiency of the whole process.
- Using the sequence numbers, entries can be inserted into the list. This is different than the access list where items can only be added to the end of the list. By default, the sequence numbers are generated automatically by the router in increments of five.
- Prefix lists are defined using names instead of numbers.

9.4.2.1 Creating a Prefix List   As an example, router J is configured with a prefix list that denies the 128.0.0.0/8 supernet. We would configure the following:

```
J(config)#ip prefix-list testlist deny 128.0.0.0/8
```

To deny all class C addresses within the 192.168.0.0/16, we would use

```
J(config)#ip prefix-list testlist deny 192.168.0.0/16 ge 24
```

To deny all supernets larger than Class B of the 192.0.0.0/8, we would configure

```
J(config)#ip prefix-list testlist deny 192.0.0.0/8 le 16
```

The testlist word is our name to define this list.

When "ge" is added to the rule, it will match any subnet mask from the ge value to 32. When "le" is added, the rule will match any subnet mask between the network address prefix number and the value following the le. If neither ge or le is specified, then the match will be exact to the network number/prefix given.

Finally, when the list has been made, it can be assigned to the BGP routing process using the following commands:

```
J(config)#router bgp 10
J(config-router)#neighbor 192.168.10.10 remote-as 10
J(config-router)#neighbor 192.168.10.10 prefix-list
testlist in
```

Here we have assigned the testlist prefix list to the specific neighbor 192.168.10.10 and to filter incoming BGP updates. Remember that prefix lists cannot be used simultaneously with distribute lists.

9.4.2.2 Manipulating and Checking the Prefix List   To enable the manual assigning of the sequence numbers in the prefix list, use the following command to disable the router's automatic assigning:

```
J(config)#no ip prefix-list sequence-number
```

When this has been done, you will have to assign the numbers by hand, when creating the list. Here's an example:

```
J(config)#ip prefix-list testlist seq 5 deny 128.0.0.0/8
```

Notice that the `seq 5` has been added here. The lower the number following `seq`, the higher in the list the rule will come. A single entry in a prefix list can be deleted by using the sequence number:

```
J(config)#no ip prefix-list testlist seq 5 deny 128.0.0.0/8
```

Here rule number 5 will be deleted from the list name's testlist. To show the list, use the following command:

```
J#show ip prefix-list testlist
ip prefix-list testlist: 2 entries
    seq 10 deny 192.168.0.0/16 ge 24
    seq 15 deny 192.0.0.0/8 le 16
```

Adding the network number or sequence number to the end will offer a more detailed view of that specific instance:

```
J#show ip prefix-list testlist seq 10
    seq 10 deny 192.168.0.0/16 ge 24 (hit count: 0,
refcount: 1)
```

9.5 Reducing the Administration Burden

As we have seen, BGP has a huge amount of configurable items. This can become overwhelming, even for the (few) well-organized companies trying to keep up with the expanding number of routers within their administration.

BGP has adapted some conveniences, however. Mostly these concern the fact that most autonomous system have a large number of general rules that apply to the entire AS or to many routers within an AS. To reduce the amount of typing and administration necessary for all these similarly configured routers, it is possible to group them together. This is the main focus of this section.

In this section we will use route maps as a way to create flexible and accurate method to allow the router to manipulate routing policies. For an in-depth look at route maps, refer to Chapter 12.

9.5.1 BGP Communities

A BGP community is formed by using the type 8 community attribute (refer to Chapter 8 for an attribute overview). Basically, the community attribute is used to group route advertisements together, and it enables routers to make decisions based on the community in which the route finds itself. It is even possible to cross the AS border and advise routers in neighboring autonomous system what to do with specific routes. For example, if you want a neighboring AS to know about the locally reachable networks in the AS, but you don't want the routes to be advertised further, then this can be simply accomplished using communities.

A destination can be grouped together with other destinations to make a community. Each destination can also be part of more than one community. All of this is up to the administrator, who defines the community and applies it to the destinations that he wants. When you have set the community parameters and want to send them to a neighboring router, you must activate the feature using the `send-community` command.

A community is defined through a number of well-known communities, which are briefly described here:

- *Internet* All routers belong to this community. It can used to be tell to advertise a route of this community to all other routers.

- *No-export* Do not pass this route using *external BGP* (EBGP). In other words, keep it in the AS.

- *No-advertise* Do not pass this route to any other router. In other words, keep it secret.

- *Local-as* This community is used in confederations and is beyond the scope of this book. Introduced in Cisco IOS 12.0, refer to Cisco CCO online to find more information on local-as.

Community values are set using route maps to provide maximum flexibility when defining them. Here we will give a few examples:

```
A#conf t
A(config)#router bgp 10
A(config-router)#neighbor 192.168.20.20 remote-as 20
A(config-router)#neighbor 192.168.20.20 send-community
A(config-router)#neighbor 192.168.20.20 route-map commtest out
```

The `send-community` command enables the sending of community variables and is defined by the route map called `commtest`. The route map can look as follows:

```
A#conf t
A(config)#route-map commtest
A(config-route-map)#match ip address 15
A(config-route-map)#set community no-export
```

Here we match all the IP network numbers that we define in access list number 15 and set the community to no-export. Doing this will result in these networks not being advertised outside the AS of the router receiving the route.

```
A#conf t
A(config)#route-map commtest
A(config-route-map)#match ip address 16
A(config-route-map)#set community 10 additive
```

Here the as path must match the as-path list, and when it does, the community attribute is set to 10. By adding the switch "additive" to the `set community 10` command, the 10 is added to the existing community attribute without replacing the existing one. The community attribute list will become a list, much like the as-path list becomes, with multiple entries per route.

In Figure 9-4, you can see an example of a community attribute. AS 10 does not want its internal networks to be advertised outside its neighboring AS 20. To do this, a route map must be made and the no-export attribute is assigned to all outgoing routes originating in AS 10.

The configuration for this is as follows:

```
A#conf t
A(config)#router bgp 10
A(config-router)#network 192.168.10.0
A(config-router)#neighbor 10.10.10.2 remote-as 20
A(config-router)#neighbor 10.10.10.2 send-community
A(config-router)#neighbor 10.10.10.2 route-map comm out
```

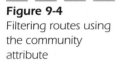

Figure 9-4
Filtering routes using
the community
attribute

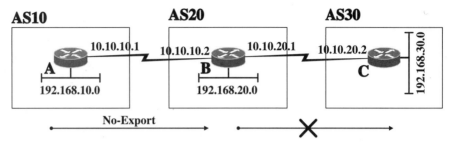

```
A(config)#route-map comm permit 10
A(config-route-map)#match ip address 15
A(config-route-map)#set community no-export

A(config)#route-map comm permit 20

A(config)#access-list 15 permit 192.168.10.0 0.0.0.255
```

It is also possible to assign a number to the community list. This number can be extracted from the incoming route information by another router and be interpreted using rules agreed on by the administrations of each router. To do this, we use the `community list` command to create a list of matches for filtering on a community attribute.

In Figure 9-5, we want the updates from AS 10 to get a weight of 10, the updates that originate from within AS20 to get a weight of 20, and the routes that have come from outside AS 20, but have traveled through it, to get a weight of 30.

In the following configuration, route map 10 matches the local ip addresses and gives those routes a community value of 20. All other routes get the value of 20 added to whatever was already in the attributes value due to the "additive" word, in router B's configuration.

Router A

```
A(config)#router bgp 10
A(config-router)#network 192.168.10.0
A(config-router)#neighbor 10.10.10.2 remote-as 30
A(config-router)#neighbor 10.10.10.2 send-community
A(config-router)#neighbor 10.10.10.2 route-map comm out

A(config)#route-map comm permit 10
```

Figure 9-5
Using community lists

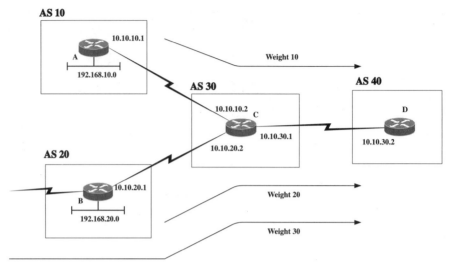

```
A(config-route-map)#match ip address 17
A(config-route-map)#set community 10

A(config)#route-map comm permit 20

A(config)#access-list 17 permit 192.168.10.0 0.0.0.255
```

Router B

```
B#conf t
B(config)#router bgp 20
B(config-router)#network 192.168.20.0
B(config-router)#neighbor 10.10.20.2 remote-as 30
B(config-router)#neighbor 10.10.20.2 send-community
B(config-router)#neighbor 10.10.20.2 route-map comm out

B(config)#route-map comm permit 10
B(config-route-map)#match ip address 20
B(config-route-map)#set community 20

B(config)#route-map comm permit 20
B(config-route-map)#set community 20 additive

B(config)#access-list 20 permit 192.168.20.0 0.0.0.255
```

In the next configuration, the route maps are numbered 10, 20, 30, and 40. They are run through and the matches are matched to the community list command. Route map 20 uses the `exact` command to match the community attribute value of 20 exactly. The next route map gives all the other routes a weight of 30. The final route map enables all the other routes to be advertised because the `permit Internet` command effectively lets everything pass.

Router C

```
C#conf t
C(config)#router bgp 30
C(config-router)#neighbor 10.10.10.1 remote-as 10
C(config-router)#neighbor 10.10.10.1 route-map comm-in in
C(config-router)#neighbor 10.10.20.1 remote-as 20
C(config-router)#neighbor 10.10.20.1 route-map comm-in in

C(config)#route-map comm-in permit 10
C(config-route-map)#match community 10
C(config-route-map)#set weight 10

C(config)#route-map comm-in permit 20
C(config-route-map)#match community 20 exact
C(config-route-map)#set weight 20

C(config)#route-map comm-in permit 30
C(config-route-map)#match community 20
C(config-route-map)#set weight 30

C(config)#route-map comm-in permit 40
C(config-route-map)#match community 3

C(config)#ip community-list 1 permit 10
C(config)#ip community-list 1 permit 20
C(config)#ip community-list 1 permit Internet
```

The greater the amount of routers attached, the greater the effect of the community attribute. If routers are added, or new ASs are attached, only a few steps are needed to add rules that will enforce the policies needed for the AS.

9.5.2 BGP Peer Groups

As BGP networks grow, administrators find that for every small change in policy, many neighbor relationships need to have the same small change made to them. To avoid this time-consuming inconvenience, *peer groups* have been defined. A number of routers that share the same policies can be configured to be part of a peer group. Policy changes are then configured to the peer group and not the individual routers. The changes will be applied to all members of that peer group. A policy defined in a peer group can be overridden, but only the policies for incoming updates. Outgoing updates will always be identical within a peer group. Let's examine the following example:

```
C(config)#no router bgp 30
C(config)#router bgp 10
C(config-router)#neighbor intra-as peer-group
C(config-router)#neighbor intra-as remote-as 10
C(config-router)#neighbor intra-as route-map inside out
C(config-router)#neighbor interas peer-group
C(config-router)#neighbor interas route-map outside out
C(config-router)#neighbor interas filter-list 1 in
C(config-router)#neighbor 10.10.10.2 peer-group intra-as
C(config-router)#neighbor 10.10.20.2 peer-group intra-as
C(config-router)#neighbor 10.10.30.2 remote-as 20
C(config-router)#neighbor 10.10.30.2 peer-group interas
C(config-router)#neighbor 10.10.40.2 remote-as 30
C(config-router)#neighbor 10.10.40.2 peer-group interas
C(config-router)#neighbor 10.10.40.2 filter-list 2 in
```

The following configurations take place in the previous code:

- The peer group is called *intra-as*. This peer group will hold all the joint configuration items for all routers that are inside the same AS as router A.
- The peer group intra-as routers are all internal, so they share the command `remote-as 10`.
- We define a route map called *inside* for applying our policies. We could define as many as we want.
- We define a second group of routers called *interas*. This will include all the routers external to the AS.

- We define another route map called *outside* and an incoming filter list.
- Two neighbors, routers B and C, are assigned and added to the peer group. They automatically inherit the `remote-as 10` command and `route-map inside out` command.
- Router D is added and, because the remote-as was not configured in the peer group, we must do this specifically for this EBGP connection.
- Router E is added and a `filter-list` command is added that will override the filter list defined for the peer group interas.

Apart from the definitions made in this example, we can define communities, the source interface for a loopback interface in IBGP communication, weights, filter lists, distribute lists, and route maps. Some points must be kept in mind though:

- Only inbound updates can be explicitly changed for individual peer group members.
- IBGP and EBGP neighbors cannot be together in a peer group.
- All EBGP peer group members must be reachable over the same interface.
- Route reflectors can be part of a peer group, but not the clients.

To check the availability of the peer groups, you can use the following command:

```
C#sh ip bgp peer-group intra-as
BGP peer-group is intra-as, peer-group leader 10.10.10.2,
internal,  remote AS 1
0
 Index 1, Offset 0, Mask 0x2
  BGP version 4
  Minimum time between advertisement runs is 5 seconds
  Update messages formatted 0, replicated 0
  Route map for outgoing advertisements is inside
```

Adding summary to the command offers an overview of all the peer groups configured.

If the peer group connections need to be cleared, after configuration it can be done using the following command:

```
A#clear ip bgp peer-group <peer group name>
```

9.6 Connecting to Multiple ISPs

In this section, we are going to examine the different ways in which an AS could be attached to an ISP. Obviously, these examples also pertain to other connection types.

Because BGP is the routing protocol of choice on Internet, one would assume that BGP is needed as soon as a router gets attached to an ISP. This is not the case, as we shall see in the following examples.

9.6.1 Using Static Routes

We will start by explaining when it is *not* necessary to use BGP to connect to another BGP network, such as the Internet. Consider Figure 9-6.

In this case, Mycompany's network has a single connection to the Internet using an ISP that runs BGP. The only concern for Mycompany is to set a static route to the ISP's router and tell its own internal network about this route.

If Mycompany uses the Class B IP range of 192.168.0.0/16 and is running an IGP, OSPF for example, the configuration on router A would be as follows:

```
C(config)#ip route 0.0.0.0 0.0.0.0 serial 0
C(config-router)#router ospf 100
C(config-router)#network 192.168.0.0 0.0.255.255 area 0
C(config-router)#default-information originate always
```

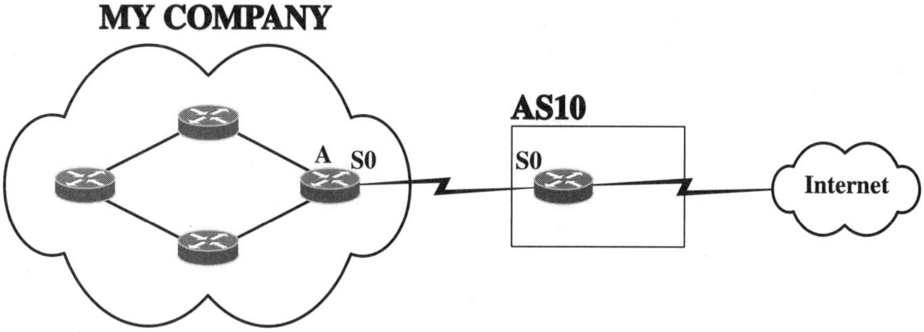

Figure 9-6
Using static routes
with BGP

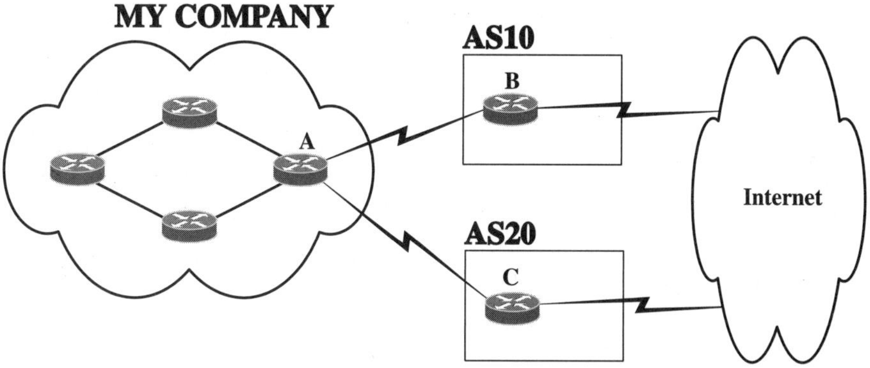

MY COMPANY

Figure 9-7
Using static routes to
connect to multiple
ISPs

MY COMPANY

The `ip route` command is the static entry. It will send all traffic to serial 0 and onto the ISP network. Here the `default-information originate always` command ensures that all OSPF routers will always advertise this default route. This method can also be used for connecting to multiple ISPs and can be used when there is a second connection to an ISP used for backup (see Figure 9-7).

The following configuration includes two static routes, each with a different distance. The one with the lowest distance is preferred. However, if this circuit fails, then the preferred route is removed from the routing table, and the backup route is used.

```
C(config)#ip route 0.0.0.0 0.0.0.0 serial 0 200
C(config)#ip route 0.0.0.0 0.0.0.0 serial 1 210
```

9.6.2 Using Dynamic BGP

When we want to use dynamic routing and guarantee loop-free routing, it can be advantageous to use BGP to route to ISPs. In this section, we will use BGP and two circuits to create a connection that is
not only redundant, but also load-balances between the circuits (see
Figure 9-8). To let the router know that it must balance the load over
multiple circuits, we use the `maximum circuits` command. In this
way, BGP can load-balance over a maximum of six circuits, but only
if they all connect to the same AS.

The configuration of router A will become as follows:

```
A#conf t
A(config)#router bgp 10
A(config-router)#no synchronization
A(config-router)#neighbor 192.168.10.2 remote-as 20
A(config-router)#neighbor 192.168.20.2 remote-as 20
A(config-router)#maximum-paths 2
```

Figure 9-8

A connection to
an ISP with load-
balancing

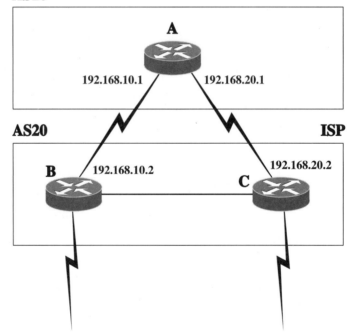

9.6.3 Multi-homing

A common use of BGP is in the case of multi-homing. Multi-homing is the word used when connection an AS to multiple ISPs.

The advantages of using multiple links to connect to the Internet are increased reliability and the possibility of using optimized paths over the various links.

There are three basic ways in which ISPs will offer routing information over connections to an AS.

1. Basic, only offer default routes.

   This method is the simplest for the AS being attached to the ISP. It requires only limited router power and memory availability.

   The ISP will offer default routes to the Internet, and the AS's internal routing protocol will decide which ISP connection to use based on the IGP's metric.

   The AS will send its routing information to the ISP, so the Internet will decide how to route information into the AS.

2. Medium routing traffic.

   In this case the ISPs offer default routes, but add specific routes to various networks. In this way the AS gets more routing information about the selected routes and can make better judgements on which ISP connection to use. The specific routes come complete with AS-path information which enables accurate routing of connections.

   This method is slightly more processor and memory intensive. As in the basic method, the routes to within the AS are determined outside the AS.

3. The obvious third method is to receive full routing information for the ISPs. Here all routes have AS-path information so the routers in the AS can determine the best path to the destination. This method is very processor and memory intensive.

9.7.1 Redistributing Routing Information into BGP

This process informs BGP which routes from within an AS should be advertised to other ASs.

This can be done in three ways.

1. Use the network command.

   This is a very safe way, as it is always known which routes are being advertised by BGP. Simply use the network command in the router bgp configuration to specify which of the AS's networks should be advertised.

2. Redistribution of static routes into BGP.

   This method uses static routes in the IGP routing table. The command redistribute static is then given in the bgp configuration to enable BGP to redistribute the routes. There is a problem in doing this, which is that if the route to the destination is lost, the static route will still exist, and BGP will continue advertising it. This can create so-called 'black holes' where a route without a destination is advertised.

3. Redistribute dynamic IGP into BGP.

   This is dangerous as IGP routing tables tend to change more than BGP routing tables. This can lead to instability in the BGP system. Also care must be taken only to distribute networks local to the AS into BGP, as the possibility of routing loops is large. To do this complex filters are used.

9.7 BGP Redistribution with IGPs

Routers running BGP will also run an IGP such as EIGRP, OSPF etc. This has been discussed in Chapter 8.

BGP keeps a routing table for its own routing, as does the IGP. These must be combined for the IGP to know which routes are available outside the AS, and for BGP to know which Internal routes are to be advertised to the outside world. The exchange of routing information is called redistribution. Chapter 12 goes into the various details of redistribution, but here we will discuss redistribution from a BGP standpoint.

9.7.2 Redistributing Routing Information from BGP into an IGP

This process sends BGP routing information into the IGP active in the AS.

If the AS is not part of an ISP then it is probable that BGP information needs to be redistributed into the IGP. If not the IGP will have no knowledge of the routes to BGP-learnt routes, and will not be able to route outside the AS.

There are two ways to distribute BGP routes into an IGP:

1. Dynamic redistribution.

   This method can overwhelm the IGP, if BGP has access to a large Internet network. Filtering is the answer here, reducing the volume of updates.

   The IGP routers will receive routing updates from the BGP router(s), containing a route metric. In this way the IGP routers can decide which is the best route to take to the remote destination network.

2. Default routes.

   As discussed earlier, it can be wise to use default routes to inform the IGP about the external routes. The downside is that the granularity of the routing metrics decreases, making optimum routing choices impossible in some cases.

The IGP routers will only know of a fixed next hop (the BGP router) to send data to.

In the case of ISPs, redistribution is usually not necessary. ISPs tend to have fully meshed IBGP networks, so all routers will know of the BGP routes. In this case the IGP is there to route local traffic and BGP is used to route external traffic. As all routers in the fully meshed network run the IGP and IBGP, there is no need to redistribute routing data.

In this case it is useful to use the 'no synchronization' command, so that BGP does not wait for the IGP to converge before using routing information. This was discussed in the previous chapter.

9.8 Chapter Summary

BGP is the protocol of choice when it comes to linking large ASs. It offers you the ability to manipulate the way you advertise your network to the surrounding areas as well as to adapt the routing information coming into your AS.

As Internetworks have become larger, ways have been found to reduce the burden of configuring and maintaining the BGP system as a whole. It is also important to remember that one should look for the simple solution first. Too often solutions are made too complicated when creative thinking can offer a simpler solution.

9.9 Frequently Asked Questions (FAQ)

Question: Inside my AS, my BGP routers talk IBGP. I also have two links to my ISP using two routers. If I list the routes learned from the IGP using the network command, will this cause a loop?

Answer: No, doing this will allow both EBGP routers to advertise the networks. BGP will choose a preferred path and in doing so will enable one router to take over if the other fails.

Question: Must I list the connected networks in BGP to make them available?

Answer: No, typically the IGP will take care of the traffic within the AS and supply the routes to the networks. If you want the networks to be directly reachable through BGP, then you can list them.

Question: If I am connected to one ISP through two links, should I worry about creating routing loops towards the provider?

Answer: No, the provider will detect this through the as-path attribute. However, it places an extra unnecessary burden on your routers and the ISP's routers. Proper configuration should send only your routes to the ISP.

9.10 Case Study

1. Question:

Create a basic bgp configuration for router C

Answer:

```
router bgp 30
neighbor 10.1.1.1 remote-as 10
neighbor 10.1.2.1 remote-as 20
neighbor 10.1.6.1 remote-as 40
neighbor 10.1.3.1 remote-as 30
neighbor 10.1.4.1 remote-as 30
```

2. Question:

Create a peer group in the following manner on router C

a. Add commands to filter incomming and outgoing updates by AS-Path for routers A,B,F.

Answer:

```
neighbor casestudy peer-group
neighbor casestudy filter-list 1 out
neighbor casestudy filter-list 2 in
neighbor 10.1.1.1 peer-group casestudy
neighbor 10.1.2.1 peer-group casestudy
neighbor 10.1.6.1 peer-group casestudy
```

b. Which command is used to define the AS-Path filter?

Answer:

```
Ip as-path access-list 1 [permit|deny] logical expression
```

c. Add the command to assign an alternative filter by AS-Path from router F

Answer:

```
neighbor 10.1.6.1 filter-list 3 in
```

3. Question:

a. Configure router C to be a route reflector for routers D and E

Answer:

```
neighbor 10.1.3.1 route-reflector-client
neighbor 10.1.4.1 route-reflector-client
```

b. Which command is needed if we want to IBGP sessions not to be reflected, but we do want router C to reflect the EBGP information?

Answer:

```
no bgp client-to-client reflection
```

Figure 9-9
Case study example

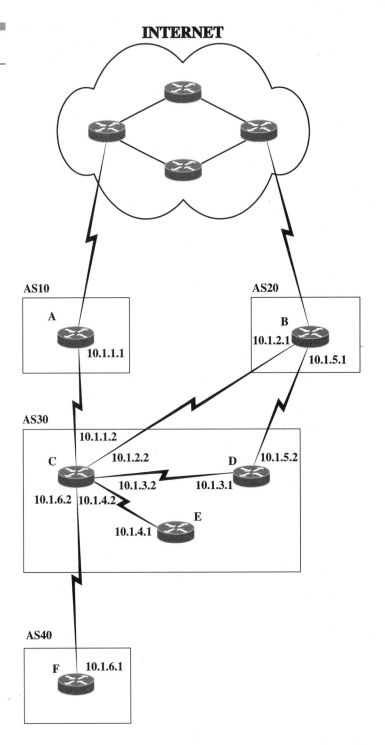

9.11 Questions

1. How do I reduce the amount of IBGP updates in my AS?

   a. By using a remote map

   b. By using route reflectors

   c. By redistributing the IGP

   d. By using the no synchronization command

2. Route reflector client routers have IBGP connections with all route reflecting routers.

   a. True

   b. False

3. Route reflecting routers have IBGP connections with all other reflecting routers.

   a. True

   b. False

4. A route reflector client can see which routers have reflected a certain path.

   a. True

   b. False

5. One AS can have multiple route reflector clusters.

   a. True

   b. False

6. A cluster only has one route reflector router.

   a. True

   b. False

7. A distribute list can be used to filter

   a. incoming BGP updates

   b. outgoing BGP updates

   c. a and b

   d. It does not filter incoming or outgoing updates.

8. Distribute lists use standard and extended access lists.

   a. True

   b. False

9. Distribute lists are easier to configure than prefix lists and are processed more quickly by the router.

    a. True
    b. False

10. A prefix list is assigned to a neighbor in the BGP router configuration.

    a. True
    b. False

11. Items in a prefix list can be erased or added at any part of the list.

    a. True
    b. False

12. Items in a distribute list can be erased or added at any part of the list.

    a. True
    b. False

13. The command used for checking the content of a prefix list is

    a. `show prefix-list <listname>`
    b. `show ip prefix-list <listname>`
    c. `show ip bgp prefix-list <listname>`

14. The common BGP community types are

    a. no-export
    b. no-import
    c. Internet
    d. Answer a + b
    e. Answer a + c
    f. Answer b + c

15. How are the rules to define communities created?

    a. Using route maps.
    b. Using prefix lists.
    c. Using route maps or prefix lists, depending on the circumstances.

16. Which command starts the community process?

    a. `neighbor <ip address> send-community`
    b. `enable bgp community`
    c. `enable ip bgp community`

17. If we have made the definitions for a peer group, we can assign a different filter for a specific neighbor for

    a. outgoing updates
    b. incoming updates
    c. a and b
    d. a or b

18. All EBGP peer group routers must be reachable over the same interface.

    a. True
    b. False

19. When connecting an AS to an ISP, it is always simpler to use BGP when the ISP also uses BGP.

    a. True
    b. False

20. If an AS needs to connect to an ISP using multiple circuits, BGP can load-balance over a maximum of ___ circuits.

    a. 2
    b. 6
    c. 64
    d. 1

9.12 Answers

1. b
2. b
3. a
4. a
5. a
6. b
7. c
8. a
9. b
10. a
11. a
12. b
13. b
14. e
15. a
16. a
17. b
18. a
19. b
20. b

CHAPTER 10

Overview of Managing Traffic and Access

10.1 Objectives Covered in This Chapter

To better understand what is needed to manage network traffic and access using Cisco routers, the following objectives will be covered.

Table 10-1

BSCN objectives

BSCN Objective
Describe causes of network congestion
List solutions for controlling network congestion using Cisco IOS services
Describe the function and applications of access lists
List solutions for optimizing routing updates

10.2 Chapter Introduction

The chapter is subdivided in three parts of which the first deals with managing traffic congestion, the second with access list concepts and usage, and the last with optimization of routing updates. Although this is an overview chapter, details of more complex issues involving access lists will be covered in the next chapter. Routing update optimization is covered in more detail in Chapter 12, "Optimizing Routing Update Operations." In a change from ACRC, Cisco decided not to include queuing in the BSCN course, but in order to prepare you for the routing exam, we felt that queuing is key information to study when dealing with traffic management issues. Therefore, queuing is covered extensively in Appendix A.

10.3 Congestion Overview

Network congestion commonly occurs when the amount of network traffic that is transmitted exceeds the bandwidth of the physical medium being used. Network congestion causes users to speak about the network being slow, while it is hard for them to comprehend why this is occurring. To most network administrators, congestion is a well-known phenomenon that tends to have a temporary or sometimes even periodical character.

Although the first can generally be expected in almost every network, the latter is usually caused by the bursty nature of network applications. The database system in a typical client-server network is shown in Figure 10-1 where the server is queried by one or more client computers. These client queries will generally pose no serious network problems. The database's server response, however, typically involves small or large portions of data to be sent back to the querying client. Although most of the time these transmissions are not sustained for long periods of time, they can significantly slow down network performance periodically. This type of congestion is referred to as *temporary congestion*. Network congestion occurs when the link's bandwidth is exceeded by the data traffic.

Another well-known example of temporary network congestion is networks slowing down in the morning and afternoon when users arrive at work and return from lunch respectively. This type of network congestion is known as *periodic congestion*, since it occurs at regular periodic intervals.

Figure 10-1
How network
congestion occurs

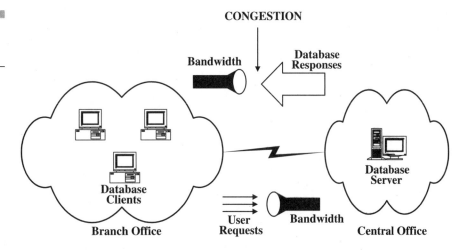

In most cases, preventing temporary or even periodic network congestion tends to be time-consuming and generally results in high costs that can't be rectified by the fairly short moments of tediousness that it causes. Chronic network congestion, however, can pose a real threat to a company's operation and should be identified and remedied in the earliest possible stage. As chronic network congestion is generally experienced on serial links, this will be our main focus in this chapter.

10.4 IP Network Traffic

When network traffic is not directly related to user applications, it is said to be *overhead traffic*. Examples of overhead traffic include routing updates and broadcast requests for a *Domain Name System* (DNS). Although an IP network can have many sources and types of data and overhead traffic, four main categories can be identified:

- User applications and user behavior
- Routing protocol updates
- DNS requests
- Transport of encapsulated protocols

10.4.1 User Applications and User Behavior

Applications using the *File Transfer Protocol* (FTP) or *Simple Mail Transfer Protocol* (SMTP), for instance, can generate lots of data traffic, especially when large files are being transferred or when lots of users use their FTP and e-mail client concurrently or a combination of both. Another example is users sending large attachments in e-mail messages, generating a lot of NetBIOS over IP (NBT) traffic. Although company policies generally prevent users from sending or receiving extremely large amounts of data, today's huge growth of intranet and Internet usage often prove to be a network administrator's nightmare when it comes to network congestion.

10.4.2 Routing Protocol Updates

Depending on the type of routing protocol used, updates are sent periodically or when topology changes in the network occur. This type of overhead traffic can become an issue when, for example, excessive updates are occurring as a result of a flapping serial link.

10.4.3 DNS Requests

With TCP/IP becoming the protocol of choice in both small and large networks, the usage of DNS and other TCP/IP-specific services has dramatically increased over the years. Since the new Windows 2000's network architecture heavily relies on DNS, this will only increase the presence of DNS traffic on most networks.

10.4.4 Transport of Encapsulated Protocols

Encapsulation is often used in situations where networks are said to be non-contiguous. These networks can be joined by encapsulating network traffic in IP packets, enabling it to cross an IP network. Logically, when two or more non-contiguous networks generate lots of data traffic, already slow links such as serial connections in the IP network can easily become congested.

10.5 Multiprotocol Network Traffic

Other than in an IP-only network, a multiprotocol network can have a multitude of different routing and routed protocols active at the same time. When we look at the characteristics of user data traffic in such as network, we see that user data traffic for each different protocol that is being used is active at the same time, resulting in many concurrent data transfers. Additionally, each protocol typically generates its own portion of overhead traffic, thereby claiming its share of the bandwidth that is to be divided in a fair and effective fashion.

Although activity on the lower layers of the OSI model can't be accounted for eating up huge portions of the available bandwidth in any given network, its role is not to be underestimated. The following is a short list of underlying types of traffic that are associated with the lower layers of the OSI model:

- Accessibility tokens
- Address Resolution Protocol (ARP) requests
- Keep-alives for maintaining connectivity

When we sum up all the different types of traffic that need to be managed or reduced in an internetwork, we can come up with the following:

- User applications
- Routing updates
- Overhead traffic
- Physical layer/data-link layer signaling

Figure 10-2 shows a multiprotocol network and its protocols.

10.6 Managing Network Congestion

Most issues related to network congestion can be summarized as, "Too much traffic within a given period of time." To resolve congestion issues, you can either *reschedule* or *reduce* the traffic. Access lists offer a variety of ways to filter application and user traffic. One of the things that traffic filters can accomplish is preventing some traffic from reaching critical links such as serial *Wide Area Network* (WAN) connections.

The next chapter discusses the configuration and operation of access lists in more detail. In the next three paragraphs, we will show you *how* and *where* access lists can be employed. We will also show you other applications for access lists that seem a bit odd at first, but that can prove to be very successful.

Figure 10-2
Bandwidth limitation
in a live multiprotocol
network

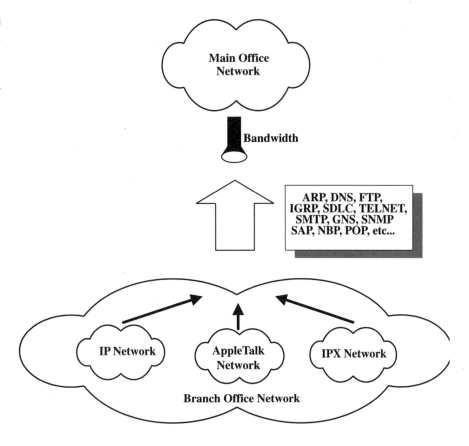

Another means of managing network congestion is filtering broadcasts. Many networked applications such as *Enterprise Resource Planning* (ERP) tools like SAP use periodic broadcasts. The transmission timers used here can be configured to lengthen the interval between broadcast transmission, thereby reducing the volume of network traffic.

To stay with the SAP example, it is also possible to adjust timers on periodic SAP announcements. When you reduce the time between the transmission of updates in a way that retains proper application operation, you can effectively reduce traffic on a link.

Experimenting with various configurations can prove to be a time-consuming effort. However, getting the network behavior of your networked application fine-tuned often results in much smoother and bandwidth-friendly operations. Moreover, using best practices to document standard procedures can help in reducing the amount of experimenting.

Another well-known technique is to incorporate static route entries in your router's routing tables. This way, you can often avoid network routes to be dynamically advertised across a link. Especially when using (slow) serial lines, you should give this idea some thought.

Chapter 12 will cover management of routing overhead traffic extensively, but we'd like to mention it here as well. Total elimination of this type of traffic is rather impossible as it is required to support the routing process(es). The keyword here is *reduction*. One method for reducing routing overhead traffic is to convert your network configuration from using distance vector protocols such as the *Routing Information Protocol* (RIP) to link-state protocols such as *Open Shortest Path First* (OSPF). When you're using RIP and suffer from its lively updating of routing information, you can also select *Enhanced IGRP* (EIGRP), which gives you part of the advantage OSPF offers but saves you from a possible administrative burden.

Section 10.9 takes reducing overhead traffic further by discussing several other techniques that can be used to reduce routing update traffic. To summarize all of this, we can say that you can control network congestion by doing the following:

- Filtering user and application traffic
- Filtering broadcast traffic
- Adjusting timers on broadcasts and periodic announcements
- Incorporating static entries in routing tables
- Controlling routing overhead traffic

Now let's examine the ways network traffic can be filtered using access lists.

10.7 Using Access Lists to Filter Traffic

Two well-known situations in which access lists are often used are backbone traffic management and managing user access. Of course, access lists are most commonly used to provide network security through traffic filtering. However, isn't filtering also the key to reducing and managing network congestion? When managing a backbone connection, the network administrator finds himself in a position where ensured delivery of the network's core-protocol (often IP) is demanded, while at the same time, other user-session traffic from the connected segments may need a timely delivery. With this situation in mind, it is not uncommon to find someone in this position tweaking and tuning router configurations all the time, as traffic tends to change over time. Building an awesome and extremely effective traffic filtering system may work this month, but chances are that within the next few months the network's traffic characteristics may change. Doesn't the new version of Quake come out in a few months? Therefore, when designing a traffic management policy and standard configuration, it is imperative that a solution not only is effective, but also flexible enough to accommodate future changes.

Security is the first word that enters our minds when the term access list is used. Although it is true that access list functionality, as it was incorporated in the Cisco IOS, was originally designed as a security mechanism, over the years additional benefits have been added. Access lists nowadays provide a great traffic filtering capability that cannot only be used as a security mechanism, but also as an effective technique to reduce unnecessary network traffic. Before access lists can be implemented as effective traffic filters, some conditions have to be met.

NOTE: *You might have found that the usage of the terms access list and traffic filter sometimes can be confusing. When we talk about a traffic filter, we are actually discussing one of the applications of an access list. The term access list itself is used to refer to the actual numbered list of addresses and wildcards. This list then can be linked to a specific application such as a traffic filter and only then such a list becomes meaningful.*

It may seem obvious that you can't throw in traffic filters at your will in your network since the result easily could be just as devastating as effective. One of the most important tasks to perform before starting to configure traffic filters is to study the character and (network) operation of the applications and its users. Different applications mean different needs and matching network requirements. Traffic flow, traffic volume, and time-critical operations are key factors here and, as a result, a compromise needs to be found to satisfy all the applications, the users, and (unfortunately last) the network itself. One important question that needs to be answered is whether the network is using a typical client/server architecture with centralized storage and processing, or is a more distributed model used that incorporates multiple workgroup servers? Both architectures use very different techniques, which are reflected in the traffic patterns, types, and directions that occur in the network.

Apart from studying traffic patterns and data types to determine *when* a traffic filter should be implemented, it is equally important to understand *where* a traffic filter should be placed in the network. A general rule of thumb here is to validate traffic as it enters the network. At least two good reasons exist for doing so:

■ The first is that the filtering of traffic should occur at devices that either reside in the access or distribution layers, presuming a hierarchical network design model is being used (as discussed in Chapter 2, "Overview of Scalable Internetworks"). Placing a traffic filter at these layers prevents unwanted traffic from reaching the high-speed switching core of the network, which is the network portion that cannot tolerate delays that are caused by long table lookups. If you will recall, the core layer of a network should be reserved for transit traffic.

- The second reason is that, depending on the access list configuration and the amount of traffic that needs to be checked, the processing of access lists can claim a lot, if not all, of the available resources, such as memory and the *Central Processing Unit* (CPU). Because a router that is configured with one or more traffic filters must be able to handle repetitive and sometimes lengthy access list checking, it should have sufficient memory and CPU resources.

Summarizing the above, we could say that

- User and application requirements should be studied and understood before applying traffic filters to optimize and secure the network.
- Make sure that adequate resources are available to satisfy the high workload that processing access lists generally causes.
- Access lists should preferably be placed at the access or distribution layers of a hierarchical network.
- Traffic should be validated as it enters the network and *not* at the time critical core layer.

10.8 Access List Application Overview

"Traffic should be validated as it enters the network and *not* at the time-critical core layer," as stated in the summary of the previous paragraph. For most companies, this means placing traffic filters at the Internet connection(s). Configuring an access list for that particular purpose generally means a compromise between blocking unsolicited inbound traffic and allowing requested traffic. This is easier when a reliable FTP is used. In this case, access lists can discriminate between unwanted requests and responses to sessions that were previously set up within the corporate network. In the latter case, the session is said to be *established,* fitting it in a category of traffic an access list can test for. Moreover, access lists provide a logging capability that can be used to record the types of activity that were rejected by the traffic filter, which is a very useful feature from a security point of view. Not only knowing what traffic was accepted, but also what was rejected is vital information when performing digital forensics after, for instance, a hacking attempt.

NOTE: *A word of caution here as the previous scenario does not imply that a single Cisco IOS device can offer complete passive and active protection against external attacks. Always make sure that a device that performs the role of the perimeter router is part of a corporate security policy that contains guidelines, dedicated firewalls, or proxy servers. This creates an overlap in areas of vulnerability that each solution carries with it, making the sum of all the different components and guidelines an acceptable security solution.*

If we take the previous application of access lists one step further, we find that applying an access list as a traffic policeman in a corporate network works conveniently as well. If we take the Corporate Management and R&D subnets in Figure 10-3, we can see that it is possible to secure one or more subnets within the same internetwork while retaining allowable communication options. The router that the access list is applied on validates the source address of arriving packets and then determines whether they are allowed to be forwarded to either of the secured subnets (R&D and Corporate Management). As an example, we could say that the Sales and Production subnets are treated as "trusted" subnets where communication with R&D and Corporate Management is allowed. Any packets originating from both of the remaining subnets, Personnel and Marketing, are not allowed to pass into the secure area. In order to retain a secure communication between two "untrusted" subnets, the network administrator can use the "established connection" that we discussed earlier.

The final step in access list security using standard Cisco IOS features and services is making use of so-called *extended IP access-lists*. Compared to the previously discussed established connection feature, extended access lists offer the additional advantage of being able to detect the originating application or protocol that generated

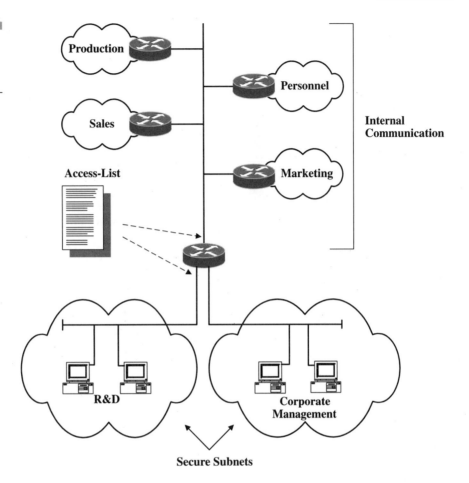

Figure 10-3
Securing individual
subnets in a network
using access lists

the traffic that is to be serviced. This technique is based on the well-known ports (that is, the port number assigned) where the port used is checked against a list of matching ports and protocols or key applications. Examples would be an FTP that uses TCP port 20 and 21 for setting up a connection and transferring data, and Telnet, which uses TCP port 23.

Figure 10-4 shows a corporate network that is connected with the Internet by a perimeter router. An access list is configured on the router, enabling communication between internal hosts and the Internet only after a session is initiated within the corporate network, using the established access list option. Unsolicited requests from hosts on the Internet are blocked by the access list.

Figure 10-4
Using an access list to
filter unsolicited
requests from the
Internet

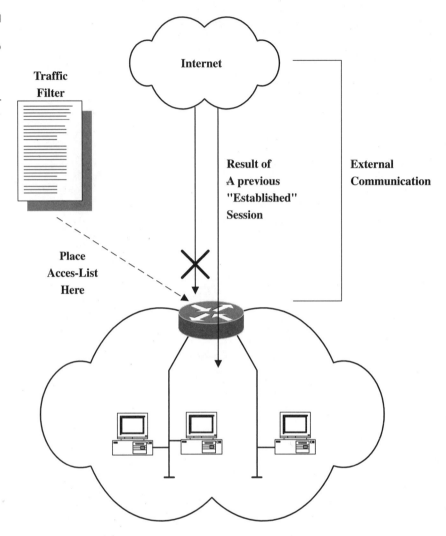

Figure 10-5 shows a company's Internetwork that features two serial interconnections that connect the Atlanta and Amsterdam corporate branch offices. An extended access list is configured on all four interfaces to route only *Simple Network Management Protocol* (SNMP), FTP, and e-mail traffic via the upper link and all network application traffic through the lower link. This way, the network administrator assures that the available bandwidth on the lower link that is used for mission-critical networked applications is not

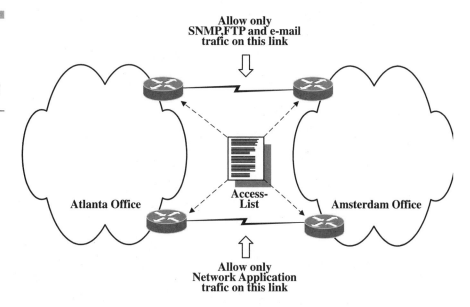

Figure 10-5
Preserving
bandwidth for
individual
applications by using
access lists

compromised by high-volume file transfers or e-mail messages. The transmission of files, e-mail, and SNMP network monitoring only takes place through the upper link.

In Appendix A, you can read how further granularity can be achieved using queuing techniques that are featured by Cisco IOS 11.2 and above. This is especially useful when only one link or several low-bandwidth links are available. The next chapter will delve much deeper into the concepts, configuration, and operation of both standard and extended access lists.

10.9 Reducing Routing Update Traffic

As we mentioned in section 10.6, configuring a link-state protocol such as OSPF instead of a distance vector protocol such as RIP dramatically reduces routing update traffic. In the OSPF and EIGRP chapters, we have seen that this is because link-state protocols only send an incremental update about a single route in case of a topology change, whereas distance-vector protocols send periodic updates containing the entire routing table. It may be obvious that the bandwidth usage on links where a link-state routing protocol is configured can decrease dramatically, especially in large networks. Table 10-1 shows various methods that can be used to reduce routing update traffic and their effects.

So how is this done? We've already discussed the link-state versus the distance-vector issues, but as you can see in the previous table, several more ways exist for reducing routing update traffic. Earlier we have seen that route summarization can be used to present a group of routes that share the same network prefix. For example, if route summarization is configured in a well-designed hierarchical OSPF network, the size of the routing table(s) in area 0 can be significantly reduced. Summarizing routes in this case namely prevents all subnets from having to be included in the routing tables, which are flooded to peer routers.

Moreover, it's possible to shrink the routing table more by configuring route filters that can be applied to filter inbound updates, but also routing updates could use some weight loss. We can use techniques such as route maps and distribute lists to control what's actually included in a routing update. Finally, in the case of a local router,

Table 10-1	Method	Effect
Methods of reducing update traffic	Create summary routes	Shrinks the size of the routing table of the receiving router(s) and reduces the number of routes that are propagated
	Use a link-state protocol instead of a distance vector protocol	Incremental updates are sent instead of periodic updates
	Filter the content of routing updates	Reduction of the number of routes that are propagated
	Configure static and default routes	Reduction of the number of routes that are propagated

it might be a good idea to configure static routes. As these entries are only relevant to the local router itself, it is not necessary to include them in the periodic announcements that are propagated to neighboring devices. These options are routing protocol-specific and should be investigated when designing the routing setup.

Which brings us to yet another point of attention: reducing the amount of routing information *before* it leaves the router. Outbound route filters can be configured to selectively remove routes from the routing update that is to be transmitted. This removal process relies on statements in the distribute list, which can be applied to one or more interfaces on which routing updates are transmitted. With this type of operation, it is typical to see more route entries in the routing table than the number of routes that are actually flooded to the neighboring routers.

Not only can the *content* of the routing update be filtered, but also the interval on which routing updates are sent can be manipulated. This can be realized by configuring a passive interface that can prevent an interface from sending regularly scheduled routing updates on behalf of the routing process(es) to which the particular interface is linked. The capability to accept incoming routing updates, however, is retained when this technique is used. These incoming updates can in turn be filtered by applying an *inbound* route filter, which essentially performs the same tasks on incoming updates.

10.10 Chapter Summary

In this chapter, we have discussed the concept and sources of traffic congestion. We have also shown you several methods to control traffic congestion such as

- Filtering user and application traffic
- Filtering broadcast traffic
- Adjusting timers on broadcasts and periodic announcements

- Incorporating static entries in routing tables
- Controlling routing overhead traffic

While covering the concepts and uses of access lists, we've discussed a number of situations in which access lists can be used to achieve a more responsive and secure network. Apart from the security point of view, access lists can be useful in many other situations. When applying access lists, the following points should be taken into account:

- User and application requirements should be studied and understood before applying traffic filters to optimize and secure the network.
- Make sure that adequate resources are available to satisfy the high workload that processing access lists generally causes.
- Access lists should preferably be placed at the access or distribution layer of a hierarchical network.
- Standard *Access Control Lists* (ACLs) should be placed closest to the traffic destination and extended ACLs should be placed closest to the traffic source.
- Traffic should be validated as it enters the network and *not* at the time-critical core layer.

The last part of this chapter dealt with optimization methods that can be used to reduce routing update traffic as well as methods that enable the network administrator to reduce the content or routing tables. Some of these methods are the following

- The creation of summary routes
- Using a link-state protocol instead of a distance vector protocol
- Filtering the content of updates
- Configuring static and default routes

Although this chapter provided an overview of access lists and optimizing route update operation issues and techniques, Chapter 11, "Configuring IP Access Lists," and Chapter 12, "Optimizing Routing Update Operations" will cover these subjects in more detail respectively.

10.11 Frequently Asked Questions (FAQ)

Question: How many access lists can I configure on my router?

Answer: There is no limit, although memory and processor resources should be checked at peak times to ensure that the router does not become overloaded. This is especially true when using extended access lists, which require considerable resources in comparison to standard access lists.

Question: How do I know when I have to tackle excessive routing update traffic?

Answer: A good network-monitoring system is the first step in managing your network. Keeping a close eye on the convergence time of the network will highlight impending problems. Checking protocol-specific warnings in logs such as EIGRP's stuck-in-active state is an example of this (see Chapter 7, "Configuring Enhanced IGRP (EIGRP)").

10.12 Case Study

The following two examples show two practical applications for IP access lists. Figure 10-6 presents network 192.168.10.0 that is not to be accessed by host 24.0.18.114. Communication with other hosts residing on the 24.0.18.0 network, however, is to be retained. The network administrator therefore configures an inbound access list on the router that interconnects both networks. The access list blocks incoming requests that have a source address of 24.0.18.114.

In Figure 10-7, we can see network 124.44.2.0 that is sitting behind a router that is configured with an extended IP access list. In the first line of the access list output shown in the figure, we can see that the network administrator has configured the router to permit TCP requests coming from any host on the 124.44.68.0 network.

The second line in the configuration example shows that all requests coming from elsewhere will be denied, except established SMTP connections with a destination address of 124.44.2.4. The blocking of all other requests occurs by the implicit *deny any* statement that ends every access list, but that is not shown in the configuration.

Figure 10-6

Blocking a single host access to a network

Figure 10-7
Allowing e-mail
transfers through a
secured connection
with the Internet

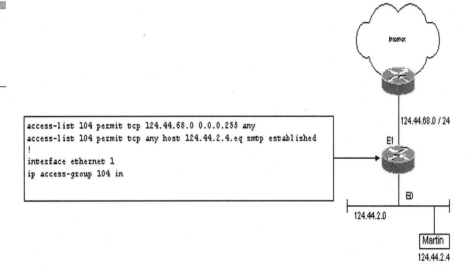

```
access-list 104 permit tcp 124.44.68.0 0.0.0.255 any
access-list 104 permit tcp any host 124.44.2.4.eq smtp established
!
interface ethernet 1
ip access-group 104 in
```

10.13 Questions

1. Which of the following sources generally does not cause excessive overhead?

    a. RIP routing protocol updates
    b. Telnet sessions
    c. Networked user applications
    d. DNS requests
    e. Encapsulated protocol transport

2. What is the biggest advantage of adding static route entries to the routing table when trying to reduce routing update traffic?

    a. Fewer router resources are used as the amount of required processing time decreases.
    b. Routes will be updated faster, as there is less data to be processed compared to dynamic routing.
    c. Static route updates are generally smaller than dynamic routing updates.
    d. It avoids the task of dyamically advertising network routes across a link.

3. Which of the following methods helps control network congestion?

    a. Reducing the number of routers in the network
    b. Controlling routing overhead traffic
    c. Upgrading all routers in the network to the latest Cisco IOS release
    d. Filtering broadcast traffic
    e. Incorporating static entries in routing tables

4. Traffic filters should be placed

    a. at the boundary of the distribution and core layers
    b. at the access layer
    c. at the distribution layer
    d. where traffic leaves the network
    e. where traffic enters the network

5. A well-configured and well-placed Cisco router can effectively provide a total network security solution.

   a. True
   b. False

6. What is the big advantage extended access lists offer over standard access lists?

   a. They are much easier to configure.
   b. They can filter both incoming and outgoing traffic.
   c. They can filter multiple protocols at the same time.
   d. They are capable of detecting the originating application or protocol that generated incoming traffic.

7. What is the effect of filtering the content of routing updates?

   a. Reduction of the number of incremental updates
   b. Reduction of the number of routes that are propagated
   c. Reduction of the router's CPU load
   d. Reduction of the number of periodic updates

8. How can you avoid routing updates to be sent to a particular connected network?

   a. By configuring the *Network Time Protocol* (NTP) on all routers in the network
   b. By configuring a lower clockrate value on serial links
   c. By configuring a passive interface
   d. By configuring an inbound route filter

9. Overhead traffic is said to be

   a. traffic that makes the router's CPU load exceed 80 percent for any given period of time
   b. traffic that is not directly related to user applications
   c. traffic that is generated by networked user applications
   d. traffic that is not directly related to router operation

10. Activity on the lower layers of the OSI model, such as keepalives, is not accountable for using any significant bandwidth.

    a. True
    b. False

11. What is the effect of creating summary routes?

    a. This shrinks the size of the routing table of the receiving router
    b. Slower convergence due to increased resource usage
    c. Reduction of the number of routes that are propagated
    d. Increased security

12. Network congestion occurs when

    a. there is insufficient space in the network cabinet to place network equipment
    b. the router is running out of memory due to lengthy queues
    c. the amount of traffic exceeds the available bandwidth
    d. too many protocols run on a single router

13. Which of the following is not one of the four categories of IP traffic?

    a. Routing protocol updates
    b. User applications
    c. SNA encapsulated in IP
    d. FTP

14. *Address Resolution Protocol* (ARP) requests reside in which layer of the OSI model?

    a. They do not reside in the OSI layer.
    b. They reside in the lower layers.
    c. They reside in the middle layers.
    d. They reside in the upper layers.

15. Access lists are only used to influence IP traffic.

    a. True
    b. False

16. Access lists can filter inbound and outbound traffic.

    a. True
    b. False

17. Long access lists performing traffic validations should be placed on the powerful core routers.

    a. True
    b. False

18. A link-state protocol produces more traffic than a distance vector protocol.

    a. True
    b. False

19. Encapsulated traffic does not add to congestion as it does not take part in the routing process.

    a. True
    b. False

20. Client computers running Windows 2000 software rely heavily on the ARP protocol.

    a. True
    b. False

10.14 Answers

1. b

2. d

3. b

4. b

5. a

6. d

7. b

8. c

9. b

10. b

11. a and c

12. c

13. d

14. b

15. b

16. a

17. b

18. b

19. b

20. a

Configuring IP Access Lists

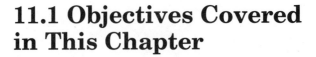

11.1 Objectives Covered in This Chapter

Upon completion of this chapter, the reader will be able to accomplish the following objectives. All these points will be covered in the subsequent sections in detail.

Table 11-1	**BSCN Objective**
BSCN objectives	Identify the key functions and special processing of IP access lists
	Configure standard IP access lists
	Configure extended IP access lists
	Control virtual terminal access with an access class
	Control Web access with an IP HTTP access class
	Control SNMP agent access with a standard access list
	Verify and monitor IP access lists
	Illustrate other applications of access lists
	Configure an alternative to access lists using a null interface

11.2 Chapter Introduction

This chapter concerns IP access lists. Access lists help us control and manage network protocol traffic in a more efficient and effective manner. Equipped with the necessary skill set or guides, we can go ahead and start configuring our networking devices. However, configuring a device is only a matter of knowing which configuration commands do what. It is how we control and manage the device in an intelligent way that is difficult. Access lists are rule-based mechanisms that enable us to do just that.

11.2 Managing IP Traffic

Access lists give the router the capability to scrutinize network traffic. With different access lists, the router can look at different Layer-3 packets such as IP, IPX, AppleTalk, VINES, DECnet, and CLNS. Also, Layer-2 access lists enable the router to look at the LLC and MAC frames and enable the NetBIOS access lists to look at the NetBIOS frames. However, this chapter will cover only IP access lists.

Access lists are rule-based and are analogous to the "if-else" conditional statements. More importantly, they give the router more control power for security, filtering decisions, and traffic management (or optimization). Access lists are universal and have a broad application base, which gives the router more leeway to customize and adapt easily to a non-standardized internetworking environment.

11.3 Configuring IP Standard and Extended Access Lists

To manage and control IP traffic, two types of access lists are defined:

- Standard access lists have numbers ranging from 1 to 99. This type of access list restricts IP traffic based on source IP addresses only.

- Extended access lists have numbers ranging from 100 to 199. This type of access list restricts traffic in a manner similar to the standard access list, except the list can be further refined with protocol numbers, destination IP addresses, and source and destination TCP/UDP port numbers.

11.3.1 Access List Overview

For an access list to take effect, it has to be applied to a router interface either in the outbound direction (for analyzing specific outgoing traffic) or the inbound direction (for analyzing incoming traffic) or both. However, outbound access lists are not designed to block traffic originating within a router.

In addition, once an IP packet matches the conditions that are stated in an IP access list, two mutually exclusive actions can take place: permit or deny the IP packet from proceeding further. The following are some guidelines to keep in mind when configuring access lists:

- Access list numbers indicate which protocol is filtered. IP standard access lists have numbers ranging from 1 to 99, and IP extended access lists have numbers ranging from 100 to 199.
- Only one access list can be applied to each interface, protocol, and direction.
- The order of access list statement controls testing should be checked so that the most restrictive statements should be at the top of the list.
- There is an implicit "deny any" as the last access list test, so a list should not have just deny statements.
- Create access lists before applying them to interfaces.
- An access list filters traffic going through the router; they do not apply to traffic originating from the router.

It is also important to remember that inbound access lists are processed before the packet in question is passed to the routing mechanism of the router. Outbound access lists are processed after having been routed to the outgoing interface. Placing access lists wisely can prevent the router from having to unnecessarily route packets through the router.

Also packets originating from within the router, such as telnet connections from the router are not influenced by the standard or extended access lists.

11.3.2 Wildcard Masking

Wildcard or reverse masking, the direct reverse of subnet masking, where the ones (ignore) are now corresponding to an IP address's host bits and the zeros (check) corresponding to its network bits, can be used to define a range of addresses. This is very useful because the number of lines that are defined in an access list will be reduced significantly, optimizing CPU cycles, and making implementation simpler. Example 11-1 illustrates how wildcard masking is used.

In this example, the test condition is to match a single IP address, that is, check all address bits. The wildcard mask 0.0.0.0 checks the bit value in all bit positions; this has the effect of matching only the specified IP host address 181.181.181.5 in all bit positions. This wildcard mask can also be abbreviated using the IP address preceded by the keyword "host" (such as host 181.181.181.5).

In Example 11-2, the test condition is to match any IP address, that is, ignore all address bits. The wildcard mask 255.255.255.255 ignores any bit value in all bit positions, which has the effect of matching anything in all bit positions. The expression 0.0.0.0 255.255.255.255 can also be abbreviated using the keyword "any."

In the next example, we look at how to create a wildcard mask to match all hosts on subnet 165.3.4.0/24 to 165.3.16.0/24. From the illustration listed in Figure 11-1, the final derived wildcard mask is 0.0.7.255.

Example 11-1

```
181.181.181.5 0.0.0.0
```

Example 11-2

```
0.0.0.0. 255.255.255.255
```

Figure 11-1
Deriving the wildcard
mask

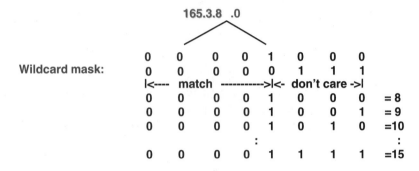

Figure 11-1
Deriving the wildcard
mask

Check for IP   subnets   165.3.   8 .0/24 to 165.3.   15 .0/24

Address and wildcard mask:

165.3.8.0 0.0.7.255

11.3.3 Configuring IP Standard Access Lists

IP access lists are rule-based mechanisms that give a router the capability and intelligence to control and manage IP traffic. They are analogous to "if-else" conditional statements. The following illustrates how a standard access list does its packet-testing using a pseudo-random "if-else" syntax:

```
If        [source_addr1]

          Execute Action {either permit or deny}

Else If    [source_addr2]

          Execute Action {either permit or deny}

Else If    [source_addr3]

          Execute Action {either permit or deny}

:

:

Else

          {Implicit deny all}
```

For IP-standard access lists, the test conditions are based on source addresses only. The global configuration command to define a standard access list is `access-list access-list-number {permit|deny} source [mask]`.

The access-list command creates an entry in a standard access list. The access-list field descriptions are as follows:

- An `access-list-number` identifies the list to which the entry belongs, a number from 1 to 99.
- A `source` is the source IP address.
- A `mask` is the wildcard mask that identifies which bits in the address field are matched. It has a 1 in position that indicates "don't care" bits and a 0 in any position that is to be strictly preserved.

Note that for an access list to come into effect, it has to be applied to an interface using the command, `ip access-group access-list-number {in | out}`.

In Example 11-3, we look at how to configure an IP standard access list. Figure 11-2 illustrates the scenario where the router denies any host on subnet 181.181.5.0 to access any host on subnet 181.181.3.0. The IP standard access list is applied on interface E0 in the outbound direction. The router configuration is as follows.

Example 11-3

```
access-list 1 deny 181.181.5.0   0.0.0.255
access-list 1 permit any
!
interface ethernet 0
  ip access-group 1 out
```

Figure 11-2
IP standard access list example

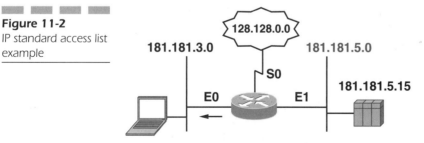

11.3.4 Configuring IP Extended Access Lists

The following illustrates how an extended access list does its packet testing using a pseudo-random if-else syntax:

```
If       [source_addr1 AND destination_addr1 AND protocol
         num1 AND port num1]

Execute Action {either permit or deny}

Else If     [source_addr2 AND destination_addr2 AND protocol
            num2 AND port num2]

            Execute Action {either permit or deny}

Else If     [source_addr3 AND destination_addr3 AND protocol
            num3 AND port num3]

            Execute Action {either permit or deny}

:

:

Else
     {Implicit deny all}
```

For IP extended access lists, the test conditions are based on source addresses, destination addresses, protocol numbers, and port numbers. The global command to define an extended access list is `access-list access-list-number {permit | deny} protocol source source-wildcard [operator port] destination destination-wildcard [operator port] [established] [log]`.

The access list field descriptions are as follows:

- `access-list-number`   A number between 100 and 199
- `protocol`   ip, tcp, udp, icmp, igrp, eigrp, ospf, and so on. If the protocol number is not listed, the protocol number between 1 and 255 may be used.
- `source`   The source IP address
- `source-wildcard`   A wildcard mask of address bits that must match. Zeros indicate bits that must match; ones are "don't care."
- `destination`   The destination IP address

- destination-wildcard The wildcard mask of address bits that must match. Zeros indicate bits that must match; ones are "don't care."

- operator This has a value of *less than* (lt), *greater than* (gt), *equal* (eq), or *not equal* (neq).

- port A port number or application name (for example, 23 or telnet)

- established This only enables established TCP sessions coming in (the ACK or RST bit must be set).

- log This generates a console message when a packet matches the access list statement.

Note that for an access list to come into effect, it has to be applied to an interface using the command ip access-group access-list-number {in | out}.

In Example 11-4, we look at how to configure an IP extended access list. Figure 11-3 illustrates the scenario where the router denies telnet from any host on subnet 181.181.5.0 out of interface E0. The router permits all other traffic. The IP extended access list is applied on interface E0 in the outbound direction. The router configuration is as follows.

Example 11-4

```
access-list 101 deny tcp 181.181.5.0   0.0.0.255
181.181.3.0 0.0.0.255 eq 23
access-list 101 permit ip any any
!
interface ethernet 0
  ip access-group 101 out
```

Figure 11-3
IP extended access list example

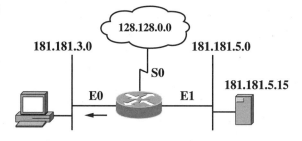

11.3.5 Extended Access list protocols

As seen in the previous section, a protocol name or number can be used to increase the granularity of the testing. Using the protocol names TCP, UDP or ICMP adds the possibility of using the names of the ports associated with the protocol to make the access lists easier to read and easier to enter into the router. Here follows some information about the protocol types and the types of filtering possible.

ICMP protocol filtering   Filtering can be done using ICMP type and code, or using the name of the ICMP message (for example, using the word 'ping' in the access list is easier than using the ICMP type and code for ping). Use the following IOS command to enter the ICMP access list:

```
access-list access-list-number {permit | deny} ICMP source
source-wildcard destination destination-wildcard [ICMP-
type[ICMP-code] | ICMP-message] log
```

See table 11.2 for an overview of the possible ICMP message names.

Table 11-2	IP extended Access List ICMP type names.
IP extended Access List ICMP type names	Administratively-prohibited
	Alternate-address
	Conversion-error
	Dod-host prohibited
	Dod-net-prohibited
	Echo
	Echo-reply
	General-parameter-problem
	Host-isolated
	Host-tos-redirect
	Host-tos-unreachable
	Host-unknown
	Host-unreachable

Information-reply

Mask-reply

Mask-request

Mobile-redirect

Net-redirect

Net-tos-redirect

Net-tos-unreachable

Net-unreachable

Network-unknown

No-room-for-option

Option-missing

Packet-too-big

Parameter-problem

Port-unreachable

Reassembly-timeout

Redirect

Router-advertisement

Router-quench

Source-route-failed

Time-exceeded

Traceroute

Ttl-exceeded

Unreachable

TCP and UDP Protocol Filtering   The syntax for the TCP and UDP filtering is not changed when using the named ports instead of the port numbers. See table 11.3 for TCP port names and table 11.4 for the UDP port names. See table 11.5 for TCP reserved port numbers and table 11.5 for UDP reserved port numbers.

Table 11-3

IP extended Access
List TCP port names

IP extended Access List TCP port names.
Bgp
Chargen
Daytime
Discard
Domain
Echo
Finger
Ftpc-control
ftp-data
Gopher
Hostmane
Irc
Klogin
Kshell
Lpd
nntp
Pop2
Pop3
Sunrpc
Syslog
Tacacs-ds
Talk
Telnet
Time
Uucp
Whois
www

Table 11-4

IP extended Access List UDP port names

IP extended Access List UDP port names.

Biff

Bootpc

Bootps

Discard

Dns

Dnsix

Echo

Mobile-ip

Nameserver

Netbios-dgm

Netbios-ns

Ntp

Rip

Snmp

Snmptrap

Sunrpc

Syslog

Tacacsds-ds

Talk

Tftp

Time

Whois

Xdmcp

Table 11-5

TCP reserved port numbers

Port number	Name	Description
0		Reserved
1-4		Unassigned
5	Rje	Remote job entry
7	Echo	Echo
9	Discard	Discard
11	Users	Active users
13	Daytime	Daytime
15	Netstat	Netstat
17	Quote	Quote of the day
19	Chargen	Character generator
20	Ftp-data	File data protocol (data)
21	ftp	File data protocol (control)
23	telnet	Terminal connection
25	Smtp	Simple mail transfer protocol
37	Time	Time of the day
39	Rlp	Resource location protocol
42	Nameserver	Host name server
43	Nicname	Whois
53	Domain	Domain name server
67	Bootps	Bootstrap server
68	Bootpc	Bootstrap client
69	Tftp	Trivial file transfer protocol
75		Private dialout service
77		Private RJE (5) service
79	Finger	Finger
95	Supdup	SUPDUP protocol
101	Hostname	NIC hostname server
102	Iso-tsap	ISO-TSAP

113	Auth	Authentication service
117	Uucp-path	UUCP path service
123	Ntp	Network time protocol
133-138		Unassigned
139	Netbios	Netbios session service
140		Unassigned
160-223		Reserved
224-255		Unassigned

Table 11-6	Port number	Name	Description
UDP reserved port numbers	0		Reserved
	1-4		Unassigned
	5	Rje	Remote job entry
	7	Echo	Echo
	9	Discard	Discard
	11	Users	Active users
	13	Daytime	Daytime
	15	Netstat	Netstat
	17	Quote	Quote of the day
	19	Chargen	Character generator
	20	Ftp-data	File data protocol (data)
	21	ftp	File data protocol (control)
	23	telnet	Terminal connection
	25	Smtp	Simple mail transfer protocol
	37	Time	Time of the day
	39	Rlp	Resource location protocol
	42	Nameserver	Host name server

continues

Port number	Name	Description
43	Nicname	Whois
53	Domain	Domain name server
67	Bootps	Bootstrap server
68	Bootpc	Bootstrap client
69	Tftp	Trivial file transfer protocol
75		Private dialout service
77		Private RJE (5) service
79	Finger	Finger
123	Ntp	Network time protocol
133-136		Unassigned
137	Netbios	Netbios name service
138	Netbios	Netbios datagram service
139-159		Unassigned
160	SNMP	SNMP
161	SNMP trap	SNMP trap
160-223		Reserved
224-255		Unassigned

11.4 Restricting Router Access

Besides the console (DCE) port and auxiliary (DTE) port, various other ways exist for accessing a Cisco router. The Cisco router can be configured as a telnet server, an HTTP server, and an SNMP manager for such accesses. However, these accesses also compromise security. As such, we might want to limit the access to these specific applications. In sections 11.4.1 to 11.4.3, we shall look at how to restrict the router's virtual terminal, HTTP, and SNMP accesses.

11.4.1 Virtual Terminal (VTY)

As discussed in section 11.3.1, outbound access lists are not designed to block traffic originating within a router. However, an access class can be used to filter incoming telnet sessions to the router's virtual terminals (0–4) and vice versa, filtering outgoing telnet sessions originating from the router's virtual terminals. To filter incoming and outgoing telnet sessions to and from the router's virtual terminals, a standard access list is used. An access class uses a standard access list to match the source address of the incoming telnet session and the destination address of the outgoing telnet session. Use the access-class-line interface configuration command to apply the standard access list to the router's virtual terminals.

Example 11-5a defines an access list that permits only hosts on network 192.168.33.0 to connect to the virtual terminals 0 through 4 on the router.

Example 11-5b defines an access list that denies connections to networks other than network 66.0.0.0 on virtual terminals 0 through 4.

11.4.2 HTTP

A Cisco router can be configured as an HTTP server using the global configuration command `ip http server`. Once the http server is enabled, the router can be accessed from a Web browser on port 80.

Example 11-5a

```
access-list 2 permit 192.168.33.0   0.0.0.255
line vty 0 4
access-class 2 in
```

Example 11-5b

```
access-list 3 permit 66.0.0.0 0.255.255.255
line vty 0 4
access-class 3 out
```

By default, the router uses port number 80 for http. To use a different port, the global configuration command `ip http port` can be used.

Example 11-6 configures the router so that you can use a Web browser via port 1600.

The global configuration command `ip http access-class` is used to control which hosts can access the Cisco HTTP server by a Web browser. Once this command is configured, the specified access list is assigned to the HTTP server. Thereafter, when the HTTP server accepts a connection, it checks the access list. If there is no match, the HTTP server does not accept the request for the connection.

Example 11-7 assigns the access list 4 to the HTTP server.

The `ip http authentication` global configuration command specifies the particular authentication method for HTTP server users. Four different authentication methods can be used:

- *AAA*   This method uses Cisco's *Authentication, Authorization, and Accounting* (AAA) facility.

- *Enable*   This method uses the enable password method, which is the default method of HTTP server user authentication.

- *Local*   This method uses the local user database (the "username" command) as defined on the Cisco router for authentication.

- *TACACS*   This method uses the TACACS authentication server to verify and authenticate the user's identity.

Example 11-6

```
ip http server
ip http port 1600
```

Example 11-7

```
ip http access-class 4
access-list 4 permit 152.15.134.0  0.0.0.255
access-list 4 permit 133.36.0.0  0.0.255.255
access-list 4 permit 50.0.0.0  0.255.255.255
```

Example 11-8 specifies local (user "mary" can access the router via http using the password "lamb") as the method of HTTP server user authentication.

11.4.3 SNMP

The *Simple Network Management Protocol* (SNMP) is an application-layer protocol running on UDP/IP that provides a message format for communication between SNMP managers and agents. The SNMP manager is a *Network Management System* (NMS). The agent and the *Management Information Base* (MIB) reside on the network device (in this case, the Cisco router). The SNMP agent contains MIB variables whose values the SNMP manager can request or change.

An SNMP community string is used to define the relationship between the SNMP manager and the agent. The community string acts as a password to permit access to the agent on the router. By default, an SNMP community string permits read-only access to all objects. An IP standard access list is used to permit specific SNMP managers to use the community string to gain access to the agent. The `snmp-server community` global configuration command is used to set up the community access string to permit access to the SNMP agent.

In Example 11-9, the router is assigned the community string `allaccess`, allowing *read-only* (ro) access to the two SNMP managers defined in the IP standard access list 5.

Example 11-8

```
username mary password lamb
ip http authentication local
```

Example 11-9

```
snmp-server community allaccess ro 5
access-list 5 permit 161.115.145.11
access-list 5 permit 135.136.17.21
```

Example 11-10

```
snmp-server community limited rw 5
```

Example 11-10 continues from the previous example, and the router is assigned the community string limited, allowing *read-write* (rw) access to the same two SNMP managers (IP addresses of 161.115.145.11 and 135.136.17.21).

11.5 Verifying Access List Configuration

To display the contents of current access lists, we can use the show access-lists EXEC command in the privileged mode. The following illustrates the output from the show access-lists command when access list 120 is specified:

```
R1# show access-lists 120
Extended IP access list 120
  deny tcp host 128.1.1.2 host 128.1.1.1 eq telnet (3
matches)
  deny tcp host 128.2.2.2 host 128.2.2.1 eq telnet (5
matches)
  permit ip any any (850 matches)
```

To clear the counters, as seen in the 'matches' of the show access-lists command, use clear access-list counters [access-list-number] command. All counters for the given access list will be set to zero.

11.6 Other Applications of Access Lists

This section outlines a variety of other access list functions including priority queuing, *dial-on-demand routing* (DDR), and route filtering.

11.6.1 Priority Queuing

Access lists can be used to define input traffic to other technologies, such as priority and custom queuing, and to control the transmission of packets on serial interfaces.

In Example 11-11, IP traffic from subnet 181.181.0.0 (defined by access-list 1) and telnet traffic are given topmost (high) priority. This is followed by traffic coming in from interface E0 (medium), followed by generic IP traffic (normal), and finally followed by all other default traffic (low).

11.6.2 Dial-on-Demand Routing (DDR)

Access lists can be used to define the interesting traffic that initiates a DDR connection.

The configuration for Router A is shown in Example 11-12.

Figure 11-4 illustrates the DDR scenario where an IP extended access list (access-list 102) is used to determine interesting traffic for a *Simple Mail Transfer Protocol* (SMTP) and telnet.

11.6.3 Route Filtering

Access lists can be used to define route filtering to restrict the contents of routing updates.

Example 11-11

```
priority-list 3 protocol ip high tcp 23
priority-list 3 ip high list 1
priority-list 3 interface ethernet 0 medium
priority-list 3 protocol ip normal
priority-list 3 default low
!
access-list 1 permit 181.181.0.0 0.0.255.255
!
interface serial 0
 priority-group 2
```

Example 11-12

```
access-list 102 permit tcp any any eq smtp
access-list 102 permit tcp any any eq telnet
dialer-list 1 list 102
!
ip route 161.8.3.0 255.255.255.0    181.10.16.2
ip route 161.8.5.0 255.255.255.0    181.10.16.2
!
interface bri 0
 ip address 181.10.16.1  255.255.255.0
 dialer-group 1
 dialer map ip 181.10.16.2  2234567 broadcast
 dialer idle-timeout 60
!
```

Figure 11-4
DDR scenario

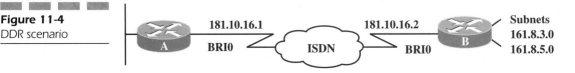

The configuration for Router B is shown in Example 11-13.

Figure 11-5 illustrates a scenario in which Router B does some route filtering using an IP standard access list (access-list 5) that enables only the route 152.168.0.0 (and not 121.0.0.0) to propagate across to network 202.202.3.0.

Example 11-13

```
router eigrp 100
 network 152.168.0.0
 network 202.202.3.0
 distribute-list 5 out s0
 !
access-list 5 permit 152.168.0.0   0.0.255.255
```

Figure 11-5
Route-filtering
scenario

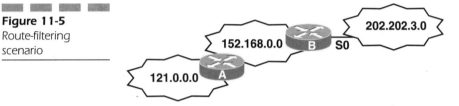

11.7 An Alternative to Access Lists

An access list takes up CPU cycles. The longer the list, the more processing cycles it requires. Hence, to save valuable CPU cycles for
other routing processes, a combination of static route and null interface can be used as an alternative to access lists.

In Figure 11-6, the static route defined in R1 would route IP traffic destined for network 202.22.6.0 to interface null 0. This is equivalent to denying all traffic going to network 202.22.6.0.

11.8 Chapter Summary

This chapter covered access lists for managing and controlling IP
traffic. Two types of IP access lists are used: standard and extended.

Figure 11-6
An alternative to
access lists

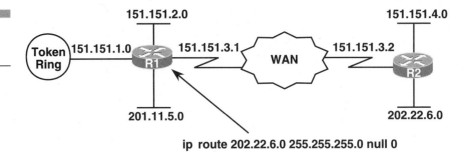

IP standard access lists range from 1 to 99 and IP extended access lists range from 100 to 199. Access lists are similiar to if-else (rule-based) statements where the condition(s) for a standard access list are IP source addresses. For an extended access list, the conditions are IP source addresses, IP destination addresses, protocol numbers, and TCP/UDP port numbers.

Access lists have universal applications. Standard access lists can be implemented to restrict telnet, HTTP, and SNMP access to a router. Access lists are also used in *Quality of Service* (QOS) mechanisms such as priority queuing, DDR, and in route filtering.

Access list processing takes up valuable CPU cycles. A combination of static route and null interface can be used to achieve the same result as an access list by routing an IP packet, going to a specific destination, to nowhere.

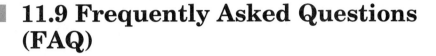

11.9 Frequently Asked Questions (FAQ)

Question: What are named access lists?

Answer: A named access list is a new approach to configuring access lists introduced with Cisco IOS Release 11.2. Named access lists accomplish the following tasks:

- Intuitively identify IP access lists using alphanumeric identifiers.

- Remove the limit on the number ranges of access lists (previously 1 to 99 for IP standards and 100 to 199 for IP extended access lists).

- Allow per-access-list-statement deletions (previously the entire numbered access list needs to be deleted as a single entity).

  The global configuration command for a named access list is as follows:

```
ip access-list {standard | extended} name
{permit | deny} {ip access list test conditions}
```

Question: When an access list is applied on an interface before the list has been defined, will implicit deny come into effect?

Answer: No, the condition is an implicit permit any when a non-existing access list is applied to an interface. However, once the list has been defined, the implicit deny will come into effect if the IP traffic does not match any of the conditions defined by the list.

11.10 Case Study

Figure 11-7 illustrates the case scenario in which H1 and H2 are in a *demilitarized zone* (DMZ). H1 is an anonymous FTP server and H2 is a SMTP mail server. Any host on the Internet is allowed to FTP into H1 and to send e-mails to H2. In addition, any host on the Internet should be able to ping H1 and H2, and likewise, H1 and H2 should be able to ping any host on the Internet. The configuration for Router A is as follows:

```
access-list 101 permit tcp any 168.18.0.0 0.0.255.255
established                        ! line 1
access-list 101 permit tcp any host 168.18.21.12 eq ftp
! line 2
access-list 101 permit tcp any host 168.18.21.12 eq ftp-data
! line 3
access-list 101 permit tcp any host 168.18.23.13 eq smtp
! line 4
access-list 101 permit icmp any any echo !          line 5
access-list 101 permit icmp any any echo-reply !    line 6
access-list 101 permit eigrp any any !              line 7
!
interface serial 0
 ip access-group 101 in
```

The first line permits H1 or H2 to enable an established TCP session coming in (that is, an ACK or RST bit must be set). For example, H1 will be able to FTP out and H2 will be able to SMTP out to other hosts on the Internet. The subsequent three lines enable any host on the Internet to FTP to H1 and SMTP to H2. Line 5 permits any host on the Internet to ping (echo) to H1 and H2. Line 6 enables H1 and H2 to ping to any host on the Internet because when any host in the Internet replies to the ICMP echo message from either of these two hosts, the incoming or returning ICMP message is echo-reply. The final line preserves the routing table by permitting all incoming EIGRP routing information.

Figure 11-7
IP extended access
list case scenario

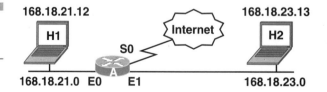

11.11 Questions

1. What are the two types of IP access lists?

2. What is the last statement in all access lists?

   a. Implicit deny
   b. Explicit deny
   c. Implicit permit
   d. Explicit permit

3. Which command do you use to apply an access list to a virtual terminal port?

   a. `ip access-group`
   b. `access-class`
   c. `named access-lists`
   d. `ip http access-class`

4. Which command do you use to control which hosts can access the Cisco router's HTTP server by a Web browser?

   a. `ip access-group`
   b. `access-class`
   c. `named access-lists`
   d. `ip http access-class`

5. For IP standard access lists, the test conditions are based on

   _____.

   a. source addresses
   b. destination addresses
   c. protocol numbers
   d. port numbers
   e. all of the above
   f. b, d

6. For IP extended access lists, the test conditions are *not* based on

   _____.

   a. source addresses
   b. destination addresses
   c. protocol numbers
   d. port numbers

 e. none of the above

 f. a, b, c, d

7. A wildcard mask of 0.0.0.0 checks the bit value in all bit positions, which has the effect of matching only the specified IP host address.

 a. True

 b. False

8. A wildcard mask of 255.255.255.255 ignores any bit value in all bit positions, which has the effect of matching anything in all bit positions.

 a. True

 b. False

9. The expression 131.131.1.1 0.0.0.0 is equivalent to host 131.131.131.1.

 a. True

 b. False

10. The expression 0.0.0.0 255.255.255.255 can also be abbreviated using the keyword host.

 a. True

 b. False

11. Outbound access lists are designed to block traffic originating within a router.

 a. True

 b. False

12. IP standard access lists have numbers ranging from _____.

 a. 1–99

 b. 100–199

 c. 200–299

 d. 600–699

 e. 700–799

 f. 800–899

 g. 900–999

13. IP extended access lists have numbers ranging from _____.

    a. 1–99

    b. 100–199

    c. 200–299

    d. 600–699

    e. 700–799

    f. 800–899

    g. 900–999

14. An IP access list can be applied at the inbound direction of an interface, and another IP access list can be applied at the outbound direction of the same interface.

    a. True

    b. False

15. The order of access list statements controls testing; thus, the least restrictive statements should be at the top of the list.

    a. True

    b. False

16. There is an implicit permit any as the last access list test; hence, a list should not have just deny statements.

    a. True

    b. False

17. There is an implicit deny any condition when a non-existing access list is applied to an interface.

    a. True

    b. False

18. Access lists are *not* used in _____.

    a. priority queuing

    b. custom queuing

    c. DDR

    d. route filtering

    e. none of the above

    f. a, b, c

19. The established keyword appended behind an IP extended access list for TCP traffic verifies which of the following TCP code bits?

    a. URG

    b. ACK

    c. PSH

    d. RST

    e. SYN

    f. FIN

20. A combination of static route and tunnel interface can be used to replace access lists.

    a. True

    b. False

11.12 Answers

1. **Standard and extended access lists**
2. a
3. b
4. d
5. a
6. e
7. a
8. a
9. a
10. b
11. b
12. a
13. b
14. a
15. b
16. b
17. b
18. e
19. b and d
20. b

11.13 References

Cisco Systems, Inc., Documentation CD-ROM, 1998.

Comer, Douglas E. *Internetworking with TCP/IP Volume 1: Principles, Protocols, and Architecture, Second Edition*. New Jersey: Prentice Hall, 1991.

Miller, M.A. *LAN Protocol Handbook*. San Mateo, California: MT&T Books, 1990.

Nam-Kee, Tan. *Configuring Cisco Routers for Bridging, DLSw+, and Desktop Protocols*. New Jersey: McGraw-Hill, November 1999.

RFC 791, Internet Protocol. DARPA Internet Program Specification. Information Science Institute University of Southern California, September 1981.

RFC 793, Transmission Control Protocol. DARPA Internet Program Specification. University of Southern California, September 1981.

Stallings, W. *Data and Computer Communications*. New York: Macmillan Publishing Company, 1991.

Tannenbaum, A.S. *Computer Networks, Second Edition*. Englewood Cliffs, New Jersey: Prentice Hall, 1988.

Optimizing Routing Update Operations

12.1 Objectives Covered in This Chapter

Upon completion of this chapter, the reader will be able to accomplish the following objectives. All these points will be covered in the subsequent sections in detail.

	BSCN Objective
Table 12-1	
BSCN objectives	Perform route summarizations
	Implement route redistributions for the varioius IP routing protocols
	Control routing update traffic between multiple routing protocols
	Verify redistribution operations
	Perform policy-based routing using route maps
	Verify policy-based routing operations

12.2 Chapter Introduction

This chapter covers the various ways of optimizing routing updates such as route summarization, route redistribution, route filtering, and policy-based routing.

12.3 Route Summarization

As routed networks grow larger, the routing information will also increase. This means more memory is required to store these additional routes in the routing table and more CPU cycles are required to process these routes. At the same time, this will result in a significant amount of route advertisement and routing information overhead.

One way to reduce the size of a routing table is through route summarization, which aggregates routing information to as few lines as possible in the routing table. Without summarization, each router in a network must have a route to every subnet in the network. With summarization, routers can reduce multiple route entries to a single advertisement, reducing the resource utilization (memory and CPU) on the router and the palpable complexity of the network. Figure 12-1a illustrates an example of route summarization in R1 in which the routes ranging from 150.150.32.0/24 to 150.150.63.0/24 inclusively coming in through R1 are summarized into a single route, 150.150.32.0/19, going out to the Internet.

Figure 12-1b illustrates how to derive the summarized route 150.150.32.0/19. From the workings, the number of common and non-common bits for the range 150.150.32.0/24 to 150.150.63.0/24 is determined and the summarization is based on the number of common bits, which is 19 bits (or a mask of 255.255.224.0) in this example.

Figure 12-1a
Summarization
example

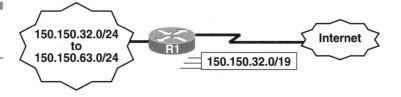

Figure 12-1b
Summarization within
an octet

150.150.32.0 =	10010110 . 10010110 .00100 000 . 00000000
150.150.33.0 =	150 . 108 .00100 001 . 0
150.150.34.0 =	150 . 108 .00100 010 . 0
: =	. . .
: =	. . .
150.150.63.0 =	150 . 108 .00111 111 . 0

Number of Common Bits = 19
Non common Bits = 13
Summary: 150.150.32.0/19

Routing protocols such as *Open Shortest Path First* (OSPF), *Enhanced Interior Gateway Protocol* (EIGRP), and *Border Gateway Protocol* (BGP) support route summarization at any bit boundary, rather than just at major network number boundaries in a network address. In order to perform bit boundary summarization, these routing protocols must also support *variable-length subnet masks* (VLSMs). Some routing protocols require manual configuration to support route summarization, while others summarize automatically. OSPF requires manual configuration, while EIGRP and BGP routes can be summarized either automatically or manually. In sections 12.2.1 to 12.2.3, we will look at how OSPF, EIGRP, and BGP summarize.

12.3.1 Route Summarization for OSPF

Route summarization is particularly important in an OSPF environment because it reduces the number of link state advertisements when there is a change in the network topology. Hence, the stability of the network is increased. If route summarization is applied here, routes within an area that has frequent topology changes do not need to propagate these changes to the backbone (Area 0) or in other areas.

Three different types of routing information can be found in an OSPF area:

- *Intra-area routes (O)*   These are explicit network or subnet routes that must be carried for all networks or subnets inside an area.

- *Inter-area routes (IA)*   These are explicit network or subnet routes that exist in this *autonomous system* (AS) but not in this area.

- *External routes (E1 or E2)*   These are the routes that are exchanged when different ASs exchange routing information.

Route summarization for OSPF can be achieved between OSPF areas and when redistributing external routes into OSPF. In OSPF, an *Area Border Router* (ABR) will advertise networks in one area into another area, that is, *inter-area* (IA) routes. If the network numbers in an area are assigned contiguously, the ABR can be configured to advertise a summary route that consolidates the individual networks or subnets within the area. To specify an address range, we can use the router configuration command: `area 6area-id7 range 6address7 6mask7`.

Figure 12-2a illustrates an OSPF inter-area route summarization example where R1 is the ABR summarizing the routes ranging from 170.170.32.0/24 to 170.170.63.0/24 on Area 0 to a single route 170.170.32.0/19 . R1 also summarizes the routes ranging from 160.160.32.0/24 to 160.160.63.0/24 on Area 160 to a single route 160.160.32.0/19. The configuration for R1 is as follows:

```
router ospf 100
 network 170.170.32.1 0.0.0.0 area 0
 network 160.160.32.1 0.0.0.0 area 160
 area 0 range 170.170.32.0   255.255.224.0
 area 160 range 160.160.32.0   255.255.224.0
```

Note that R1's interface address to Area 160 is 160.160.32.1 and R1's interface address to Area 0 is 170.170.32.1.

When redistributing routes (refer to section 12.3) from other protocols into OSPF, each route is advertised individually in an external *link state advertisement* (Type 5 LSA), which is either E1 or E2

Figure 12-2a

OSPF inter-area route summarization example

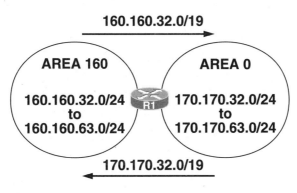

routes. External link state advertisements are originated from an *Autonomous System Border Router* (ASBR) and they describe routes to a destination external to the AS. These LSAs are flooded to all areas except stub areas. To reduce these advertisements and to decrease the size of the OSPF link state database, all the redistributed routes can be consolidated into a single route using the router configuration command, `summary-address 6ip-address7 6mask7`. This command is effective only on ASBRs performing redistributions into OSPF.

Figure 12-2b illustrates an OSPF external route summarization example where R1 is the ASBR summarizing the EIGRP routes ranging from 190.190.32.0/24 to 190.190.63.0/24 to a single external route 190.190.32.0/19. The configuration for R1 is as follows:

```
router ospf 100
  summary-address 190.190.32.0 255.255.224.0
  redistribute eigrp 80 metric 200 subnets
```

Figure 12-2b
OSPF external route summarization example

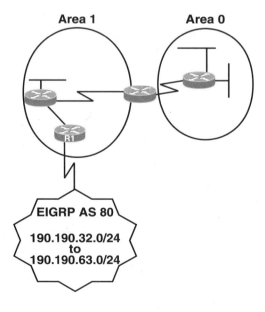

12.3.2 Route Summarization for EIGRP

In IP EIGRP environments, route summarization is used to reduce the size of routing tables, to generate fewer updates, and to narrow the scope of query boundaries when EIGRP goes into an active state (diffusing computation). Implementing route summarization for EIGRP can be done using two different methods:

- *Auto summarization* This is implemented on major network boundaries where networks are summarized to the major networks. Auto summarization is turned on by default in EIGRP.

- *Manual summarization* This is configurable on a per-interface basis in any router within a network using the interface configuration command, `ip summary-address`. When EIGRP summarization is configured on an interface, the router immediately creates a route pointing to null zero (a loop-prevention mechanism) with an administrative distance of five. The best metric of the specific routes is used as the metric of the summary route. The summary is deleted when the last specific route of the summary no longer exists.

Figure 12-3 illustrates an EIGRP manual route summarization example where R1 summarizes the EIGRP routes ranging from 180.180.32.0/24 to 180.180.63.0/24 in AS 90 to a single route180. 180.32.0/19 out of interface S0. The configuration for R1 is as follows:

Figure 12-3
EIGRP manual route summarization example

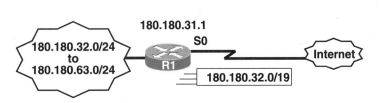

```
interface s0
  ip address 180.180.31.1 255.255.255.0
  ip summary-address eigrp 90 180.180.32.0 255.255.224.0
```

12.3.3 Route Aggregation for BGP

BGP supports *classless inter-domain routing* (CIDR). CIDR eliminates the concept of IP classes (Class A, B, C, and so on). For example, network 202.202.0.0/16 is an illegal Class C network number,
but when represented in CIDR notation, it is a legal supernet. The
/16 is equivalent to 202.202.0.0 to 255.255.0.0.

CIDR makes it easy to aggregate routes. Aggregation (or summarization) is the process of combining several different routes in such
a way that a single route can be advertised, which minimizes the size
of routing tables.

Figure 12-4 illustrates a BGP aggregation example where R2
aggregates the four routes ranging from 202.202.24.0/24 to 202.202.
27.0/24 to a prefix route (or supernet), in this case, 202.202.24.0/22.
Without the summary-only keyword, R2 advertises the prefix route
together with the four specific routes. To propagate the prefix route

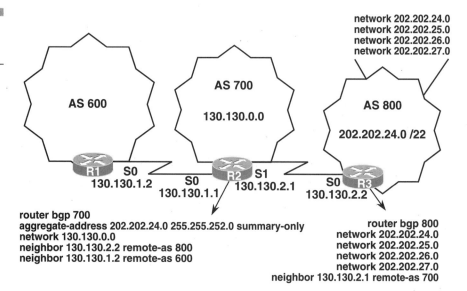

Figure 12-4
BGP aggregation
example

only, the summary-only keyword is used. Note that R3 advertises the four specific routes to R2 using the "network" router configuration command.

12.4 Route Redistribution

In some cases id might be advantageous to run multiple routing protocols in an Internetwork. Obviously the routing protocols will have to share information between each other in order for all routers to have complete routing tables. This process is called route redistribution.

Some reasons for running multiple protocols in a single Internetwork have been summarized in the following list:

- *Migration from one (usually older) routing protocol to another* Imagine a company running RIP on older routers, which is migrating to Cisco routers using EIGRP. In this case it would be wise to set up a redistribution strategy to allow some time for a comfortable migration.
- *Boundaries within an Internetwork* You might experience a company that has different strategies for security and routing for different divisions. In this case it can be advantageous to set up a separate routing mechanism for the differing groups, so as to keep the two apart.
- *Incompatibility* Sometimes a network has evolved using non-Cisco routers or hosts with routing capabilities that require a certain routing protocol to be used. In this case the routing protocol can often be redistributed from into the Internetwork's routing strategy.

Different routing protocols have different characteristics. For example, in order for a periodic update routing protocol to "talk" to an incremental link-state routing protocol, there must be some form of translation between the periodic update protocol and the incremental link-state protocol. This ability to translate among heterogeneous routing protocols, different routing metrics, and update information is known as *route redistribution*.

One must remember that redistribution is a powerful tool, and requires quite a lot of planning to implement properly. Due to the differences in routing information, such as metrics, differences in convergence time and the increased risk of loops between the redistributing partners, it is important to fully understand the needs and differences of each protocol that is to be redistributed.

12.4.1 Route Redistribution for OSPF

Redistributing routes into OSPF from other routing protocols or from static routes causes these routes to become OSPF external routes. To redistribute routes into OSPF, the router configuration command used is `redistribute protocol [process-id] [metric value] [metric-type value] [subnets]`. The protocol and process-id are the protocols that we are injecting into OSPF and its process-id, if it exits. The metric is the cost we are assigning to the external route. If no metric is specified, OSPF puts a default value of 20 when redistributing routes from all protocols except BGP routes, which gets a metric of 1. When redistributing routes into OSPF, only routes that are not subnetted are redistributed if the subnets keyword is not specified.

Figure 12-5 illustrates the redistribution of RIP routes into an OSPF AS. The partial configuration that is listed indicates a metric (cost) of 100 being associated with the redistributed routes from network 198.198.198.0/24. The OSPF AS considers these routes as E2 routes (which are the default external route types).

External routes fall under two categories: external type1 and external type 2. The difference between the two is the way the cost (metric) of the route is calculated. The cost of a type 2 (E2) route is always the external cost, irrespective of the interior cost to reach that router. A type 1 (E1) cost is the addition of the external cost and internal cost used to reach that route. A type 1 route is always preferred over a type 2 route for the same destination.

In Figure 12-6, if we use the E2 external routes, the cost associated with these redistributed external routes will all be of cost 1,562, regardless of the router's perspective.

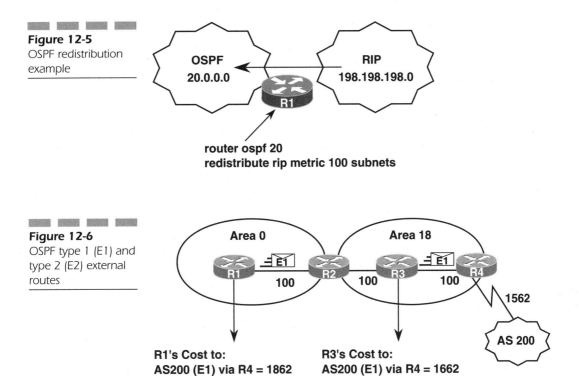

Figure 12-5
OSPF redistribution example

router ospf 20
redistribute rip metric 100 subnets

Figure 12-6
OSPF type 1 (E1) and type 2 (E2) external routes

However, if we change the external route type to E1, the cost associated with the redistributed routes from AS 200 will be different for all the routers because the cost for an E1 route is the addition of the external cost and internal cost used to reach that route. For example, the cost for R1 to reach AS 200 is 1,862 and the cost for R3 to reach AS 200 is 1,662.

12.4.2 Route Redistribution for EIGRP

Two types of IP EIGRP routes exist: internal and external. Internal EIGRP routes are any routes that originate from their own EIGRP AS and have an administrative distance of 90 (refer to section 12.4.2). External EIGRP routes are any routes that are being redistributed into an EIGRP AS from another routing protocol or EIGRP AS. They also have an administrative distance of 170 (refer to section

12.4.2). Note that EIGRP and IGRP with the same AS number will be automatically redistributed into each other.

Figure 12-7 illustrates the redistribution of OSPF routes into EIGRP AS 150. The partial configuration indicates a default metric in the form of bandwidth delay reliability loading the *maximum transmission unit* (MTU). Here bandwidth is the minimum bandwidth of the route in kilobits per second, delay is the route delay in tens of microseconds, and reliability is the likelihood of a successful packet transmission expressed as a number between 0 and 255 (the value 255 = 255/255 × 100 percent reliability; 0 means no reliability). Loading is the effective bandwidth of the route expressed as a number from 0 to 255 (the value 1 = 1/255 × 100 percent loading), and MTU is the *maximum transmission unit* size of the route in bytes. In this example, these correspond to a composite metric of 56 1000 255 1 1500 being associated with the redistributed routes from network 128.128.0.0/16. The EIGRP AS will consider these routes as EIGRP external routes (or DX routes).

12.4.3 Route Redistribution for BGP

One way to advertise a network or a subnet originating from an AS is through redistribution. Typically, IGP routes such as static, EIGRP, OSPF, and so on are redistributed into BGP. The BGP origin attribute will be reflected as incomplete (?) when a route is redistributed into BGP.

Figure 12-7
EIGRP redistribution example

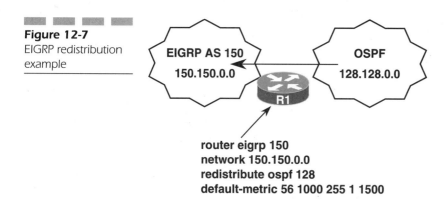

```
router eigrp 150
network 150.150.0.0
redistribute ospf 128
default-metric 56 1000 255 1 1500
```

Figure 12-8 illustrates the redistribution of EIGRP routes from AS 1000 into BGP AS 2000. The partial configuration that is listed indicates a *Multi-exit Discriminator* (MED) metric of 200 being associated with the redistributed routes from network 178.178. 0.0/16 (the name of this metric for BGP Versions 2 and 3 is INTER_AS).

12.5 Controlling Routing Update Traffic among Multiple Routing Protocols

This section focuses on controlling routing update traffic among routing protocols. Here we'll examine filters, administrative distances, and different kinds of metrics.

12.5.1 Filters

Filters are used to prevent other routers from learning a particular device's interpretation of one or more routes. When redistribution is being done in more than one router, it is crucial to beware of potential feedback loops. To prevent other routers from learning one or more routes, we can use distribute-list filters for blocking routes that are redistributed back into the originating network.

Figure 12-8
BGP redistribution
example

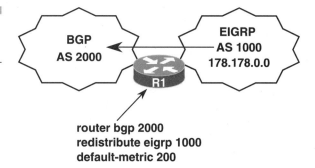

An outbound distribute list can be used on an ASBR to filter redistributed routes into other ASs. However, filtering information with link-state protocols such as OSPF can be tricky because an inbound distribute list stops routes from being inserted into the routing table but does not prevent link-state advertisements from being propagated. This means the downstream OSPF routers would still have the routes. Therefore, to prevent loops, it would be better to implement filtering on the other routing protocols besides OSPF.

Figure 12-9 illustrates an example of avoiding redistribution loops. The partial redistribution-filtering configuration on R2 is as follows:

```
router rip
 network 129.129.0.0
 redistribute ospf 20 metric 100
 distribute-list 11 out ospf 20
 passive-interface s1
!
access-list 11 deny 129.129.129.0 0.0.0.255
access-list 11 permit any
!
```

The distribute list 11 prevents the route 129.129.129.0/24 (which originates from the RIP AS) from redistributing back again from the OSPF AS, thus avoiding a redistribution loop between the two routing processes. Hence, the RIP routing process in R2 advertises all redistributed routes from the OSPF routing process except the route 129.129.129.0/24.

Note the `passive-interface` router configuration command is used to disable the sending of RIP routing updates on interface S1. This prevents native RIP updates in R2 from propagating into the

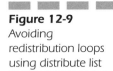

Figure 12-9

Avoiding redistribution loops using distribute list

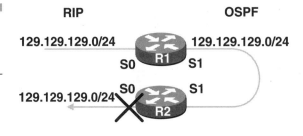

OSPF AS back to R1. Likewise, the `passive-interface` router configuration command should also be implemented on interface S1 in the RIP routing process of R1 to prevent native RIP updates in R1 from propagating into the OSPF AS back to R2.

12.5.2 Administrative Distance

An administrative distance is used to compare routes coming from two or more different routing protocols. Table 12-2 illustrates the default administrative distance defined for some of the more common IP routing protocols. This is done to prioritize routing information from different sources, because some pieces of routing information may be more accurate than others.

An administrative distance is a rating of the trustworthiness of a routing information source, such as an individual router or a group of routers. In a large network, some routing protocols and some routers can be more reliable than others as sources of routing information. Also, when multiple routing processes are running in the same router for IP, it is possible for the same route to be advertised by more than one routing process. By specifying administrative distance values, you enable the router to intelligently discriminate

Table 12-2

The default administrative distance for the common routing protocols

Route Source	Default Distance
Connected Interface	0
Static Route	1
Enhanced IGRP Summary Route	5
External BGP	20
Internal Enhanced IGRP	90
IGRP	100
OSPF	110
IS-IS	115
RIP	120
EGP	140
External Enhanced IGRP	170
Internal BGP	200
Unknown	255

between sources of routing information. The router will always pick the route whose routing protocol has the lowest administrative distance (which will also be the highest ranking).

Figure 12-10 illustrates an administrative distance example. In this scenario, a mutual redistribution between two different routing processes is performed at R3. From the perspective of R1, all the routes (171.171.21.0/24, 171.171.22.0/24, 171.171.31.0/24, and 171.171.32.0/24) will be learned via IGRP 171, instead of RIP, because IGRP has a better administrative distance of 100 as compared to RIP, which has a larger administrative distance of 120. As a result, the leased line between R1 and R3 will be less utilized as compared with the leased line between R1 and R2.

Supposedly, we want R1 to learn the routes 171.171.31.0/24 and 171.171.32.0/24 via RIP so that any traffic originating from these two subnets will choose the leased line between R1 and R3 instead. To achieve this, we can change the IGRP administrative distance in R1 for these two routes to a larger value (of 121) than RIP:

```
router igrp 171
 network 171.171.0.0
 distance 121 0.0.0.0 255.255.255.255 17
!
access-list 17 permit 171.171.31.0 0.0.0.255
access-list 17 permit 171.171.32.0 0.0.0.255
!
```

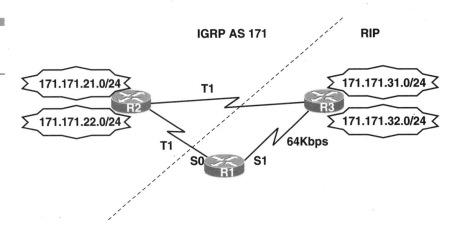

Figure 12-10
An administrative
distance example

The distance router configuration command changes the IGRP administrative distance for routes 171.171.31.0/24 and 171.171.32.0/24 to 121 by using access list 17.

12.5.3 Metric

Metrics are used to compare routes coming from the same routing protocol. In the case of multiple paths to the same destination, the router always chooses the path with the best metric. However, we might not always want the router to choose the best path. We can explicitly modify the metric for a specific path to become the best path to the destination, thus coaxing the router to choose this route instead. In the following subsections, we shall examine the respective metrics used by OSPF, EIGRP, and BGP.

12.5.3.1 OSPF Cost   The OSPF cost (or metric) is based on the bandwidth of a given media or interface type. The cost of an interface is inversely proportional to the bandwidth of this specific interface. This implies that a lower bandwidth will result in a higher cost. The formula used to calculate OSPF cost is 10^8/bandwidth. The metric for a route is the aggregate of the cost for all the links in the route. By default, the cost of a link is automatically calculated based on the bandwidth of the link media. We can explicitly change the cost of an interface by using the `ip ospf cost interface` configuration command.

12.5.3.2 EIGRP Composite Metrics   EIGRP's metric is calculated using the following formula:

$$\text{k1} \times \text{Bandwidth} + (\text{k2} \times \text{Bandwidth})/(256 - \text{Load}) + \text{k3} \times \text{Delay}] \times \text{k5} / (\text{Reliability} + \text{k4})$$

By default, k1 = k3 = 1 and k2 = k4 = k5 = 0. This means EIGRP computes the metric for a route by using the minimum bandwidth of each hop in the path and adding a media-specific delay for each hop. The composite metrics used by EIGRP are as follows:

- *Bandwidth*   Here bandwidth is equal to 10^7/bandwidth of the media type. The bandwidth of a media or interface type can be modified with the `bandwidth interface` configuration command.

- *Delay*   Here delay equals the delay of media type/10. Each media type has a latency or delay associated with it. Changing this value is a useful way to optimize routing in networks using satellite links. This delay can be modified using the `delay interface` configuration command.

- *Reliability*   This metric is dynamically calculated as a rolling weighted average over five seconds.

- *Load*   This metric is dynamically calculated as a rolling weighted average over five seconds.

12.5.3.3 BGP Path Selection Criteria   BGP is somewhat special when it chooses the best path. It uses a wide range of attributes to select the most optimal path in the following order:

1. If the path specifies a next hop that is inaccessible, discard the update.

2. Prefer the path with the greatest weight.

3. If the weights are the same, prefer the path with the greatest local preference.

4. If the local preferences are the same, prefer the path that was originated by BGP running on this router.

5. If no route was originated, prefer the route that has the shortest AS_PATH.

6. If all paths have the same AS_PATH length, prefer the path with the lowest origin type (where IGP is less than EGP is less than Incomplete).

7. If the origin codes are the same, prefer the path with the smallest MED attribute.

8. If the paths have the same MED, prefer the external path to the internal path.

9. If the paths are the same, prefer the path through the nearest IGP neighbor.

10. Prefer the path with the lowest IP address, as specified by the BGP router ID.

12.6 Verifying Redistribution Operations

We can verify redistribution operations by examining the contents of the IP routing table using the exec command, `show ip route`. In addition, the exec command `trace` can be used to track the path an IP packet takes.

12.7 Policy-based Routing Using Route Maps

Policy routing is another form of routing where the router matches all incoming packets using a route map and implements whatever actions are defined by the route map before routing them out. The route map tells the router which packets will be routed to which subsequent router. Therefore, policy routing is more flexible and customizable than plain destination routing. Some common applications for policy routing are to provide load-balancing and equal access, to provide source versus destination-oriented routing, to provide interactive versus batch traffic routing, and to optimize routing traffic across low-bandwidth links. Creating and using a route map are mandatory for implementing policy routing. The route map itself specifies the match criteria and the resulting action if all of the match clauses are met.

To enable policy routing on an interface, the interface configuration command `ip policy route-map` is used. All packets arriving on the particular interface where this command is present will be subject to policy routing. The `ip policy route-map` command identifies a route map to use for policy routing. Note this command disables fast switching of all the packets arriving on this interface. To enable fast switching for policy routing, the interface configuration command `ip route-cache policy` is used.

In addition, packets that are originated by the router are not policy-routed. To enable local policy-routing for such packets, the global configuration command `ip local policy route-map` is used and thus all packets originating on the router are then subject to local policy routing.

Each route map command has a list of associated match and set commands. The match commands specify the match criteria, or the conditions under which policy routing is allowed for the interface. The set commands specify the set actions, or the particular policy routing actions to execute if the conditions defined by the match commands are met.

Figure 12-11 illustrates an example of policy routing where traffic coming from subnet 184.195.161.0/24 is to be routed some other way than the obvious shortest path. In this case, the traffic coming from subnet 184.195.161.0/24 is rerouted via the next hop address of 184.121.13.30 instead of 184.121.13.20 (the preferred path because of the lower cost metric). Since the Frame Relay *virtual circuit* (VC) between R1 and R3 is underutilized, and the batch traffic from subnet 184.195.161.0/24 is routine and not mission-critical, we can redirect traffic coming from 184.195.161.0/24 to R3 to utilize the capacity of the R1-R3 VC. The resulted latency will be minimal, as R3 can reach R2 and the HQ network via ATM. Nevertheless, traffic coming from subnet 184.195.160.0/24 is not rerouted because the traffic from this particular source is both interactive and time-sensitive. Diverting the batch traffic over to the R1-R3 VC also helps to ease the congestion or overload situation on the R1-R2 VC. Example 12-1 illustrates the partial configuration in R1 for implementing this scenario.

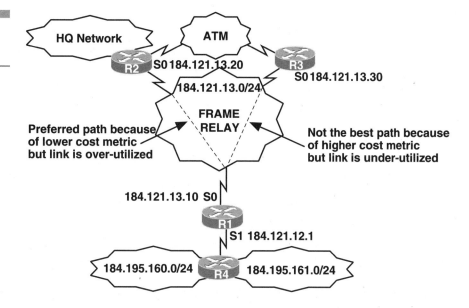

Figure 12-11
Policy routing
example

Example 12-1

```
interface serial 1
 ip address 184.121.12.1 255.255.255.0
 ip policy route-map test
!
route-map test
 match ip address 10
 set ip next-hop 184.121.13.30
!
access-list 10 permit 184.195.161.0 0.0.0.255
```

12.7.1 Route Map Syntax

The route map statements form a route list similar to an access list. The list is processed top-down, as illustrated in Figure 12-12. If a route matches the condition specified by the match statements, then the set statements are performed and the route is permitted or denied according to the route map permit or deny keyword. Thus, no further searching is required for this route. However, if a particular route map statement does not match a route, then the next route map statement is verified and this continues until a match is found. If no matches are found after the last route map statement, the route is implicitly denied. Note a sequence number is used for each route map statement.

In Example 12-2, line 1 is the start of the first route map statement. Line 2 and 3 define the conditions whereby a route must match the conditions specified either by access-list 11 *or* access-list 12, *and* the route must have a next-hop address that matches that defined by access-list 21. Notice the deny keyword in line 5 means

Figure 12-12
Route map syntax

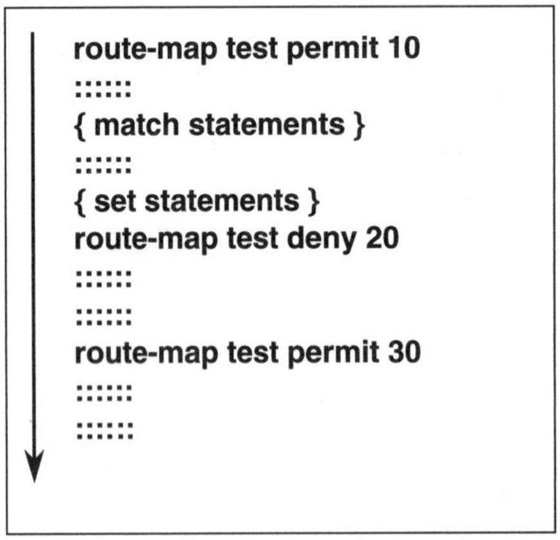

```
route-map test permit 10
::::::
{ match statements }
::::::
{ set statements }
route-map test deny 20
::::::
::::::
route-map test permit 30
::::::
::::::
```

Example 12-2

```
router rip
 redistribute ospf 10 route-map my_ospf
 !
route-map my_ospf permit 10          !line 1
 match ip address 11 12               !line 2
 match next-hop 21                    !line 3
 set metric 3                         !line 4
 !
route-map my_ospf deny 20            !line 5
 match ip address 31                  !line 6
 !
route-map my_ospf permit 30          !line 7
 match ip address 51                  !line 8
 set metric 16                        !line 9
 !
```

that the routes that match the conditions defined in access-list 31 (line 6) will not be distributed. All routes that do not match the conditions specified in the previous two route map statements will come to line 7, which is the start of the third and last route map statement. Routes that match the conditions defined by access list 51 (line 8) are set to a hop count of 16, which means RIP will advertise these routes as unreachable. This example demonstrates how complicated, powerful, and flexible a route map can become through simple logical constructs.

12.8 Verifying Policy-Based Routing Operations

We can use the `show ip policy` exec command to display the route map used for policy routing, and use the `show ip local policy` exec command to display the route map used for local policy routing. The `trace` exec command can also be used here to track which path an IP packet takes.

12.9 Chapter Summary

This chapter discusses the different ways of optimizing routing updates. The routing information overhead and the size of a routing table for OSPF, EIGRP, and BGP can be reduced significantly using route summarization or route aggregation. With summarization, routers can aggregate multiple route entries to a single advertisement, reducing the resources utilization (memory and CPU) on the router and the complexity of the network. The ability to translate among heterogeneous routing protocols, different routing metrics, and update information is known as *route redistribution* and this chapter has covered the route redistribution for OSPF, EIGRP, and BGP in detail.

Filters, administrative distance, and metrics can be used to control routing update traffic between multiple routing protocols, but the most powerful and flexible way to manage and control routing information is through route maps. A router can perform policy routing using a route map to specify conditions that match all incoming packets and implements whatever actions are defined by the route map before routing them out. The route map tells the router which packets will be routed to which subsequent router. As a result, policy routing is more flexible and customizable than plain destination routing.

12.10 Frequently Asked Questions (FAQ)

Question: What cost must I use for a media type that is faster than the *fastest default media* (FDDI) configurable for OSPF?

Answer: An example of media faster than FDDI is ATM. By default, a faster media will be assigned a cost equal to 1. Thus, given an environment with both FDDI and a faster media type, configure the FDDI with a cost greater than 1 and the faster link with a cost less than the assigned FDDI link cost.

Question: Under what circumstances will internal EIGRP routes be preferred over IGRP routes?

Answer: This occurs when both EIGRP and IGRP have different AS numbers. In this case, an administrative distance of 90 versus 100 is taken into consideration and the internal EIGRP routes (administrative distance of 90) will be preferred.

Question: Under what circumstances will external EIGRP routes be preferred over IGRP routes?

Answer: This occurs when both EIGRP and IGRP have the same AS number and the same scaled route metric. In this case, the administrative distance is not considered.

12.11 Case Study

Figure 12-13 illustrates an example of manipulating the BGP MED using route maps. In this example, AS 1000 is deliberately indicating to AS 2000 the preferred route to the AS 1000 networks. R11 is advertising networks 201.201.11.0/24 and 201.201.12.0/24 to AS 2000 with a MED value of 100. All other networks (201.201.21.0/24 and 201.201.22.0/24) are set to a MED value of 200. Likewise, R12 is advertising networks 201.201.21.0/24 and 201.201.22.0/24 to AS 2000 with a MED value of 100. All other networks (201.201.11.0/24 and 201.201.12.0/24) are set to a MED value of 200.

Figure 12-13
Manipulating
BGP **Multi-exit**
Discriminator (MED)
using route maps

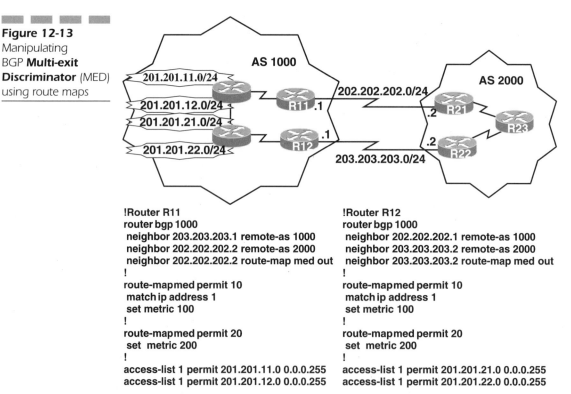

```
!Router R11                                      !Router R12
router bgp 1000                                  router bgp 1000
 neighbor 203.203.203.1 remote-as 1000           neighbor 202.202.202.1 remote-as 1000
 neighbor 202.202.202.2 remote-as 2000           neighbor 203.203.203.2 remote-as 2000
 neighbor 202.202.202.2 route-map med out        neighbor 203.203.203.2 route-map med out
!                                               !
route-map med permit 10                          route-map med permit 10
 match ip address 1                              match ip address 1
 set metric 100                                  set metric 100
!                                               !
route-map med permit 20                          route-map med permit 20
 set  metric 200                                 set  metric 200
!                                               !
access-list 1 permit 201.201.11.0 0.0.0.255      access-list 1 permit 201.201.21.0 0.0.0.255
access-list 1 permit 201.201.12.0 0.0.0.255      access-list 1 permit 201.201.22.0 0.0.0.255
```

The router, such as R23, in AS 2000 would choose the smallest MED to the networks in AS 1000. R23 would send packets going to networks 201.201.11.0/24 and 201.201.12.0/24 to R11 and packets going to networks 201.201.21.0/24 and 201.201.22.0/24 to R12. Note the assumption for this example is that BGP selects a path using MED only if Weight and Local Preference values are the same.

12.12 Questions

1. For OSPF inter-area summarization, we can use the router configuration command: `area 6area-id7 range 6address7 6mask7`.

   a. True
   b. False

2. For OSPF external route summarization, we can use the router configuration command: `summary-address 6ip-address7 6mask7`.

   a. True
   b. False

3. OSPF routes can be summarized either automatically or manually.

   a. True
   b. False

4. EIGRP routes can be summarized either automatically or manually.

   a. True
   b. False

5. EIGRP routes can be manually summarized using the interface configuration command: `ip summary-address`.

   a. True
   b. False

6. BGP routes can be aggregated to a supernet using the router configuration command: `aggregate-address`.

   a. True
   b. False

7. When redistributing routes into OSPF, only routes that are subnetted are redistributed if the subnets keyword is not specified.

   a. True
   b. False

8. An E2 external route is the default external route type when redistributing this route from an external AS into OSPF.

   a. True
   b. False

9. An E2 route is always preferred over an E1 route for the same destination.

   a. True
   b. False

10. Internal EIGRP routes are any routes that originate from their own EIGRP AS and they have an administrative distance of 170.

    a. True
    b. False

11. External EIGRP routes are any routes that are being redistributed into an EIGRP AS from another routing protocol or EIGRP AS and they have an administrative distance of 90.

    a. True
    b. False

12. EIGRP and IGRP with the same AS number will be automatically redistributed into each other.

    a. True
    b. False

13. An inbound distribute list does not prevent OSPF link-state advertisements from being propagated to the downstream OSPF routers.

    a. True
    b. False

14. A metric is used to compare routes coming from two or more different routing protocols.

    a. True
    b. False

15. An administrative distance is used to compare routes coming from the same routing protocol.

    a. True

    b. False

16. We can create a floating static route by changing its administrative distance to 255.

    a. True

    b. False

17. What is the default OSPF cost for a 64-kbps serial link?

    a. 1,785

    b. 1,562

    c. 65

    d. 48

    e. 10

    f. 1

    g. None of the above

18. What is the default OSPF cost for a 155-Mbps ATM link?

    a. 1785

    b. 1562

    c. 65

    d. 48

    e. 10

    f. 1

    g. None of the above

19. Packets that are originated by the router are not policy-routed. To enable policy routing for such packets, we can use the global configuration command: `ip policy route-map`.

    a. True

    b. False

20. If a particular route map statement does not match a route, then the next route map statement is verified and this continues until a match is found. If no matches are found after the last route map statement, the route will be implicitly permitted.

    a. True

    b. False

12.13 Answers

1. a
2. a
3. b
4. a
5. a
6. a
7. b
8. a
9. b
10. b
11. b
12. a
13. a
14. b
15. b
16. b
17. b
18. f
19. b
20. b

APPENDIX A

Coltun, R. "OSPF: An Internet Routing Protocol." *ConneXions: The Interoperability Report.* Vol. 3, No. 8: August 1989.

Comer, Douglas E. *Internetworking with TCP/IP Volume 1: Principles, Protocols, and Architecture, Second Edition.* New Jersey: Prentice Hall, 1991.

Garcia-Luna-Aceves, J.J. "Loop-Free Routing Using Diffusing Computations." *IEEE/ACM Transactions on Networking.* Vol. 1, No. 1, 1993.

Giles, Roosevelt. *Cisco CCIE Study Guide*, New Jersey: McGraw-Hill, 1998.

Halabi, Bassam. *Internet Routing Architectures.* Indianapolis: Cisco Press, 1998.

Huitema, Christian. *Routing in the Internet.* New Jersey: Prentice Hall, 1995.

Lewis, Chris. *Cisco TCP/IP Routing Professional Reference.* New Jersey: McGraw-Hill, 1999.

Medin, M. "The Great IGP Debate Part Two: The Open Shortest Path First (OSPF) Routing Protocol." *ConneXions: The Interoperability Report.* Vol. 5, No. 10: October 1991.

Miller, M.A. *LAN Protocol Handbook.* San Mateo, California: MT&T Books, 1990.

Pepelnjak, Ivan. *IGRP Network Design Solutions.* Indianapolis: Cisco Press, 2000.

Nam-Kee, Tam. *Configuring Cisco Routers for Bridging, DLSw+, and Desktop Protocols.* New Jersey: McGraw-Hill, November 1999.

Rossi, Louis D., Louis R. Rossi, and Thomas Rossi. *Cisco and IP Addressing.* New Jersey: McGraw-Hill, 1999.

Slattery, Terry and Bill Burton. *Advanced IP Routing in Cisco Networks.* New Jersey: McGraw-Hill, 1999.

Stallings, W. *Data and Computer Communications.* New York: Macmillan Publishing Company, 1991.

Tannenbaum, A.S. *Computer Networks, Second Edition*. Englewood Cliffs, New Jersey: Prentice Hall, 1988.

Thomas II, Thomas M. *OSPF Network Design Solutions*. Indianapolis: Cisco Press, 1998.

RFCs and Other Sources

Cisco CCO Internet pages, `www.cisco.com` (no mention is made of specific pages due to their changeable character).

Documentation CD-ROM, Cisco Systems, Inc., 1998 and 1999.

RFC 791, Internet Protocol, DARPA Internet Program Specification. Information Science Institute, University of Southern California,
September 1981.

RFC 793, Transmission Control Protocol, DARPA Internet Program Specification. University of Southern California, September 1981.

RFC 1518, An Architecture for IP Address Allocation with CIDR. T.J.
Watson Research Center, IBM Corporation, Cisco Systems, September 1993.

RFC 1519, Classless Interdomain Routing (CIDR): An Address Assignment and Aggregation Strategy. BARRNet, MERIT, Cisco Systems, OARnet, September 1993.

RFC 1771, A Border Gateway Protocol 4 (BGP-4). T.J. Watson Research Center, IBM Corporation, Cisco Systems, March 1995.

RFC 1774, BGP Version 4 Protocol Analysis. Cisco Systems, March 1995.

RFC 2178, OSPF Version 2. Cascade Communications Corporation, July 1997.

APPENDIX B

Password Recovery

There will be times when, for whatever reason, you do not have the password(s) to configure your Cisco router. This appendix describes the process of password recovery.

Any password recovery procedure for a Cisco access server has six main steps. Although the actual commands used to implement these steps may differ from device to device, the logical progression of events is the same, with the exception of the Cisco 700 series. In that series, routers do not run Cisco IOS, so password recovery uses a different procedure.

Password Recovery Procedure

The password recovery procedure is as follows:

1. Configure the router to boot without reading NVRAM (config file).
2. Reboot the Cisco access server.
3. Obtain access to the enable mode.
4. Modify the configuration so that you know the required password(s).
5. Configure the router to read NVRAM (config file) when booting
6. Reboot the Cisco access server.

NOTE: *The version of HyperTerminal that comes with Windows NT does not support the use of ctrl-break. Therefore, if you are using Windows NT, you need a terminal emulator that implements the ctrl-break sequence correctly. Many can be used, but we recommend the upgraded version of HyperTerminal and TeraTerm Pro.*

Cisco 2000, 2500, 3000, 4000, and 7000 Series Routers Password Recovery

In order for this password recovery method to work, your Cisco router must have a ROM of 10.0 or later.

1. Using a rolled cable, connect a COM port on your PC to the console port on your Cisco Router.

2. Hit Enter several times until you are in user mode.

3. Use `Router>show version`. Make note of the configuration register as in Example B-1.

4. Reboot the Cisco router.

5. Within 30 seconds after the router is powered up, hit the ctrl-break. The router will respond as shown in Example B-2. If you wait too long, the Cisco router will not register the key sequence.

6. `>o/r 0x42` instructs the router to boot from flash and skip the configuration file.

7. `>i` instructs the router to reboot boot from flash.

8. When prompted, answer no to the setup questions. This keeps from running through Cisco's auto-configuration wizard.

9. `Router>ena` enables us to enter enable mode. There is no enable password at this point because it has been bypassed.

Example B-1
Output from the
show version
command

```
TestRouter>show version
Cisco Internetwork Operating System Software
IOS (tm) 2500 Software (C2500-IS56-L), Version 12.0(8), RELEASE
SOFTWARE (fc1)
Copyright (c) 1986-1999 by cisco Systems, Inc.
Compiled Mon 29-Nov-99 17:32 by kpma
Image text-base: 0x0303F638, data-base: 0x00001000

ROM: System Bootstrap, Version 4.14(9.1), SOFTWARE

TestRouter uptime is 2 minutes
System restarted by power-on
System image file is "flash:c2500-is56-l_120-8.bin"

cisco 2500 (68030) processor (revision D) with 16384K/2048K bytes
of memory.
Processor board ID 01739404, with hardware revision 00000000
Bridging software.
X.25 software, Version 3.0.0.
1 Ethernet/IEEE 802.3 interface(s)
2 Serial network interface(s)
32K bytes of non-volatile configuration memory.
8192K bytes of processor board System flash (Read ONLY)

Configuration register is 0x2102
```

Example B-2
Output during a
reboot when ctrl-
break has been
executed

```
System Bootstrap, Version 11.0(10c), SOFTWARE
Copyright (c) 1986-1996 by cisco Systems
2500 processor with 6144 Kbytes of main memory

Abort at 0x1098B26 (PC)
>
```

NOTE: *If we want to view the password, we can use the* show con-
fig *command. However, if the enable password is encrypted, we will
not be able to view it.*

10. `Router#configure memory` copies the configuration file in NVRAM into memory. Because we are already in enable mode, we have effectively bypassed the enable password. If we fail to do this step, when we save our changes in step 15 we will overwrite NVRAM with a generic configuration file (except for the password).

11. Use `Router#configure terminal`. Enter the global configuration mode.

12. Use `Router(config)#enable secret password`. This command sets the enable secret password.

13. Use `Router#config-register *config-register-value*`. Use the value found in step 3. Typically, this will be 0x2102, but it could be a different value.

14. Use `Router(config)#exit` and exit global configuration mode.

15. Use `Router#write memory` and save the configuration file with your new enable password into NVRAM.

16. Use `Router#reload`. If you have followed the previous steps, this reboots the router with only the enable password changed.

Cisco 3600, 4500, 4700, 7200, and 7500 Series Routers Password Recovery

1. Using a rolled cable, connect a COM port on your PC to the console port on your Cisco router.

2. Hit Enter several times until you are in user mode.

3. Use `Router>show version`. Make note of the configuration register as shown in Example B-3.

4. Reboot the Cisco router.

Example B-3
Output from the
show version
command

```
TestRouter#show version
Cisco Internetwork Operating System Software
IOS (tm) 3600 Software (C3640-IS-M), Version 12.0(3)T3,  RELEASE
SOFTWARE (fc1)
Copyright (c) 1986-1999 by cisco Systems, Inc.
Compiled Thu 15-Apr-99 21:46 by kpma
Image text-base: 0x600088F0, data-base: 0x60AD6000

ROM: System Bootstrap, Version 11.1(19)AA, EARLY DEPLOYMENT
RELEASE SOFTWARE (fc1)

TestRouter uptime is 13 minutes
System restarted by power-on
System image file is "slot0:c3640-is-mz_120-3_T3.bin"

cisco 3640 (R4700) processor (revision 0x00) with 28672K/4096K
bytes of memory.
Processor board ID 10705813
R4700 CPU at 100Mhz, Implementation 33, Rev 1.0
MICA-6DM Firmware: CP ver 2310 - 6/3/1998, SP ver 2310 -
6/3/1998.
Bridging software.
X.25 software, Version 3.0.0.
Basic Rate ISDN software, Version 1.1.
1 Ethernet/IEEE 802.3 interface(s)
4 ISDN Basic Rate interface(s)
12 terminal line(s)
Integrated NT1's for 4 ISDN Basic Rate interfaces
DRAM configuration is 64 bits wide with parity disabled.
125K bytes of non-volatile configuration memory.
4096K bytes of processor board System flash (Read/Write)
8192K bytes of processor board PCMCIA Slot0 flash (Read/Write)

Configuration register is 0x2102
```

5. Within 30 seconds after the router is powered up, hit ctrl-break. The router will respond as shown in Example B-4. If you wait too long, the Cisco router will not register the key sequence.

6. >confreg 0x42 instructs the router to boot from flash and skip the configuration file.

7. >reset instructs the router to reboot.

8. When prompted, answer no to the setup questions. This keeps from running through Cisco's auto-configuration wizard.

Example B-4
Output during a
reboot after ctrl-break
has been executed

```
System Bootstrap, Version 11.1(19)AA, EARLY DEPLOYMENT RELEASE
SOFTWARE (fc1)
Copyright (c) 1998 by cisco Systems, Inc.
C3600 processor with 32768 Kbytes of main memory
Main memory is configured to 64 bit mode with parity disabled


monitor: command "boot" aborted due to user interrupt
rommon 1 >
```

9. `Router>ena` enables us to enter enable mode. There is no enable password at this point because it has been bypassed.

NOTE: *If we want to view the password, we can use the* show con-fig *command. However, if the enable password is encrypted, we will not be able to view it.*

10. `Router#configure memory` copies the configuration file in NVRAM into memory. Because we are already in enable mode, we have effectively bypassed the enable password. If we fail to do this step, when we save our changes in step 15 we will overwrite NVRAM with a generic configuration file (except for the password).

11. Use `Router#configure terminal` and enter the global configuration mode.

12. Use `Router(config)#enable secret password`. This command sets the enable secret password.

13. Use `Router(config)#config-register config-register-value`. Use the value found in step 3. Typically, this will be 0x2102, but it could be a different value.

14. Use `Router(config)#exit` and exit global configuration mode.

15. Use `Router#write memory`. Save the configuration file with your new enable password into NVRAM.

16. Use `Router#reload`. If you have followed the previous steps, this reboots the router with only the enable password changed.

Cisco 700 Series Router Password Recovery

Because the Cisco 700 series does not run Cisco's IOS, the password recovery technique used is completely different. The system password provided on the Cisco 700 series router is for remote access protection only (such as login and Telnet). Instead of bypassing the configuration file as we do with the 2500, 2600, 3600, and 4000, we need to upload a new firmware into flash to recover from a lost password. This is not difficult, but it can be done:

1. Using the light blue nine-pin male and female cable that comes with your Cisco 700 series router, connect the male end to the Cisco 700 series router and the female end to a COM port on your PC.

2. Power up the Cisco 700 series router.

3. Use `>version` to display the version of software used by your Cisco 770 series router as in Example B-5.

Example B-5
Output from the
`version` command

```
> version
Software Version c760-i.b.US 4.2(2) - May 26 1998 17:39:36
Cisco 776
ISDN Stack Revision US 2.10 (5ESS/DMS/NI-1)
Copyright (c) 1993-1998 by Cisco Systems, Inc.  All rights
reserved.
Software is used subject to software license agreement contained
with this product. By using this product you agree to accept the
terms of the software license.
Hardware Configuration:
    DRAM:  1.5MB
    Flash: 1.0MB
    POTS:  Type 0 (Rev. 73-1797-05-C0)
    NT1:   Installed
    ROM:   2.1(2)
```

4. Download the appropriate version of the software required for your Cisco 700 series router. The two choices are 750 or 760. In Example B-3, the Cisco 700 series router is using the 760 firmware. You can download the appropriate firmware from the following URLs:

```
www.cisco.com/warp/public/779/smbiz/service/knowledge/
general/750erase.hex
```

```
www.cisco.com/warp/public/779/smbiz/service/knowledge/
general/760erase.hex<f$>
```

5. Reboot the Cisco 700 series router.

6. Within 30 seconds after the router is powered up, hit the Esc key several times. The router will respond, as shown in Example B-6. This will put the router into software load mode. If you wait too long, the Cisco 700 series router will not register the key sequence.

7. Select the baud rate in which to upload the firmware, which will be uploaded through your terminal emulator. Therefore, you should use option 5 to upload the firmware. Once selected, you will see the output shown in Example B-7.

8. At this point, you will need to configure your local terminal emulator to upload the image. Verify that the Line Delay and Character Delay are set to zero. These attributes can be found in HyperTerminal under File, Properties, Settings Tab, ASCII Setup.

9. Select "Send line ends with line feeds" found on the same page as Line Delay and Character Delay from Step 5 above.

10. Click the OK button on both configuration screens.

11. Select Send Text File from the Transfer menu.

12. Locate and select the firmware file in the Send Text File window.

13. Select the Open button. At this point, the file will transfer to the Cisco 700 series router. The only indication that the file is transferring is the flashing of the LINE LED on the front of the router. The file transfer should take approximately 12 minutes with a 9600-baud connection. Once the firmware is downloaded, you will need to reconfigure the Cisco 700 series router.

Example B-6

Output during a reboot in which escape has been executed

```
Boot version 2.1(2) 11/07/97 16:06
Copyright (c) 1993-1997.  All rights reserved.

POST ........... OK (1.5MB).
Validating FLASH ... OK.
Waiting ...

Ready to upload new firmware into flash. Select baud rate:

    1 -     300 baud
    2 -    1200 baud
    3 -    2400 baud
    4 -    4800 baud
    5 -    9600 baud
    6 -   19200 baud
    7 -   38400 baud
    8 -   57600 baud
    9 - 115200 baud
```

Example B-7

Output after selecting the baud rate in which the firmware will upload

```
Begin ascii upload at 8n1/9600 baud.
```

APPENDIX C

OSI Model

The OSI Model is used to describe how information from one application on one computer can move to an application on another computer. Developed by the *International Organization for Standardization* (ISO) in 1984, it is the primary architectural model for internetworking communications. The OSI Model has seven layers:

- Physical layer
- Data link layer
- Network layer
- Transport layer
- Session layer
- Presentation layer
- Application layer

We will now take a look at their purposes within the OSI Model and give an example of a technology that correlates to that particular layer.

Layer 1: The Physical Layer

The definition of the physical layer is that it is Layer 1 of the OSI Reference Model. The physical layer defines the electrical, mechanical, procedural, and functional specifications for activating, maintaining, and deactivating the physical link between end systems. It is comprised of three components. These components, in some instances, are the same in *Local Area Network* (LAN) and *Wide Area Network* (WAN) environments. They are cables or wires, connectors, and encoding.

Cables and Wires

The majority of the cable in place today falls into three types: *Unshielded Twisted Pair* (UTP), coaxial, and fiber optic. The majority of modern internal cable plant wiring is UTP. However, coaxial cable is still used today for specific LAN applications as well as for some high-speed WAN applications. Finally, the high-speed cable of choice is fiber. Fiber is used as the backbone for all high-speed LAN and WAN connections today.

Unshielded Twisted Pair (UTP)   UTP has many uses. It is used for voice communication, key card readers, alarm systems, and data communications. The first distinction in the type of UTP that can be used is the rating of the cable. UTP cable is rated for *either* or *plenum* use. If an area is a plenum or air return space, plenum rated cable must be used. Otherwise, standard cable is acceptable for use.

NOTE: *Plenum-rated cable is approximately twice the cost of standard UTP cable.*

The next distinction, and probably most important, is the category designator. The category, often abbreviated as CAT, levels officially run from Category 1 to Category 5:

- *CAT 1*   Here cable performance is intended for basic communications and power-limited circuit cable. No performance criteria exist for cable at this level.

- *CAT 2*   Low performance UTP. Typical applications are voice and low-speed data. This is not specified in the *Electronic Industries Association/Telecommunications Industry Association* (EIA/TIA) 568A for data use.

- *CAT 3*   This is data cable that complies with the transmission requirements in the EIA/TIA 568A. It has a maximum transmission speed of 16Mbps. In current installations, this is the grade most often used for voice cabling.

■ *CAT 4* An infrequently used category. It has a maximum transmission speed of 20Mbps.

■ *CAT 5* The most commonly used UTP category. Its maximum transmission speed is 100Mbps.

Coaxial cable The coaxial cable used in networks is a relative of the coax cable used in many households for cable TV reception. Just like UTP, there can be both PVC and plenum-rated varieties for each variation. Many variations of this cable exist, but only three are used for data communications. The impedance or resistance of the cable is the item that differentiates the specific cables. RG58, RG59, and RG62 have approximately the same diameter, but each cable has a different amount of impedance. Table C-1 summarizes the coax categories, as follows:

■ *RG58* Also called ThinNet. Rated for 10MHz transmissions over a distance of 185 meters.

■ *RG8* Also called ThickNet. Rated for 10MHz transmissions over a distance of 500 meters.

■ *RG62* Used for IBM controller cabling.

■ *RG59* Not used for data transmissions. Used primarily for video transmissions and household cable TV.

Fiber optic cable Fiber optic cable is the cable of choice for high-speed, long-distance communications. Simply put, a light source such as a low-powered laser is used to generate the optical or light signals down this type of cable. These cables are constructed out of

Table C-1

Coaxial Cable
Variations

Type of Coaxial Cable	Impedance	Cable Diameter	Usage
RG8	50 Ohm	10mm	10Base5, Thick Ethernet
RG58	50 Ohm	5mm	10 Base2, Thin Ethernet
RG59	75 Ohm	6mm	Video
RG62	93 Ohm	6mm	IBM 3270, Arcnet

small, thin strands of glass that look like fibers. The distance limitation of fiber is often measured in kilometers. Fiber optic cable, like UTP and coax, is rated either for PVC or plenum use. Two different types of fiber optic cable exist:

- *Multimode Fiber (MMF)*   Multimode fiber enables light to travel over one of many possible paths. Light, for example, could bounce under various angles in the core of the multimode cable. Because of the larger diameter of the core, it is much easier to get the light within it, allowing for less expensive electronics and connectors. The maximum distance for MMF is two km.

- *Single Mode Fiber (SMF)*   This offers the light only one route to travel through. SMF has a much smaller core than MMF (eight micron for SMF versus 50 or 62.5 micron for MMF). The smaller core enables much longer distances than MMF. Telephone companies interconnect their network equipment with SMF. The typical distance is between five and 1,000 miles. Simply put, if you want more distance, use a stronger laser.

NOTE: *SMF equipment is much more expensive than the equipment for MMF.*

Physical Terminations and Connectors

Without connectors and terminations, cables would have to be "hard-wired" to the end device. This would make quick disconnects and reconnects impossible. Connectors usually vary depending on the media type.

UTP   Four basic modular jack styles are used in UTP. Figure C-1 shows the eight-position and eight-position keyed modular jacks. These jacks are commonly and incorrectly referred to as RJ45 and keyed RJ45 respectively.

The six-position modular jack is commonly referred to as RJ11. Using these terms can sometimes lead to confusion since the RJ designations actually refer to specific wiring configurations called *Universal Service Ordering Codes* (USOC).

The designation RJ means "registered jack." Each of these three basic jack styles can be wired for different RJ configurations. For example, the six-position jack can be wired as an RJ11C (one-pair), RJ14C (two-pair), or RJ25C (three-pair) configuration. An eight-position jack can be wired for configurations such as RJ61C (four-pair) and RJ48C. The keyed eight-position jack can be wired for RJ45S, RJ46S, and RJ47S.

The fourth modular jack style is a modified version of the six-position jack (modified modular jack or MMJ). It was designed by *Digital Equipment Corporation*® (DEC) along with the *modified modular plug* (MMP) to eliminate the possibility of connecting DEC data equipment to voice lines and vice versa.

Cable Termination Practices for UTP Two primary wiring standards exist. One set of standards is set by the EIA/TIA; the other is set by the USOC. The various pinouts are detailed in Figure C-2.

Two wiring schemes have been adopted by the EIA/TIA 568-A standard. They are nearly identical, except that pairs two and three are reversed. T568A is the preferred scheme because it is compatible with one or two-pair USOC systems. Either configuration can be used for *Integrated Services Digital Network* (ISDN) and high-speed data applications.

Figure C-1
UTP jacks

8-position   8-position
keyed

6-position   6-position
modified

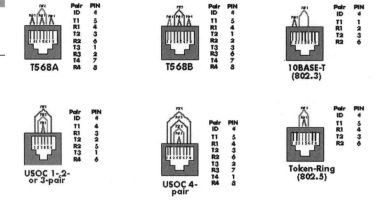

Figure C-2
EIA/TIA and USOC
jack pinouts

USOC wiring is available for one-, two-, three-, or four-pair systems. Pair 1 occupies the center conductors; pair 2 occupies the next two contacts out, and so on. One advantage to this scheme is that a six-position plug configured with one or two pairs can be inserted into an eight-position jack and maintain pair continuity.

Ethernet uses either of the EIA/TIA standards in an eight-position jack. However, only two pairs are used. On the other hand, Token Ring wiring uses either an eight-position or six-position jack. The eight-position format is compatible with T568A, T568B, and USOC wiring schemes. The six-position format is compatible with one- or two-pair USOC wiring.

Coaxial connectors Coaxial cables use two different connectors. One type is used specifically for ThickNet. All other types of coax use the same type of connector.

All ThinNet and other coax cables, except RG8 (ThickNet), use the *Bayonet Neil-Concelman* (BNC) connector, shown in Figure C-3. The acronym BNC has also been purported to mean British Naval Connector and Bayonet Nut Connector, but those references are incorrect.

Figure C-3
BNC connector for
coaxial cable

NOTE: *If the connector is not firmly connected to the cable, the connection will have intermittent connection issues. This is not acceptable for DS3 WAN circuits.*

ThickNet (RG8) uses an *Attachment Unit Interface* (AUI) connector to connect devices to the cable. The AUI connector itself is a standard male DB-15M with studs instead of mounting screws; the female is a DB-15F with a slide-clip that attempts to lock onto the studs. Table C-2 lists the pinouts for an AUI connector as well as an RJ45-pinned connector.

Fiber optic connectors   Five popular types of fiber connectors exist. They can be used for both MMF and SMF. The most common types of connectors, ST, SC, and MIC, are pictured in Figure C-4. The less common connector types are ESCON and MT-RJ. The following is a brief description of each of the connectors:

- *ST*   A commonly used connector in the earlier days of fiber installations.

- *SC*   The most commonly used connector type today. Almost every connector on Cisco equipment uses an SC connector.

- *MIC/FSD*   The *Medium Interface Connector/Fiber Shroud Duplex* (MIC/FSD) connector is used for fiber-based Fiber Distributed Data Interfaces (FDDI) connections. It is polarized so that TX/RX are always correct.

Table C-2

AUI and RJ45
Pinouts

AUI Pin No.	Ethernet V2.0	IEEE 802.3	RJ45 (EIA/TIA568A) Pin #
1	Shield	Control in Shield	
2	Collision Presence +	Control in A	
3	Transmit +	Data out A	1
4	Reserved	Data in Shield	
5	Receive +	Data in A	3
6	Power Return	Voltage Common	
7	Reserved	Control out A	
8	Reserved	Control out Shield	
9	Collision Presence −	Control in B	
10	Transmit −	Data out B	2
11	Reserved	Data out Shield	
12	Receive −	Data in B	6
13	Power	Voltage	
14	Reserved	Voltage Shield	
15	Reserved	Control out B	
Connector Shield ―――――――――――――――			Protective Ground

Figure C-4
Common types of
fiber connectors

A) ST Connector   B) SC Connector

C) MIC Connector

- *ESCON* This is used to connect to IBM equipment as well as channel interface processors.

- *MT-RJ* A new fiber connector that is able to fit into a standard 110 patch panel. It almost doubles the port capacity of an SC module.

Physical Encoding Methods

An encoding method is the method that a device uses to put data on the media. Although the media and connectors for LANs and WANs are similar, the encoding variations for LANs and WANs are different.

LAN encoding   Four basic LAN encoding schemes exist. The first encoding scheme is the foundation for all the other encoding schemes. Thus, it is important that you understand the basic encoding scheme that everything is based on, the *Non-Return To Zero-Level* (NRZ-L). Figure C-5 shows how the various encoding methods reduce the binary numbers to electrical or optical signals.

The common encoding methods are as follows:

- *Non-Return to Zero-Level (NRZ-L)*   This is the basic type of encoding upon which all others are based. A *one* is positive voltage; a *zero* is no voltage. The problem with this is that timing information cannot be retrieved from a string of zeros. Thus, other encoding methods have been developed to overcome this problem.

- *Non-Return to Zero Inverted (NRZI)*   Used in 100Base-Fx fiber networks, NRZI uses a change in signal to represent a one.

- *Manchester*   Used in Ethernet, this encoding is based on the signal transition in the middle of the bit. An upward transition is a one. A downward transition represents a zero.

Figure C-5
Common encoding
methods

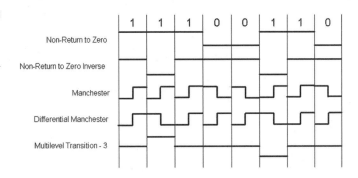

■ *Differential Manchester*   Used in Token Ring networks, this always has a transition in the middle. However, the encoding is based on the transition at the bit boundaries. A transition indicates a zero. No transition indicates a one.

■ *MLT-3*   Used in Fast Ethernet Networks. Instead of two voltage levels (voltage and no voltage), MLT-3 uses three layers: positive voltage, no voltage, and negative voltage. Changing the voltage represents a one. For instance, a series of ones would be represented as $0,1,0,-1,0,1,0.-1$.

WAN connectors   Remember that the same types of media are used in WANs as LANs. However, the connectors used in WANs differ depending upon their use. Too many WAN connectors exist for us to cover every type, but the most common WAN connectors terminate T1 and E1 lines. Table C-3 displays the pinouts of T1 and E1 Lines.

NOTE: *The use of the terms tip and ring are typically not used today. Their usage is historical in perspective when testing was done with a tone tester. This test would allow a different tone to be present depending on which tip or ring was tested.*

Table C-3

The Pinouts of T1 and E1 Lines

Eight Position Jack Pinouts	T1/EI
1	Receive (tip)
2	Receive (ring)
3	Not used
4	Transmit (tip)
5	Transmit (ring)
6	Not used
7	Not used
8	Not used

WAN encoding   Before the topic of WAN encoding can be addressed, the concept of the digital hierarchy must be familiar to the reader. The digital hierarchy is a classification of circuit speeds. In North America, it is called the North American Digital Hierarchy. In Europe and the majority of the world, it is called the CCITT Digital Hierarchy. Both begin at the DS0 level with a single 64Kbps circuit. Then differences appear in the two systems.

In the North American Digital Hierarchy, this DS0 circuit is multiplied 24 times into a DS1 circuit with a speed of 1.544Mbps. This DS1 is then multiplied 28 times into a DS3 circuit with a speed of over 44Mbps.

The CCITT Digital Hierarchy combines 30 DS0s into an E1 circuit with a speed of 2.048Mbps. Next, 16 E1 circuits are combined to form an E3 circuit with a speed of over 34Mbps.

The WAN media type used depends on the circuit speed. T1 and E1 circuits generally use UTP. DS3 and E3 circuits use coax. However, all speeds above DS3/E3 require the use of fiber optic cables. The terms *North American Synchronous Optical Network* (SONET) and *International Synchronous Digital Network* (SDH) identify the circuits in this range. Table C-4 denotes the various circuit names and speeds.

The variations in WAN encoding first occur at the DS1 level. When a DS1 line is ordered, it is necessary to specify the framing and line coding. These settings must match the Channel Service Unit/Data Service Unit (CSU/ DSU) and the other end of the circuit.

Table C-4

Various Circuit
Names and Speeds

Optical Circuit	Speed
OC-1	51.8Mbps
OC-3	155.5Mbps
OC-12	622.1Mbps
OC-48	2488.3Mbps

NOTE: One of the most difficult issues to troubleshoot is the incorrect encoding of a circuit. More that once, I have seen a service provider finally determine that the cause of a line fault is improper encoding at one end of the circuit.

The two frame types available for DS1s are *D4 / Super Frame* (SF) and *Extended Super Frame* (ESF). The two frame types for E1s are CRC4 and no CRC4.

The available line codings for DS1s are *Alternate Mark Inversion* (AMI) and *Bipolar Eight-Zero Substitution* (B8ZS). The only available line codings for E1s are AMI and *High-Density Bipolar 3* (HDB3).

Conclusion

The physical layer may be seen as the most trivial or least important of the seven layers. After all, no fancy things like routing or switching happen at this layer. No addresses are used at the physical layer. However, many of the issues faced in the networking world are solved at the physical layer. A UTP cable might run too close to a fluorescent light or an OC-3 fiber patch cord might get accidentally crushed. When troubleshooting network problems, one of the most effective methods is to follow the OSI Model and troubleshoot by layers. Thus, you would start at the physical layer and move up once you have determined each layer is operating correctly.

Layer 2: The Data Link Layer

Layer 2 of the OSI Reference Model is the data link layer. Figure C-6 shows the placement of the network layer in the OSI Reference Model.

Figure C-6
The data link layer in
the OSI Reference
Model

7	Application Layer
6	Presentation Layer
5	Session Layer
4	Transport Layer
3	Network Layer
2	**Data Link Layer**
1	Physical Layer

The data link layer is responsible for describing the specifications for topology and communication between local systems. Many examples of data link layer technology exist:

- Ethernet
- Fast Ethernet
- Token Ring
- Frame Relay
- HDLC
- Point-to-Point Protocol (PPP)
- Serial Line Interface Protocol (SLIP)

All of these services describe how conversations take place between two devices on the same media. Remember that the data link layer implementation used is independent of the physical layer. For example, Ethernet can use UTP or coaxial cable. It does not matter which physical layer media it uses; the rules that govern the technology are the same. This is the beauty of the OSI Model: any layer can be replaced without concerns about the lower or upper layers.

Communication at the data link layer is between two hosts on the same network. Those two hosts can be a desktop computer communicating with a local file server or a local host sending data to a router that is destined for a remote host (see Figure C-7).

Data Link Layer Example

The following section focuses on Ethernet, one of the most commonly used data link layer standards. If we look at the frame format of an Ethernet frame, we can get a better understanding of each component's purpose. In Figure C-8, we see a standard IEEE 802.3 Ethernet frame format. If we look at each component, we can easily see its purpose.

Figure C-7
An example of data link layer conversations

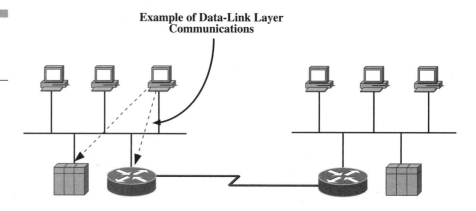

Figure C-8
Ethernet frame format

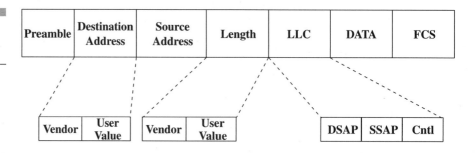

Preamble   The preamble is an alternating pattern of ones and zeros. It tells the other stations on the media that a frame is coming. The IEEE 802.3 preamble ends with two consecutive ones, which serves to synchronize the frame reception of all stations on the LAN.

Data link layer addressing (Destination and source address)
The capability to distinguish one host from another is critical when multiple hosts have access to the same media. Compare that to point-to-point connections in which the capability to distinguish the end point is irrelevant because there is only one other node on the network that can hear the data.

The address used by end hosts to identify each other is called the *Media Access Control* (MAC) address. It is often referred to as the physical address, burned-in address, or hardware address. The MAC address of each Ethernet *Network Interface Card* (NIC) is by definition unique. It is a 48-bit address built into the NIC that uniquely identifies the station. It is generally represented in one of three formats:

- 00-60-94-EB-41-9F

- 00:60:94:EB:41:9F

- 0060.94EB.419F

If we look closely at the MAC address, we will see that it can be broken down into two distinct components: the vendor's address and a unique host identifier. The first three octets (24 bits) identify the vendor. Using the example listed above, we can look up 00-60-94 at `http://standards.ieee.org/regauth/oui/oui.txt`.

We can see that this NIC was manufactured by IBM. This can be useful when attempting to locate a device on the network that is malfunctioning.

Length   The Length field indicates the number of bytes contained in the Data field. Although all of the other fields are of a predetermined length (the Destination and Source addresses are six bytes) the Data field can be up to 1,500 bytes. If the data in the frame is insufficient to fill the frame to a minimum 64-byte size, the frame is padded to ensure at least a 64-byte frame.

Logical Link Control (LLC)   The IEEE 802.2 *Logical Link Control* (LLC) header is used to specify which upper layer protocol is contained in the data. Without the capability to distinguish which upper layer protocol a packet belongs to, it is impossible to carry multiple network layer protocols over a data link layer implementation. For example, because Novell's 802.3 RAW frame format does not have a method to distinguish between network layer protocols, it could only carry a single network layer protocol. This is one of the reasons why Novell's 802.3 frame format is generally not employed.

Another example of a data link layer technology not using a type field is SLIP. Even though it enjoyed some success in the late '80s and early '90s as a dialup protocol, its incapability to distinguish between different network layer protocols has allowed PPP to become the standard dialup protocol.

The following fields all play a part in LLC identification:

- *DSAP*   The *Destination Service Access Point* (DSAP) is a one-byte field that acts like a pointer in the receiving station. It tells the receiving NIC which buffer to put this information in. This function is critical when users are running multiple network layer protocols.

- *SSAP*   The *Source Service Access Point* (SSAP) is identical to the DSAP, except that it indicates the source of the sending application.

- *Control*   This one-byte field is used to indicate the type of LLC frame of this data frame. Three different types of LLC frames exist:

  - *LLC1*   An unacknowledged connectionless service. It uses unsequenced information to set up communication between two network stations. This type of LLC is generally used with Novell's *Internetwork Packet Exchange* (IPX), TCP/IP, and Vines IP.

  - *LLC2*   A connection-oriented service between two network stations. This type of service is generally used in SNA and NetBIOS sessions.

  - *LLC3*   A connectionless but acknowledged-oriented service between two different stations. This type of service can be used by SDLC.

Data   The Data field in an IEEE 802.3 frame can be between 43 and 1,497 bytes. However, depending upon the type of frame being used, this size can vary. For example, an Ethernet II frame can hold between 46 and 1,497 bytes of data, while a frame using Novell's RAW 802.3 frame format can hold between 46 and 1,500 bytes of data.

Frame Check Sequence (FCS)   The last four bytes of a IEEE 802.3 frame are used to verify that the frame is not corrupt. By using a complex polynomial, the NIC can detect errors in the frame. If errors are detected, then the frame is discarded and it never reaches the memory buffers.

Now that we understand the frame format of an IEEE 802.3 frame, we need to discuss how those frames get on the wire.

Carrier Sense Media Access with Collision Detection (CSMA/CD)   Ethernet is one of the most common network topologies. The basic rule behind Ethernet communication is called *Carrier Sense Multiple Access with Collision Detection* (CSMA/CD). If we break down each phrase, we can interpret its meaning:

- *Carrier Sense*   All Ethernet stations are required to listen to the network to see if any other devices are sending data. This serves two purposes: one, it keeps the station from sending data when someone else is sending data and, two, it enables the station to be ready when another station wants to send it data.

- *Multiple Access*   This means more than two stations can be connected to the same network at the same time and that all stations can transmit data whenever the network is free. In order for data to be transmitted, the station must wait until the Ethernet channel is idle. Once the channel is idle, the station can transmit a frame, but it must listen to see if there is a collision.

- *Collision Detection*   If there is a collision, then both stations must immediately back off and use a backoff algorithm to randomly determine how long they should wait before trying to transmit again. It is important that a random number be generated for this timer, because if some standard number were used, then both stations would wait the same length of time and then attempt to transmit again, thus causing another collision.

NOTE: *A collision is the simultaneous transmitting of a frame by two different stations. A station can detect a collision within the first 64 bytes of the transmission.*

Conclusion

Many different types of data link layer technologies exist, and Ethernet is one of those technologies. Although a data link layer technology can theoretically use any physical layer implementation, generally the actual implementation of a data link layer technology goes hand in hand with the physical layer implementation. For example, PPP is generally used over dialup networks or WAN networks, while Ethernet and Token Ring are used in LAN environments. This means that you probably won't see very many implementations of PPP using CAT 5 cable for its wiring infrastructure. Likewise, you probably won't see Token Ring being deployed from a corporate office to a telecommuter's home using the Telco's wiring infrastructure.

Layer 3: Network Layer

Layer 3 of the OSI Reference Model is the network layer. Figure C-9 shows the placement of the network layer in the OSI Reference Model.

This layer is responsible for providing routing for the network. Routing, in a generic sense, is simply finding a path to a destination. In the context of the network layer, routing means finding a path to a destination that is a member of a different Layer 2 network than the source. Physical networks can be connected together with bridges to form larger Layer 2 networks. Unfortunately, Layer 2 networks cannot scale to an infinite size. As these networks grow, more bandwidth is used to transmit broadcast packets that flood the entire Layer 2 network. These broadcast packets are used to find the destination host.

■■■■ ■■■■ ■■■■ ■■■■

Figure C-9
The network layer
and the OSI
Reference Model

7	Application Layer
6	Presentation Layer
5	Session Layer
4	Transport Layer
3	**Network Layer**
2	Data Link Layer
1	Physical Layer

Routing enables Layer 2 networks to be broken into smaller segments, enabling the network to grow to support more hosts. Figure C-10 shows the concept of routing.

The data link control layer passes packets up to the network layer. These packets have headers to define the source and destination addresses and other network layer parameters of the data in the packet. The network layer only uses the data in the network layer packet header for information to perform its functions. This maintains the modularity of the network layer. Therefore, there is no dependency on the information from the data link control layer headers and the transport layer headers.

Network layer communication is not guaranteed. This means that there is no mechanism to determine if the destination node received the network layer packets. Guaranteed delivery is maintained at other layers in the OSI Reference Model. The most obvious reason for not implementing guaranteed delivery at the network layer is because this layer has no concept of end-to-end delivery. It would be more appropriate for upper layer protocols that implement more connection-oriented services to make sure that the data reaches its destination. The network layer routes data on a packet-by-packet basis.

Figure C-10
Routing between
Layer 2 networks

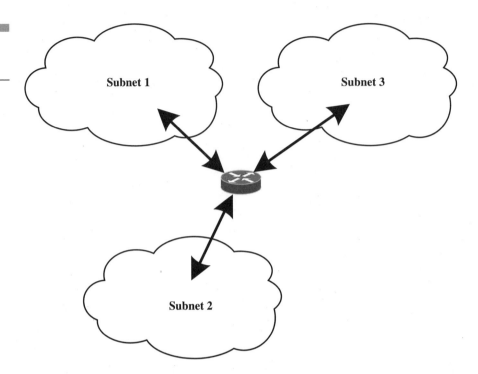

Only one network layer process exists for each network node. Several data link control layer processes may be found below the network layer, depending on the number of physical interfaces in the node, and several transport layer processes may be found above the network layer, depending on the number of connection-oriented streams terminating at the node. Several network layer protocols may be running on a node, but each of these protocols corresponds to a separate logical internetwork and they do not intercommunicate.

A special node called a *gateway* connects logical networks formed by network layer addressing schemes. Gateways have a special sublayer in the upper portion of the network layer called the *Internet sublayer*. This sublayer handles the intercommunication between subnets. When a packet arrives from one subnet that is destined for another, the packet will be passed from the network layer to the Internet sublayer. The Internet sublayer in turn determines the destination subnet and forwards the packet back down to the lower portion of the network layer to the destination subnet. This is the basic idea behind routing. Figure C-11 illustrates the concept of a network node.

Figure C-11
Network node model

3	**Internet Sublayer**
	Network Layer
2	Data Link Layer
1	Physical Layer

Each network layer process at each node is a peer process. These peer processes work together to implement distributed algorithms. These distributed algorithms are the routing algorithms corresponding to various routing protocols. These protocols provide a means to automatically discover and transmit routing information between gateways.

The Internet Protocol (IP)

The most familiar protocol that operates at the network layer is the *Internet Protocol* (IP). IP is by far the most widely deployed network layer protocol due to the success of the Internet. This protocol is the foundation of the Internet in terms of addressing and packet routing. The Internet employs multiple protocols in the other OSI Reference Model layers, but it only uses IP in the network layer.

Another example of a network protocol is Novell's *Internet Packet Exchange* (IPX). Novell has since refined NetWare to use IP as the native network layer protocol instead of IPX.

IP Node Operation

If an IP host wants to communicate with another IP host, the transmitting IP source must determine if the destination IP address is in the same subnet or not. If the destination is in the same subnet, the host must send an *Address Resolution Protocol* (ARP) request packet to obtain the MAC address of the destination, assuming the destination MAC address isn't already in its ARP table. If the destination is not in the same subnet as the source, the source must send the packet to the MAC address of the gateway for that subnet. Most IP hosts have one IP address to send their packets to if they are destined for any subnet other than their own. This is called the *default gateway* or *default router address*. The user configures the default gateway address.

Once the default gateway (router) gets the packet and sees that the packet is destined for its own MAC address and at the same time destined for another IP host, the router knows that it must forward the packet to another interface to move the packet closer to its destination.

The mechanism for determining if the destination IP host is in the same subnet is as follows. The subnet mask is bitwise ANDed with both the source IP address and the destination IP address. The logic table for the AND operation is shown in Table C-5.

The result of these two functions is exclusively ORed (XORed). If this final result is not zero, then the destination IP address is in another subnet. The logic table for the XOR operation is shown in Table C-6.

Here is an example of determining if the destination address is in the same subnet as the host:

Table C-5

Logic table for AND operations

	1	0
1	1	0
0	0	0

Table C-6

Logic table for OR operations

	1	0
1	0	1
0	1	0

Source IP address:

$(100.1.43.1)_{\text{dotted-decimal}}$
$(01100100.00000001.00101011.00000001)_{\text{binary}}$

Subnet mask:

$(255.255.255.0)_{\text{dotted-decimal}}$
$(11111111.11111111.11111111.00000000)_{\text{binary}}$

Destination IP address:

$(100.1.44.2)_{\text{dotted-decimal}}$
$(01100100.00000001.00101100.00000010)_{\text{binary}}$

Source IP address ANDed with subnet mask:

01100100.00000001.00101011.00000001
<u>11111111.11111111.11111111.00000000</u>
01100100.00000001.00101011.00000000

Destination IP address ANDed with subnet mask:

01100100.00000001.00101100.00000010
<u>11111111.11111111.11111111.00000000</u>
01100100.00000001.00101100.00000000

The two results XORed:

01100100.00000001.00101011.00000000
<u>01100100.00000001.00101100.00000000</u>
00000000.00000000.00000111.00000000

The result of the XOR function is not zero. Therefore, the destination IP address is in another subnet than the source and the packet must be sent to the default gateway to be routed to the destination subnet.

When the router gets a packet to be forwarded to another subnet, the router must manipulate the MAC and IP header fields to ensure that the packet is forwarded toward its destination.

Three things must happen when the router forwards the packet at the network layer:

- The interface to forward the packet to must be determined.

- The destination MAC address must be updated with the MAC address of the next-hop router or destination host.

- The *Time to Live* (TTL) field must be decremented in the IP header.

The interface that the packet is forwarded out of is determined by looking through the route table that the router maintains. This route table associates a route to a destination with a physical interface.

The destination MAC address must be updated with the MAC address of the destination IP host if the host is directly connected to the router. If the destination host is not directly connected to one of the ports of the router, the router must forward the packet to the next router to move the packet toward the destination IP host. In either case, if the router doesn't know the MAC address of the next hop toward the destination, it must ARP for the MAC address.

The TTL field is then decremented. This field provides a mechanism for the packet to be removed from the network if it gets caught in a loop. Without such a mechanism, the packet may be forwarded for as long as the routing loop is active. The packet is removed by a router if its TTL field is zero.

Internetwork Packet Exchange (IPX) Operation

Another example of a Layer 3 protocol is the IPX protocol. The IPX protocol was developed by Novell NetWare. Novell NetWare is a *Network Operating System* (NOS) that provides network file and print services. IPX is quickly being replaced by IP since NetWare now provides native IP support, but there remains a large installed base of IPX networks in campus networks.

Unlike IP, IPX has no concept of multiple subnets per the Layer 2 network. Instead, IPX has only one address per physical network called a *network number*. The full network layer address for a network device is made of two parts: the 32-bit network number and the node's 48-bit MAC address.

Some argue that the combination of Layer 2 and Layer 3 addresses to form a Layer 3 address undermines the modularity of the OSI Reference Model. This is due to the fact that IPX (Layer 3) network numbers depend on the Layer 2 addressing scheme. This argument is purely academic since the MAC address scheme is so prevalent. The real limitation to IPX is its inability to logically subnet hosts on the same physical network.

Layer 4: Transport Layer

Layer 4 of the OSI Reference Model is the transport layer. Figure C-12 shows the placement of the network layer in the OSI Reference Model.

Figure C-12
The transport layer and the OSI Reference Model

7	Application Layer
6	Presentation Layer
5	Session Layer
4	**Transport Layer**
3	Network Layer
2	Data Link Layer
1	Physical Layer

The transport layer is responsible for data transfer issues such as reliability of the connection, establishing error detections, recovery, and flow control. In addition, this layer is responsible for delivering packets from the network layer to the upper layers of the OSI Model.

If we think of the network layer as responsible for delivering packets from one host to another, the transport layer is responsible for identifying the conversations between two hosts. For example, Figure C-13 shows an example of how the transport layer keeps the conversations between the different applications separate.

Two different variants of transport layer protocols are used. The first provides a reliable, connection-oriented service, while the second method is a best-effort delivery. The difference between these two protocols dictates the paradigm in which they operate. When using TCP/IP, the two different protocols are TCP and UDP. Inside an IP packet is a protocol number that enables the host to identify whether the packet contains a TCP message or a UDP message. The TCP protocol value is 6 and for UDP it is 17. Many other (~130) protocols types exist, but these two are commonly used to transport user messages from one host to another.

Transport Layer Protocol Examples

In this section, we'll examine some examples of transport layer protocols.

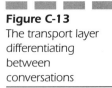

Figure C-13
The transport layer differentiating between conversations

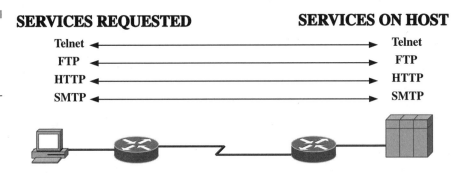

SERVICES REQUESTED   SERVICES ON HOST

Telnet ←————————————————————→ Telnet
FTP ←————————————————————→ FTP
HTTP ←————————————————————→ HTTP
SMTP ←————————————————————→ SMTP

Transmission Control Protocol (TCP) The TCP described in RFC 793 provides applications with a reliable connection-oriented service. Three basic instruments are used to make TCP a connection-oriented service:

- Sequence numbers
- Acknowledgments
- Windowing

In order for data to be handed down to the network layer, the data must be broken down into messages. These messages are then given a sequence number by TCP before being handed off to the network layer. The purpose of the sequence number is so that in case the packets arrive out of order the remote host can reassemble the data using the sequence numbers. This only guarantees that the data is reassembled correctly.

In addition to sequence numbers, acknowledgements are used by the remote host to tell the local host that the data was received, guaranteeing the delivery of data. If, for whatever reason, a packet gets dropped along the way, the remote host can see that it is missing a message and request it again, as shown in Figure C-14.

Although windowing enables TCP to regulate the flow of packets between two hosts, this minimizes the chances of packets being dropped because the buffers are full in the remote host.

In order for a TCP connection to be established, a three-step handshake is exchanged between the local host and the remote host. This three-way handshake starts with the local host initiating a conver-

Figure C-14
Using
acknowledgements
for guaranteed
delivery

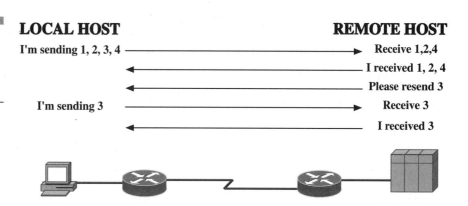

sation by sending a *Synchronize Sequence Numbers* (SYN) packet to the remote host, as shown in Figure C-15.

The remote host acknowledges the SYN and sends an SYN acknowledgement back to the local host. The local host responds by sending an acknowledgement and then starts sending data. The purpose of this handshake is to synchronize the sequence numbers that identify the proper order used to reconstruct the messages throughout the conversation.

User Datagram Protocol (UDP)   The UDP, as described in RFC 768, provides applications with a connectionless best-effort delivery service. Because there is no time wasted setting up a connection, applications that utilize UDP are very fast. Applications that send short bursts of data can take advantage of UDP's speed, but if the messages get delivered out of order or a message gets dropped, then the entire message fails.

Well-Known Ports   We've seen how we can guarantee the delivery of a packet through the use of TCP and how we can improve throughput by using a connectionless delivery service, but how are discrete conversations between two hosts handled? Both TCP and UDP utilize a mechanism called a port (also known as a socket). By utilizing a source port and a destination port, two hosts can distinguish between multiple conversations.

In order to provide services to unknown callers, a host will use a well-known port number. Well-known port numbers are assigned by the *Internet Assigned Numbers Authority* (IANA). By adhering to the well-known port numbers published by the IANA, we can make sure that various services do not utilize the same port. Both TCP and

Figure C-15

Three-way handshake to initiate a connection

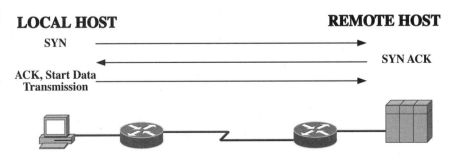

LOCAL HOST   REMOTE HOST

SYN   ——————————————————————▶

◀——————————————————————   SYN ACK

ACK, Start Data ——————————————————————▶
Transmission

UDP use port numbers and when a service can utilize both TCP and UDP, the port number is identical. Table C-7 shows us a sampling of the well-known port numbers.

Until recently, the assigned port range was from 0 to 255. However, the range has been expanded from 0 to 1,023.

Conclusion

The transport layer protocol helps end devices distinguish between simultaneous conversations between the same two hosts. The protocol that is used, connection-oriented or connectionless, is dependent upon the needs of the upper layer application. Some applications want the speed of UDP and will implement their own form of reliability-checking in an effort to speed up the transmission of the data. Although this obviously adds a lot of overhead to the programmer's job, it can be worth it, depending upon the applications requirements.

Layer 5: Session Layer

Layer 5 of the OSI Reference Model is the session layer. Figure C-16 shows the placement of the session layer in the OSI Reference Model.

Table C-7

Well-Known Port Numbers

Port Number	Service
20	FTP (Data)
21	FTP (Control)
23	Telnet
25	SMTP
42	Host Name Server
53	Domain Name Service
80	HTTP

Figure C-16
The session layer and
the OSI Reference
Model

7	Application Layer
6	Presentation Layer
5	**Session Layer**
4	Transport Layer
3	Network Layer
2	Data Link Layer
1	Physical Layer

The session layer is responsible for providing such functions as directory service and access rights. The session layer has a defined role in the OSI Reference Model, but its functions are not as critical as the lower layers to all networks. For example, a network without the physical layer, the data link layer, network layer, or the transport layer would be lacking basic functionality that would make the network useful. Until recently, the session layer has been ignored or at least not seen as absolutely necessary in data networks. Session layer functionality has been seen as a host responsibility, not a network function. As networks become larger and more secure, functions such as directory services and access rights become more necessary.

Access rights functionality deals with a user's access to various network resources such as computer access and authentication, file access, and printer access. Devices providing the service such as file and print servers have typically implemented access rights. There has been a shift in responsibility for these functions in recent years. Authentication can now be distributed using authentication services such as Kerberos. File and print service access control is moving to network directory services such as Novell's *Network Directory Service* (NDS) or Microsoft's *Active Directory Services* (ADS). These services control what resources a host may access.

Directory services are services that find resources on the network. Typically, a user would have to have prior knowledge of a service to gain access to the service. Some services have the capability of broadcasting their presence, but that methodology does not scale well in a large network with many hosts and many services. True directory services act as a redirection point for hosts to be given addressing information to find a particular resource. Novell's NDS or Microsoft's ADS can act as directory services as well as define a user's access rights, as mentioned above.

The session layer has no hard and fast rules for interfacing with the presentation layer since the presentation layer is optional in many cases. The session layer services are typically accessed via TCP or UDP port numbers, therefore defining the interface to the transport layer.

Layer 6: Presentation Layer

Layer 6 of the OSI Reference Model is the presentation layer. Figure C-17 shows the placement of the network layer in the OSI Reference Model.

Figure C-17
The presentation layer and the OSI Reference Model

7	Application Layer
6	**Presentation Layer**
5	Session Layer
4	Transport Layer
3	Network Layer
2	Data Link Layer
1	Physical Layer

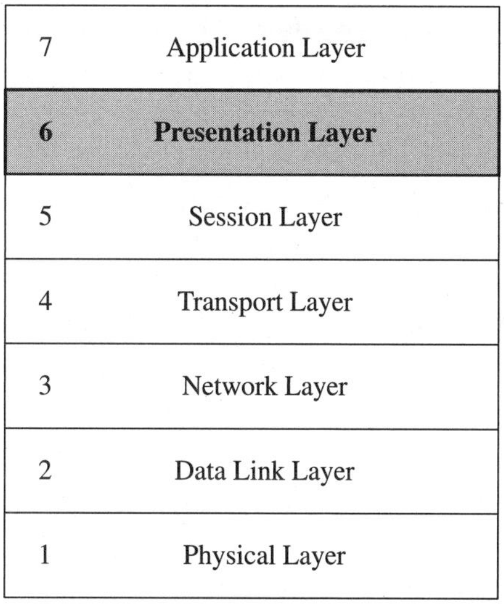

The presentation layer is responsible for providing data encryption, data compression, and code conversion. The functions in this layer have not been considered a function of the network and have been handled by various applications. In recent years, data encryption, compression, and code conversion have moved into the mainstream of the network protocol functionality.

Data encryption is moving to the forefront of networking since networks are carrying more sensitive data. Encryption can be handled in a number of ways. The easiest and most secure method for encrypting data is to encrypt all the data on a particular link. This requires a device on both ends of a path to encrypt and decrypt the payload of each packet that passes over the link. This requires that sensitive data always pass over a path installed with an encryption device. This does not scale well for a large network. The more scalable method for encryption is for the applications at both ends of a session to set up a means for encrypting the data. This method of encryption requires that a device have more processing power to handle the application and the data encryption in real time.

Data compression conserves bandwidth over a link. Like data encryption, data compression can be done on both ends of a path through a network. This requires an external device to compress the network data. This method does not scale well in large networks where there can be many paths through a network. A more scalable method for data compression is to allow the application at both ends of a session to compress the data. The tradeoff in this method is more processing power is required on the host to support the application and real-time compression/decompression.

Code conversion involves converting a set of data or a data stream from one format to another. Data formats can be for character sets, video formats, graphics formats, and presentation formats. Examples of character set formats are ASCII and EBCDIC, video formats are MPEG and MJPEG, graphics formats are GIF, TIFF, JPEG, and bitmap, and presentation formats are HTML, XML, and SHTML.

No hard and fast rules define the interface between the presentation layer and the session layer since the session layer may be optional for a particular network. The presentation layer communicates to the application layer by addressing the application with an appropriate transport layer (session) address such as a TCP port number.

Layer 7: Application Layer

The final layer, Layer 7, of the OSI Model is the application layer. This section will define the application layer and examine in moderate detail what takes place at Layer 7.

The application layer consists of an application that requires the use of a network to perform its task. Communication between applications takes place at Layer 7. As with the previous layers, Layer 7 exchanges messages with Layer 7 only. Restated, an application communicates with only a peer application. Figure C-18 depicts this layer-to-layer communication.

An example application could be something as simple as a *chat* program. The application connects to its peer application and sends characters that are entered on the keyboard. It also displays characters received from the peer application. The applications communicating at Layer 7 use the lower layers and the services they provide to send and receive application-specific information.

Furthermore, it is common for applications to further define the contents of the data that is being exchanged. Even with the simple chat program, a protocol is defined: "Each message received from a peer application contains a single character." This creates a challenge for troubleshooting network-related problems.

Although only a handful of protocols are used at the lower layers, the protocols are usually well specified. As you can see, anyone can define a new protocol for his or her specific application. This makes

Figure C-18
Layer 7 application
communication

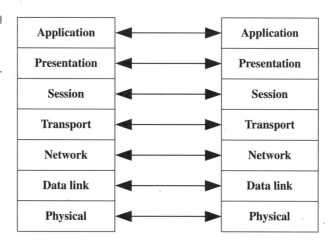

it difficult for vendors that develop network analyzers to provide the capability of troubleshooting application, or Layer 7, problems.

As you can see, this layer can be any application that requires network communication. The application communicates with its peer application at Layer 7, and an application may arbitrarily define a protocol that specifies application-to-application communication.

Conclusion

It is important to remember that the OSI Model is only for reference. Not all protocols and technologies have a direct correlation to one of the seven layers. Frequently, a protocol may straddle different layers, such as ARP, which is used when a computer knows the IP address it needs to communicate with (network layer) but it doesn't know its MAC address (data link layer). ARP enables a computer to map an IP address to a MAC address. So is ARP a data link layer-protocol or a network-layer protocol? Technically, it straddles both layers, so it doesn't really fit the OSI Model, but without it IP communication on a LAN couldn't happen.

APPENDIX D

D.1 Traffic Management Using Queuing

Not only access lists are used to prevent Internet congestion. Another technique is called *queuing*, which allows designated traffic to be forwarded before other traffic. Queuing is mostly used on low bandwidth serial links where certain traffic easily clogs up the link causing time-outs, bringing time-critical sessions such as SNA or audio/video to its knees. Cisco supports three types of queuing: weighted fair queuing, priority queuing and custom queuing.

Weighted Fair Queuing.	Ensures satisfactory response time for time-critical user applications by prioritizing interactive traffic (such as SNA sessions) over file transfers. Weighted fair queuing is *enabled by default.*
Priority Queuing.	Ensures timely delivery of a specific protocol or traffic type by transmitting it before all others
Custom Queuing.	Allocates bandwidth for each different traffic type

Before IOS version 11.1, the standard queuing policy used to manage and control incoming/outgoing traffic was *First-In, First-Out* (FIFO) queuing. When FIFO is used, packet transmission occurs in the order they are received. FIFO queuing was the default for all router interfaces, so if a company needed different traffic handling, another queuing policy was established. When dealing with time-critical traffic, FIFO queuing is not the preferred method. When the FIFO queuing process has filled all interface buffers, the router is indiscriminate about which packets to drop until interface buffer memory is freed.

By using one of the previously mentioned queuing strategies, network staff is able to either let the router itself decide on which packets to drop first (weighted fair queuing), or decide for themselves what traffic has priority (priority queuing or custom queuing).

To better understand queuing, look at the concept of *traffic prioritization* in the following text.

D.2 Prioritizing Traffic

When more and more new protocols were introduced and used in the internet scene, it became evident that some protocols reacted differently than others.

Different protocols have different characteristics and therefore can sometimes display different behaviour in multiprotocol environments. This behaviour severely impacts the performance of other protocols, thereby slowing down or disabling some connections. Prioritizing packets arises from such situations.

The question if users experience serious network performance degradation totally depends on the application type in use and the available bandwidth. If there is plenty of available bandwidth, delay sensitive traffic such as telnet sessions, SNA sessions or desktop videoconferencing may not experience any performance degradation, even on a busy network. But more often this situation is reversed. Due to high WAN bandwidth prices and the increasing amount of traffic crossing the Internet, not enough bandwidth is available to satisfy all applications in a timely manner.

Another type of popular traffic, desktop videoconferencing, requires a specified amount of bandwidth to perform acceptably. This traffic type relies heavily on being able to send and receive acknowledgements, which makes it very sensitive to delay. When used in a multiprotocol network where all traffice shares a single datapath, prioritization may be required.

As we've mentioned earlier, traffic prioritization is only effective when used on slow links. If users do not experience network delay when using WAN links, there is no reason to use traffic prioritization as this lays a heavy claim on router resources. Moreover, implementing prioritization on a link that is not congested will reduce overall network performance.

Therefore, don't consider prioritization or queuing as the wonder medicine for constantly congested WAN links. In most cases, adding more bandwidth is the smarter option. When the WAN link averages 80 percent or greater utilization, adding bandwidth is a better solution to accomodate the traffic needs than queuing is (See Figure D-1).

Figure D-1
Queuing can be used to provide WAN access to certain traffic on heavy-utilized WAN links.

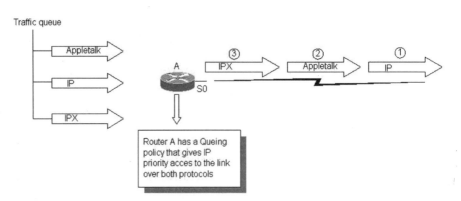

D.3 Queuing Policy

Two challenging issues for most network management staff are keeping all users happy when it comes to available bandwidth and controlling expensive WAN link costs. While the "lower layers" are screaming for more bandwidth, the "upper layers" demand explanations for huge bills by the WAN link provider. Without a good corporate queuing policy it is impossible to provide users with an appropriate service level while supporting mission-critical applications and services concurrently. To meet the demands from both sides network managers can implement queuing on their network so that valuable network resources can be put efficiently to use. This provides for a workaround in a situation where multiple traffic types can be integrated and migrated in already bandwidth hungry environments without creating additional WAN cost.

In the following text we look at how to choose the most appropriate queuing option from the three that Cisco IOS offers. However, before doing so it is obvious that network managers recognize the need for queuing, in addition to the network and corporate staff agreeing upon a queuing policy. Prioritization policies tend to have their share of political importance as well.

D.4 Selecting a Queuing Option

When determining what the best queuing option is in a given situation, consider the following guidelines which also map to Figure D-2:

1. Determine if one or more WAN links are congested.

2. Analyse where and when congestion occurs. If the maximum transmission capability is almost constantly exceeded, there is no need to implement queuing—this only slows down traffic handling even more because of its router resource usage. Adding more bandwidth is the only solution of choice. However, if the incoming load only exceeds the maximum transmission capability during peaks, queuing might be an option to solve the problem.

3. There are two issues that must be decided upon—is strict control over traffic prioritization necessary, and can automatic configuration be acceptable? When the answer to the latter question is "yes", *weighted fair queuing* comes into play.

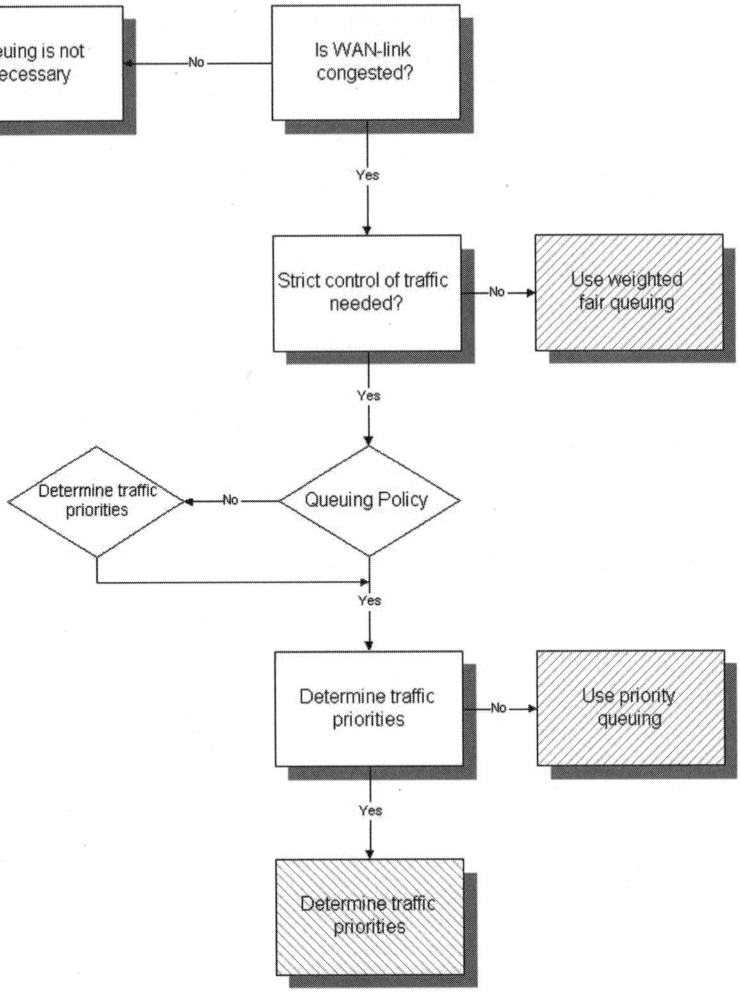

Figure D-2
Making queuing
decisions

Weighted fair queuing doesn't require any configuration of queue
lists to determine what can be considered as priority traffic on an
interface. Its algorithm sorts traffic into *messages* that are part of a
conversation in a dynamic matter.

Configuring queuing should not be underestimated as something
that is done between 8 A.M. and lunch. In order for the network
manager to establish an effective queuing configuration, he must
analyze the network to get a good view on the types traffic it handles
and give each one a relative priority in the process. Using the
analysis outcome as a baseline, he must install the appropriate

filters and again measure the effects they have on the baseline situation. While this may work out well the first time, these must be repeated periodically as traffic patterns tend to change over time.

4. After the analysis of traffic patterns and the determination of relative traffic priorities is completed, a queuing policy must be established.

5. The final necessary step is to determine whether any of the previous identified traffic patterns can tolerate delay.

D.5 Differentiating between Queuing Options

The characteristics of weighted fair queuing are pretty straightforward. While both other options must explicitly be configured on an interface, weighted fair queuing is enabled by default. In contrary to priority queuing and custom queuing it does not use queue lists as a means of differentiating between traffic. Weighted fair queuing dynamically sorts incoming traffic into messages that are part of a conversation instead, using the fair-queue algorithm. Next, it queues the messages for low-volume conversations such as interactive traffic and gives it priority over high-volume, bandwidth-intensive conversations like FTP or SMTP (large attachments) sessions. In the event of concurrent transmissions, weighted fair queuing ensures a balanced priority for each so the available bandwidth is comparable for all sessions.

When looking at the operational aspects, the primary difference between priority queuing and custom queuing is that priority queuing is less flexible in a multiprotocol environment. If, for instance, you have to deal with a serial link that has limited bandwidth available while high volumes of (time) critical traffic have to be serviced, priority queuing does the job for that particular traffic but may cause other traffic to choke completely. In the case of custom queuing, traffic is serviced in a round-robin fashion so even when dealing with heavily loaded WAN links, all traffic can count on some level of service.

Table D-1 presents a convenient overview of the available queuing options in Cisco IOS. Combined with Figure D-2 on the previous page, this table helps to make a well informed decision on what queuing option to use in a particular situation.

Table D-1
Overview of Cisco
queuing options

Weighted Fair Queuing	Priority Queuing	Custom Queuing
Does not use queue lists	4 queues	16 queues
Low volume is given priority	High queue is serviced first	Services in a round-robin fashion
Interactive traffic is given priority	Only critical traffic makes it trough	Allocates available bandwidth
Conversation dispatching	Packet dispatching	Treshold dispatching
Balances file-transfer access	Designed for low-bandwidth links	Designed for higher speed low-bandwidth links
Enabled by default	Must be configured	Must be configured

D.6 Weighted Fair Queuing

If we consider a WAN link that not only services user application traffic and routing updates but also videoconferencing sessions, it may be obvious that leaving these traffic types unmanaged will not only result in clear video and zero-delay speech (dependent on the bandwidth) but also in a very angry group of users that face a clogged up Internet. Clogging up networks is exactly what high-bandwidth sessions such as video conferencing or large file transfers tend to do when left alone to play. Therefore on low-bandwidth serial links that have to bear these types of traffic, weighted fair queuing comes into its own. We can thus state that when weighted fair queuing is used, all traffic is provided fair bandwidth allocation. What then is the added advantage of configuring weighted fair queuing when traffic management is necessary, but extreme granularity should be avoided due to, for instance, administration overhead? This question can best be answered by looking at the pre-IOS 11.1 period, when all traffic was handled in a *First In – First Out* (FIFO) fashion.

If FIFO is used, all traffic is transmitted in the same order as it was received. Bandwidth consumption and the associated delays are not taken into account. This can be fatal if you consider that, for an example, large file transfers generate a series of packets that contain associated data. These packets are often referred to as packet trains. If a packet train of considerable size would be received by a router that was configured to process packets in a FIFO fashion, the result is obvious—all other packets have to wait before the

Figure D-3
FIFO giving
precedence over the
high-volume packet
train because it was
received before the
low-volume packet
train

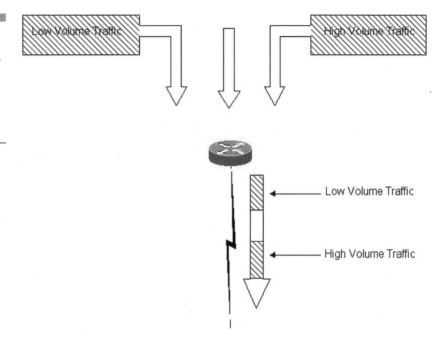

packet train is processed, resulting in possibly fatal delays, dying TTL timers and other data slaughter. Consider Figure D-3 showing FIFO processing.

This is exactly where weighted fair queuing's added advantage kicks in—it breaks the packet train up so that the (often sensitive) timing of low-volume packets is assured. This prevents the packet train from consuming all bandwidth at the expense of other traffic. Moreover, low-volume traffic such as telnet sessions is given a higher priority over high-volume traffic such as SMTP bursts or FTP sessions. When concurrent transfers of this high-volume traffic need to be serviced, balanced use of link capacity is given.

Thus, weighted fair queuing lacks the finer granularity tuning options that priority queuing and custom queuing can offer. It is the queuing option of choice for use with slow serial links in situations where added administration capacity is unavailable. In addition, it is also enabled by default on physical interfaces where bandwidth is less than or equal to 2.048 Mbps, and also on interfaces that *do not* use compressed PPP, X.25, LAPB or SDLC encapsulation.

Weighted fair queuing is not an option for high-speed links because it gives low-volume traffic precedence over high-volume traffic. High capacity networks might experience crippling delays if this type of queuing were to be used.

D.6.2 Weighted Fair Queuing Operation

When receiving traffic that needs to be serviced, the weighted fair queuing algorithm starts arranging the traffic into "conversations" where packet header addressing is used as the discriminator between the different types of traffic. These discriminators can be either a Source or Destination MAC address.

After the weighted fair queuing algorithm has finished arranging the traffic into various conversations, the packets that make up these conversations are placed in the *fair queue*. The virtual delivery time of the last bit of each arriving packet is used to determine the removal order of packets from the fair queue. As you've learned, small low-volume packets are given precedence over large, high-volume packets. After servicing low-volume conversations, the weighted fair queuing algorithm gives fair link capacity or alternative transmission time slots to high-volume conversations.

Consider Figure D-4 which shows weighted fair queuing at work. The high-volume conversation packets that make up both file transfers are queued in arrival order. The low-volume e-mail packet is serviced first, even though it arrived later then the first high-volume packet. After the low-volume packet is queued and serviced, the remaining packets are alotted a fair amount of bandwidth, rather than the first high-volume conversation eating up all the bandwidth when using the standard FIFO. Here you can see the fair-queue reflecting weighted fair queuing's operation by first queuing small, low-volume packets that do not need much bandwidth before servicing high-volume conversations.

Figure D-4
Weighted fair
queuing at work

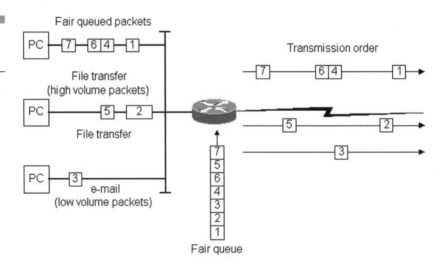

D.6.3 Configuring Weighted Fair Queuing

To enable weighted fair queuing on interfaces you only have to use one command which should be used in interface configuration mode: `fair queue` It can have three optional parameters, `congestive-discard-threshold`, `dynamic-queues` and `reservable-queues` of which the individual functions are listed in Table D-2. To disable weighted fair queueing for an interface, use the `no` form of this command.

The full syntax for this command is:

```
fair-queue [congestive-discard-threshold [dynamic-queues
[reservable-queues]]]
no faizr-queue
```

D.6.4 Example of Weighted Fair Queuing

Consider Figure D-5 showing two networks interconnected by a Frame Relay network. The link attached to interface S1 is configured for a 56kbps link speed. In the example configuration, you can see that the network administrator configured the congestive-discard-threshold-number to 128.

Table D-2

Fair-queue parameter descriptions

Fair-queue parameter	Description
congestive-discard-threshold	(Optional) Number of messages allowed in each queue. The default is 64 messages, and a new threshold must be a power of 2 in the range 16 to 4096. When a conversation reaches this threshold, new message packets are discarded.
dynamic-queues	(Optional) Number of dynamic queues used for best-effort conversations (that is, a normal conversation not requiring any special network services). Values are 16, 32, 64, 128, 256, 512, 1024, 2048, and 4096. The default is 256.
reservable-queues	(Optional) Number of reservable queues used for reserved conversations in the range 0 to 1000. The default is 0. Reservable queues are used for interfaces configured for features such as Resource Reservation Protocol (RSVP).

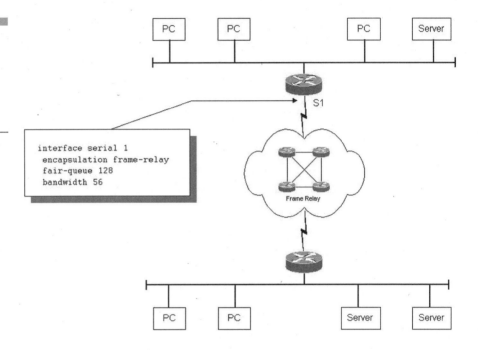

Figure D-5
Configuration of a
discard treshold
prevents a single
conversation
clogging up a
slow link.

```
interface serial 1
  encapsulation frame-relay
  fair-queue 128
  bandwidth 56
```

This creates a congestive treshold after which messages for high-volume conversation traffic will no longer be queued.

This discard policy only affects high-volume conversations with more than one message in the queue, preventing long packet trains to monopolize the link. In the event of one conversation queue contains more messages than the configured or default congestive discard threshold, that conversation cannot have any new messages queued until the queue content drops below one-fourth of the configured congestive-discard value. In our case, this would be 128/4 = 32 entries.

D.7 Priority Queuing

When strict control is needed over which traffic is to be forwarded, priority queuing is extremely useful. Priority queuing is the oldest type of queuing discussed, and before weighted fair queuing came in the picture, it was typically used to prioritize interactive traffic such as Telnet sessions over bulk traffic like high volume file transfers. Today, weighted fair queuing is the favorable option for this job. In contrary to priority queuing, it needs little

Figure D-6
Priority queuing
categorizes and
priotizes traffic arriving
at interface S0.

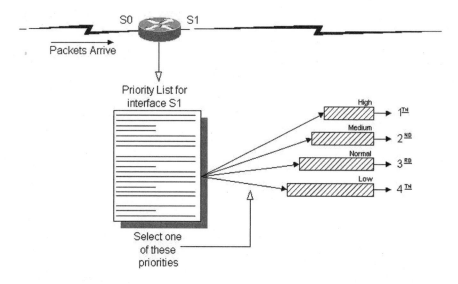

or no configuration at all. Priority queuing is still used in most cases due to its capability of guaranteeing timely delivery of mission-critical traffic. Traffic crossing an interface on which priority queuing is configured, categorized and prioritized, is seen in Figure D-6.

Depending on the protocol or TCP port number used or on the router interface they enter, the traffic can be assigned to the various queues. Mission critical traffic, or time-senstive traffic such as SNA and DEC LAT, can be controlled by prority queuing on low-bandwidth links. Traffic selection occurs by configuring a prioritly list that contains entries stating which traffic should be assigned to which queue. Similar to access list configuration, priority lists are manually maintained and must be linked to an interface. Four types of queues can be used with priority queuing, are listed:

■ High queue

■ Medium queue

■ Normal queue

■ Low queue

This is also the order in which these queues are emptied. It may seem obvious that, large amounts of traffic in the high-queue can result in traffic in the lower queues which cannot be forwarded in a timely fashion or even at all. While this offers the best assurance for a timely delivery of certain traffic, great care should be taken before configuring this type of queuing.

There's also a default queue where packets not matching the priority list will end up. A rule of thumb here is that priority queuing should only be used when guaranteed delivery of certain traffic is required, and as much of the available bandwidth should be alotted to this traffic as possible.

In contrary of weighted fair queuing, priority queuing cannoy compensate for low-bandwidth for all traffic that has to be serviced. Moreover, it should only be used on low-bandwidth serial lines, as it's strategy would be unacceptable for use on higher-speed interfaces.

D.7.1 Priority Queuing Operation

To get a grasp on how priority queuing's internals do their work, look at Figure D-7 showing a flowchart of the priority queuing operation. An incoming packet is matched against the priority list and is assigned to a queue, depending on the outcome of the match. The next match is to see whether the selected queue is full or not. If the queue is full, the packet will be discarded (which is exactly why care should be taken when configuring the queue size). If there is room available in queue, the packet is placed there. Although before being dispatched, a check is done on timeouts, as some protocols such as IP check the *Time To Live* (TTL) or other timer-fields before they forward the packet.

As we've seen earlier, the high-priority queue is emptied first before servicing any other queue. When this is done, the other queues are serviced in order of importance. Before a packet can be dispatched, the *dispatching algorithm* makes sure that the high-priority contains no packets, making sure mission or time critical traffic is always serviced first.

NOTE: *Packets that fail to match against any of the configured statements in the priority list will be sent to a default queue, which must explicitly be configured. The role of "default queue" must be assigned to either one of the four other queues.*

NOTE: *While at first it is tempting to be uncompromising when defining traffic belonging in the high queue because it always gets serviced first, it could result in the high queue being full all the time, causing packets in other queues to remain there waiting for their timers to expire.*

Figure D-7
Priority queuing
operation

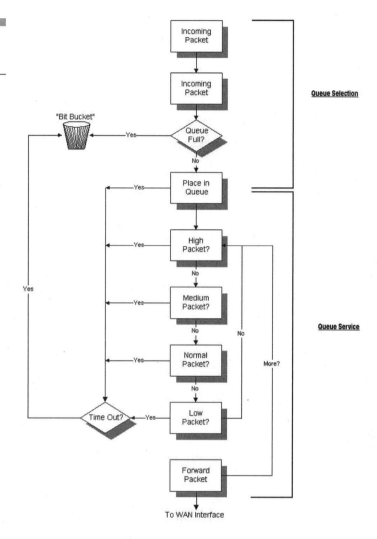

Figure D-7
Priority queuing
operation

D.7.2 Configuration Tasks

To configure priority queuing, perform the following tasks:

1. Configure an output priority queuing list.

   A priority list is a set of rules that describes how packets should be assigned to priority queues. You can establish queuing priorities based on the protocol type or the packets entering from a specific interface. All Cisco-supported protocols are allowed. In Figure D-8, the priority queue list is TCP (High), IPX and AppleTalk (Medium), and IP (Normal).

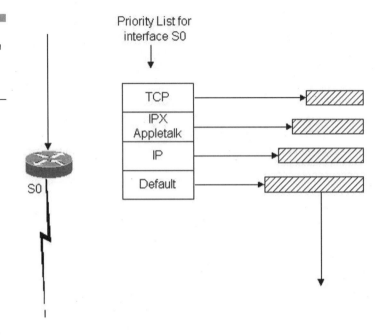

Figure D-8
Packets are placed in
a specific queue as
configured in the
priority list

A priority list is like an access list and so only IP traffic that is not
carrying TCP will fall through to the normal queue.

To define a priority list of protocols, you should use the global
configuration command:

```
priority-list [list number 1-16] protocol [protocol name] [priority
high, medium, normal or low] [other, protocol dependant options]
```

When using the incoming interface as a way to assign priorities, use
the following global configuration command:

```
priority-list interface [list number 1-16] [interface type and
number i.e. S1] [priority, which is high, medium, normail or low]
```

2. Define a default queue.
   One of the queues must be defined as the default queue so that
   packets that don't match any of the statements configured in the
   priority list are placed in a certain queue. To do this, use the
   following global configuration command:

```
priority-list [list number 1-16] default [high, medium, normal or
low]
```

In Figure D-7, the default queue is lowest priority. SNA traffic for
example, would be placed in the default queue.

Table D-3

Maximum number of allowable packets per queue default values

Queue	Maximum number of packets that can be stored
High	20
Medium	40
Normal	60
Low	80

3. Specify the queue sizes. (Optional)

You can specify the maximum number of allowable packets in each queue. In general, it is not recommended that the default queue sizes be changed, unless high-priority traffic monopolizes the link, causing timeouts for other communications. The defaults are listed in Table D-3.

To change the maximum number of packets that each queue can accept, use the following global configuration command:

```
priority-list [list number 1-16] queue-limit [high value] [medium
value] [normal value] [low value]
```

4. Apply the priority list number to an interface.

The final step is to apply the queue to an outgoing interface using the global configuration command:

```
priority-group [list number 1-16]
```

Only one list can be assigned per interface. Once assigned, the priority list rules are applied to all traffic that passes through the interface.

D.8 Custom Queuing

Custom queuing's operation is somewhat comparable to priority queuing in that the same filtering technique is used to match packets against a list which decides packets placement in a certain queue. Custom queuing's filters inspect the packets for characteristics such as source, destination, transport protocol, or application in order to be able to make a queuing decision. Next, the packets are placed in the appropriate queue by the queuing algorithm. While both custom priority queuing use queuing algorithms at the interface, the algorithms differ.

As seen in priority queuing, it could be possible that packets in the high-priority queue can prevent other queues from being emptied as they claim all of the available bandwidth. Custom queuing on the other hand offers more granularity by assigning queue space on a per-protocol or per-interface basis. It hereby effectively eliminates potential queuing problems caused by a dominating priority configuration.

D.8.1 Custom Queuing Operation

Let's take a closer look on how custom queuing works. Custom queuing allocates a certain percentage of bandwidth for every configured traffic type. Filters can be used to assign these traffic types to 1 of 16 possible queues. These queues are serviced in a sequential fashion by the router, where it transmits a pre-configured amount of traffic from each queue before handling the next one. This method prevents traffic received on a particular interface from eating up all bandwidth. Extreme granularity can be achieved because the number of bytes transmitted from the queue each time it is serviced can be configured. This way, you can fine tune the percentage of the interface's bandwidth used by each queue.

NOTE: *By now it may be obvious that custom queuing is the queuing option of choice when you have to deal with time-critical protocols such as DEC LAT and SNA that rely heavily on timely responses.*

Apart from the 16 queues we have mentioned earlier, there's also a "Queue 0". This queue is dedicated for handling system packets such as keepalives. It is always serviced before the other queues. Some examples of traffic that use queue 0 because timely response is required include

- DECnet hellos
- ISIS hellos
- ISO IGRP hellos
- ESIS hellos
- SLARP address resolution
- Enhanced IGRP hellos
- OSPF hellos
- Router syslog messages
- Spanning Tree keepalives

Figure D-9
The custom queuing dispatching algorithm at work

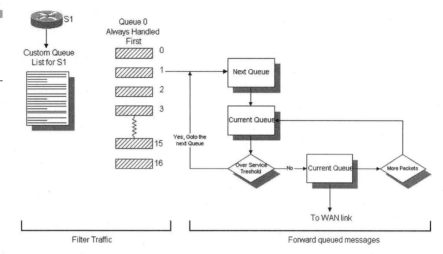

When you consider these traffic types are arriving at a router interface that has the priority queuing configured, they are treated as low-volume. As a result, its bandwidth share in a system utilizing priority queuing is not too impressive and possibly causes havoc on the network. If you compare this to weighted fair queuing, this traffic type is given more priority as it is considered as low-volume traffic.

Consider Figure D-9 showing custom queuing at work. After the received packets are placed in the queues as result of the traffic filtering process, queued message forwarding is handled by a round-robin dispatching algorithm. This algorithm assures that every queue continues packet transmission until the configured threshold, which corresponds with a forwarded byte-count, is reached. The next queue is serviced only after either this configured byte count is reached, or if the queue is empty.

D.8.2 Custom Queuing Configuration

Custom queuing can be configured using the following order:

1. Configure custom queue filtering for a protocol or an interface.

   You can configure custom queuing to filter for an interface or a protocol. As an example, you could configure custom queuing to do any of the following:

   a. Send all IP traffic to custom queue 2

   b. Send all traffic from Ethernet interface 1 to custom queue 5

   c. Send all IPX traffic to custom queue 3

d. Send all AppleTalk traffic to custom queue 4

e. Send all SNA traffic to custom queue 6

To create the queue use the following global configuration command:

```
queue-list [list number 1 to 16] protocol [protocol name] [queue
number 1 to 16] [queue keyword can specify an access list etc.]
```

To create a queue from an interface use the following global
configuration command:

```
queue-list interface [list number 1 to 16] [interface type and
number i.e. S1] [queue number 1 to 16].
```

2. Configure a default custom queue. You can configure a queue for those
    packets that failed all matches in the custom queuing filtering process

    To assign a default queue that all undefined packets will be placed
    in, use the following command:

```
queue-list [list number 1 to 16] default [queue number 1 to 16].
```

3. Configure queue capacity. You can configure the maximum number
    of packets that a queue can contain. (Optional configuration step)

    To change the number of packets that can be in any queue at any
    one time use the following global configuration command:

```
queue-list [list number 1 to 16] queue [queue-number 1 to 16]
limit [number of packet 0 to 32767 (default = 20)]
```

4. Configure the transfer rate per queue. To allocate more bandwidth to a
    protocol's traffic from an interface, the queue size can be changed.

    To change the minimum amount of bytes that are transferred from
    any queue, use the following global configuration command:

```
queue-list [list number 1 to 16] queue [queue number 1 to 16]
byte-count [minimum number of bytes to be transferred (default =
1500)]
```

5. Apply the custom queue list to an interface. The filters of the queue
    list are applied to all traffic that passes through the interface.

    To apply the custom queue to an outgoing interface use the following
    interface configuration command:

```
custom-queue-list [list number 1 to 16]
```

D.8.3 Custom Queuing Configuration Commands

These are six commands used to configure custom queuing. Each command is listed in Table D-4 with the configuration mode it used.

Table D-4
Custom queuing configuration commands

Command	Configuration Mode	Explanation
queue-list *list-number* protocol *protocol-name* queue-number queue-	Global	This defines which protocol *keyword keyword value* is to be placed into which queue. It can be very specific, identifying application or packet size in some instances.
queue-list *list-number* interface *interface-type* *interface-number* *queue-number*	Global	This is included in the custom-list command and identifies an incoming interface. All traffic from that source interface on the router whose traffic is destined out of the interface to which this custom list is applied will be placed in the defined queue.
queue-list *list-number* default *queue-number*	Global	This states what is to be done for all traffic that does not find a match in the custom list.
queue-list *list-number* queue *queue-number* limit *limit-number*	Global	The default is set to 20 packets for each queue. This command enables you to change this parameter.
queue-list *list-number* queue *queue-number* byte-count	Global	This is the command that sets the threshold on the queue, determining how traffic can be transmitted before it is required to visit the next queue.

continues

Table D-4
Continued

Command	Configuration Mode	Explanation
Custom-queue-list *list-number*	Interface	This applies the custom queue list to the interface. The custom queue will not take effect until the list is applied to the interface.

Summary

For easy study reference, remember the following facts on the various queuing options:

- Weighted fair queuing
  - Low volume traffic such as Telnet is given priority.
  - Interactive traffic gets higher priority than long file transfers.
  - High bandwidth usage traffic such as long file transfer traffic gets equal priority with other high bandwidth use traffic.
  - Groups of conversations are based on both source and destination to allow each conversation to get fair access.

- Priority queuing
  - Best used on low bandwidth links such as serial connections
  - Assigns one of four priorities to traffic—high, medium, normal or low
  - High traffic is given priority over all others—these possibly might never get access.

- Custom Queuing
  - Has 16 queues which are serviced in a round robin fashion
  - Full control over which traffic gets what percentage of bandwidth
  - Allocates full bandwidth
  - Suitable for high bandwidth links
  - System packets are handled by a separate, dedicated queue, Queue 0

INDEX

ABOUT THE CD-ROM ▨ ▨ ▨ ▨ ▨ ▨ ▨

FastTrakExpress™

FastTrak Express provides interactive certification exams to help you prepare for certification. With the enclosed CD, you can test your knowledge of the topics covered in this book with over 200 multiple choice questions.

To Install FastTrak Express:

1. Insert the CD-ROM in your CD-ROM drive.
2. From your computer, choose Run. Select the CD-ROM drive and Run the file called "setupfte.exe." This will launch the Installation Wizard.
3. When the Setup is finished, you may immediately begin using FastTrak Express.
4. To begin using FastTrak Express, enter your license key number: 312272746981

FastTrak Express offers two testing options: the Adaptive exam and the Standard exam.

The Adaptive Exam

The Adaptive exam style does not simulate all of the exam environments that are found on certification exams. You cannot choose specific subcategories for the adaptive exam and once a question has been answered you cannot go back to a previous question.

You have a time limit in which to complete the adaptive exam. This time varies from subject to subject, although it is usually 15 to 25 questions in 30 minutes. When the time limit has been reached, your exam automatically ends.

To take the Adaptive Exam:

1. Click the Adaptive Exam button from the Main window. The Adaptive Exam window will appear.
2. Click the circle or square to the left of the correct answer.

NOTE: *There may be more than one correct answer. The text in the bottom left corner of the window instructs you to Choose the Best Answer (if there is only one answer) or Mark All Correct Answers (if there is more than one correct answer.*

3. Click the Next button to continue.
4. To quit the test at any time, click the Finish button. After about 30 minutes, the exam exits to review mode.

After you have completed the Adaptive exam, FastTrak Express displays your score and the passing score required for the test.

- ■ Click Details to display a chapter-by-chapter review of your exam results.
- ■ Click on Report to get a full analysis of your score.

To review the Adaptive exam   After you have taken an Adaptive exam, you can review the questions, your answers, and the correct answers. You may only review your questions immediately after an Adaptive exam. To review your questions:

1. Click the Correct Answer button.
2. To see your answer, click the Your Answer button.

The Standard Exam

After you have learned about your subject using the Adaptive sessions, you can take a Standard exam. This mode simulates the environment that might be found on an actual certification exam.

You cannot choose subcategories for a Standard exam. You have a time limit (this time varies from subject to subject, although it is usually 75 minutes) to complete the Standard exam. When this time limit has been reached, your exam automatically ends.

To take the Standard exam:

1. Click the Standard Exam button from the Main window. The Standard Exam window will appear.
2. Click the circle or square to the left of the correct answer.

▬ ▬

NOTE: *There may be more than one correct answer. The text in the bottom left corner of the window instructs you to Choose the Best Answer (if there is only one answer) or Mark All Correct Answers (if there is more than one correct answer).*

3. If you are unsure of the answer and wish to mark the question so you can return to it later, check the Mark box in the upper left hand corner.
4. To review which questions you have marked, which you have answered, and which you have not answered, click the Review button.
5. Click the Next button to continue.
6. To quit the test at any time, click the Finish button. After about 75 minutes, the exam exits to review mode.

After you have completed the Standard exam, FastTrak Express displays your score and the passing score required for the test.

■ Click Details to display a chapter-by-chapter review of your exam results.
■ Click on Report to get a full analysis of your score.

To review a Standard Exam   After you have taken a Standard exam, you can review the questions, your answers, and the correct answers.

You may only review your questions immediately after a Standard exam.

To review your questions:

1. Click the Correct Answer button.
2. To see your answer, click the Your Answer button.

Changing Exams   FastTrakExpress provides several practice exams to test your knowledge. To change exams:

1. Select the exam for the test you want to run from the Select Exam window.

If you experience technical difficulties please call (888) 992-3131. Outside the U.S. call (281) 972-3131. Or, you may e-mail brucem@bfq.com. For more information, visit the BeachFrontQuizzer site at www.bfq.com.

SOFTWARE AND INFORMATION LICENSE